To Ella

C000126983

AN ALLIANCE
ACROSS THE ALPS

Britain and Italy's Waldensians

R.D. Kernohan

R.D. Kernohan (signature)

All rights reserved. No part of this publication may be reproduced, stored in a retrieval system, or transmitted in any form by any means, electronic, mechanical, photocopying, recording or otherwise, without the prior permission of The Handsel Press Ltd

British Library Cataloguing in Publication Data:
A catalogue record for this publication
is available from the British Library

ISBN   1 871828 64 3

© The Handsel Press 2005

Typeset in 11 pt. Garamond

Printed by Polestar Wheaton, Exeter

Thanks are expressed
to the Drummond Trust of 3 Pitt Terrace, Stirling,
to the Europe Committee
of the Church of Scotland World Mission Council,
and to the Hope Trust
for assistance with the publication of this book

CONTENTS

ACKNOWLEDGMENTS

In addition to people and books mentioned in the text or bibliography I owe more thanks than I could record. Among those who have been especially helpful or put upon are Iain Douglas, Ray Sawers, and Malcolm Ritchie of the Scottish Waldensian Missions Aid Society and the society's secretary, David Lamb, who opened the society's archive to me and traced additional material. Sinclair Horne of the Scottish Reformation Society enabled me to consult the books on Waldensian themes collected by Malcolm Ritchie and held in the Magdalen Chapel, Edinburgh. Iain Maciver of the National Library of Scotland introduced me to the Scottish-Waldensian, Free Church, and related or subsequent material held in its manuscripts division. Shirley Fraser drew my attention to valuable privately published work by Daisy Ronco about Italian Protestants and the Risorgimento. Colin Forrester-Paton gave me access to the Donald Miller papers.

In Italy I am indebted to Gabriella Ballesio, the Waldensian archivist; to the Waldensian Cultural Centre; to pastors in Torre Pellice, Turin, Florence, Pinerolo; to Pastor Luca Baratto; and to various others, some of whom knew they were helping me with a book and others who merely answered tiresome questions.

I owe all those and many others heartfelt thanks, as I do to Jock Stein for his immense help, advice, and understanding when I sought a publisher; to Margaret Stein for the two maps; to my son Neil for help with the electronics of modern authorship; and to my wife for patience, understanding, and help. Of course the opinions in the book are mine, and not necessarily theirs - in some cases probably not theirs!

Edinburgh, June 2005

The light shines in the darkness, and the darkness has never put it out.

La luce splende nelle tenebre, e le tenebre non l'hanno sopraffatta.

St John's Gospel, 1.5, as in The Good News Bible and the modern Italian translation of the Genevan Bible Society.

ITALY

(with the Waldensian Valleys shaded)

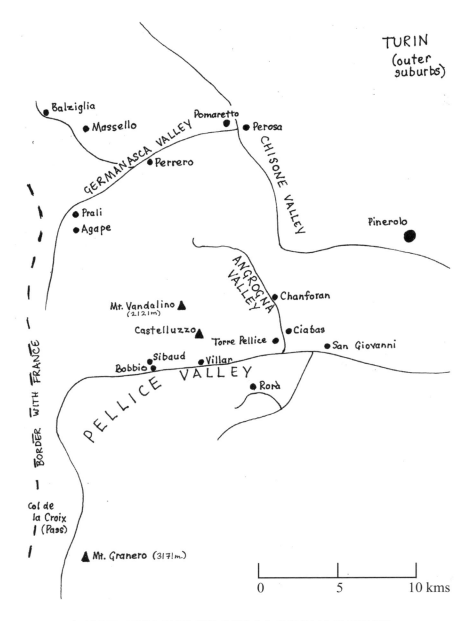

THE WALDENSIAN VALLEYS

(a rough sketch showing some peaks and main rivers)

Prologue:

ABOUT HISTORY, DISCOVERY AND TESTIMONY

This is a prologue or prelude in the most literal sense of the terms. I began to write while the book was no more than a series of notes and some introductory pages. But it was a book that had to be started and which I hope emerges as a book that deserved and needed to be completed.

In one important respect I believe it differs from most modern books in English about the Waldensians which I have encountered. For them the last 150 years tend to be treated as an important postscript to the glorious origins and long tribulations of the Waldensians. I concentrate on how that story continues through the *Risorgimento* (literally, the revival or resurgence) and in modern Italy, though I necessarily explain who this remarkable people are, whence they came, and what they endured. I also try to set them in the wider context of modern Italian Protestantism, within which they are a minority.

The book is history, discovery and testimony. It is an account of British encounters with the Waldensian Church and people in Italy rather than a theological or historical treatise. Some of the encounters are recent or contemporary. Some are not only with Waldensians but with other Italian Protestants.

Some encounters are my own. But many are those of people in times past, whose labours and enthusiasms in Alpine Piedmont and other parts of Italy are almost unknown in modern Britain. They were labours of love as well as faith and hope, and will not be lost, for they are surely well-recorded in the minute-books and archives of Heaven.

This is not mainly a history of Waldensian Christianity, that senior branch of the Reformed sector of the universal or truly catholic Church in Europe, but of its British and Irish connections. If it has an emphasis on the Scottish threads in that connection, this is not through any desire to minimise the achievement of such English enthusiasts as W.S. Gilly and the incomparable Charles Beckwith or to ignore the Irish Protestant contribution, but because the Scottish role has recently been neglected - not by the Waldensians but by the Scots themselves.

This book is not a call for some 'Glorious Return' - the aptness of that phrase will become apparent to those who read the book - to the styles and expectations of the past. The testimony is not only to some historical glories, many sufferings, various difficulties, and only partially-fulfilled expectations. It is to the contribution that the British Protestant tradition, apparently so

1

undervalued in our contemporary culture, and the Italian Protestant minority, apparently so negligible an influence in its increasingly pluralist society, can make to both countries, to Europe, and to truly ecumenical Christianity.

For these contributions will not only be to their own countries, even though different traditions and cultures will be far more tenacious and resilient than arch-enthusiasts for European integration believe. Closer European political and economic union, whatever its structures and treaty-relations may be, will encourage many kinds of new social and personal contacts. It will create new climates of opinion, even in religious and cultural matters. One of the likeliest climate-changes might seem to be consolidation of the claims of the Bishop of Rome not only to hold the most powerful Christian office in Europe but to be Christ's vicar for what remains of 'Christendom', a concept which an otherwise benevolent Christian publisher once suggested I delete from a book on grounds of obsolescence. Another trend might seem to be consolidation of the secular rationalist predominance which has been the greatest force in Continental European culture since the 'Enlightenment' and the French Revolution.

But things are not necessarily so. There is, if the politicians have not spoiled the term, a third way - a revived Christianity in which reason and intellect are guided and inspired by the authority of the Bible and the biblical and evangelical traditions of the universal Church. These transcend all denominational boundaries, as they do today both in Britain and in Italy. The Roman Church will be touched by them too. But among the most valuable of them are those of the British reformed and reforming Churches (Anglican as well as Presbyterian or 'free church') and of minority churches such as French Huguenots and the Italian Waldensians who, in spite of the fallibility of all denominations, kept and keep a pure, clear light shining in the darkness. And as a children's hymn says, 'Many kinds of darkness in the world are found'.

This book owes debts to many people and many earlier authors, most of them long out of print and largely out of mind. The bibliography at the end is also a vote of thanks. But it has been directly inspired by one book which I encountered in Italy, an account by several scholars, with the Waldensian historian Giorgio Tourn as editorial preses, of the experiences of British travellers, English and Scottish, in the Waldensian valleys: *Viaggiatori Britannici alle Valli Valdesi, 1753-1899* (Claudiana, Turin, 1994).

I was grateful I had enough Italian to follow the narrative and the translations of extracts from the travellers' first-hand accounts. I was then rather shamed that some of those who had written so vividly in my own tongue, and being dead yet spoke to me through Italian translation, were merely names to me and that others were wholly unknown. But grateful though I was to the translators, and impressed by the affectionate respect in which they held my British countrymen, both Scots and English, I felt an urge to encounter the travellers in our own language and then a call to share some of their experience.

My next modern labour of love was to try to supplement the experience of these principal British travellers to the valleys with the experience of others who encountered the Waldensians or other Italian Protestants, either there or elsewhere in Italy. Some, like Charles Beckwith and Robert Walter Stewart, gave the best of their lives to Italy. Far more were visitors who made up for a relatively brief stay by the intensity of their experience. Others were British expatriates and temporary residents in Italy.

The age of the *Risorgimento*, which led to and followed the creation of the united Kingdom of Italy, and the end of the temporal power of the Papacy, coincided with one of the most vigorous ages of travel-writing in English, with Americans as well as British involved. It was also a time of great cultural and literary interest in Italy. This was the age which gave us Garibaldi biscuits, Venetian blinds, and Robert Browning's home thoughts from abroad. It is therefore possible to put the experiences and evangelical hopes of enthusiastic Protestants in a wider context, with comments and evidence from literary and other tourists. These ranged from the sympathetic majority through the indifferent to the hostile, which category included many Roman Catholics, either attracted to Italy or repelled by it, some feeling both emotions at the same time. Anyone looking for unkind but not untrue comments on Italian life before the *Risorgimento* is by no means confined to Protestant sources and is well served by John Henry Newman.

For this was the age when the old British Roman Catholic remnant, which had many Italian connections, as well as Jacobite memories and close ties with the Scots and English colleges in Rome, was reinforced by the volunteers from that part of the Oxford Movement which deserted Anglicanism. They had taken the road to Rome and naturally wanted to look around their destination - some with mixed feelings, some ready to idolise the indefensible. Perhaps the older strain in British Roman Catholicism found it easier to take the Italians just as they found them. It was certainly able to behave just as flamboyantly as any Whig nobleman or romantic poet, for example when Charles Waterton, later celebrated as naturalist and explorer, climbed the lightning conductor on the top of St Peter's and then balanced on one foot on the head of an angel decorating the Castel Sant' Angelo above the Tiber.

As I developed the book I became convinced that the links between Britain and Italy were wider and deeper in the nineteenth century than at any other time in our history. They combined the classical inheritance with a romantic enthusiasm, and the pursuit of the past and its antiquities with a zestful enjoyment of the present, as well as evangelical missionary zeal, Protestant solidarity, or Roman Catholic piety. These Victorians also spoke and read Italian far more widely than even highly educated British travellers do today and learned it much more quickly, helped by their schooling in Latin and stimulated by the practical needs of travel in a country where English was not yet widely spoken.

This book does not try to assess all these cultural or religious connections. It is about the evangelical and Protestant strands in a very complex relationship whose visible symbols include the Canova monument in St Peter's to the last of the Stuarts, as well as the British Protestant graves in the Piedmontese valleys and the poets' memorials in the Protestant cemeteries of Rome and Florence. But the nineteenth-century Protestant connection can only be fully understood in the context of those wider associations and especially of what was happening in the golden age of over-optimistic liberalism and idealistic nationalism, which was also a great age of mission and evangelism. In part, it was a religious dimension of the Victorian belief in progress. This is why at times I depart from the doings of denominations and evangelists to those of ideologies and politicians, some of whom I may occasionally refer to as statesmen.

Thereafter our countries sometimes drifted apart. Yet even Mussolini's ambitions and ill-judged leap into the Second World War never caused any profound estrangement, though many an inoffensive ice-cream shop had its windows broken by British hooligans in June 1940. But perhaps the phrase which Robert Browning, so much part of the Italian connection, applied when William Wordsworth displeased him could also apply to the British-Italian relationship: it would be 'never glad confident morning again'. That makes it all the more important to appreciate what was so remarkable in the relationship and to sustain it new ways for a new age.

I have also supplemented the notable travellers of the nineteenth century with some account of developments in the next one and of some recent and contemporary hopes and uncertainties in Italy. It is a country very different not just from the one Victorians knew but from any one they could have imagined. In this I am not claiming any special authority or expertise, only enough understanding to recognise the difficulties as well as the demands of the subject.

To speak with authority on all that Waldensian history and contemporary witness involves would demand an astonishing depth of scholarship and breadth of versatility, covering not only theology and Church history but medieval social history, international diplomacy, and Italian politics or sociology. I had visited Italy several times before the Waldensians were anything more to me than a name, a footnote in history, and the memory of a Milton sonnet from my schooldays. I had been on the committee of the Scottish society encouraging links with the Waldensians for years before I got round to visiting their heartland. I fear that till then my main contribution to the cause had been as editor of the Church of Scotland's magazine *Life and Work*, giving lunch to the occasional fraternal Italian visitor, still known by the Victorian style of 'deputy', and constructing an encouraging news story from the conversation over the Chianti.

Maybe that played its part in equipping me to handle the discovery of the triumphs and tragedies of Waldensian history and to set them in the context of a changing Italy, a new ecumenical outlook, probable future convulsions in the Roman Church, and continuing uncertainties in the mainstream Protestantism of Northern Europe and America. For all their remarkable history, the Waldensians are a people of the present and future, and part of a modern Italy more European-minded that at any time in its history since the Roman Empire. As a minority under pressure, but a committed and steadfast minority witnessing to the majority around them and seeking to serve it, they may also have lessons for the rest of the world's Christian minority.

Most of my bibliographical debts are acknowledged at the end of the book, but in addition to the Giorgio Tourn book mentioned above and another of his works, *You are my Witnesses*, I have often relied on the balanced modern English study of 'faith, intolerance, and survival' in Waldensian history by Prescot Stephens, *The Waldensian Story*. It is not only a history but a critical appreciation of the Waldensians, rich in sympathy and solidarity but free from the hagiographical tendencies of some earlier British work and performing the essential tasks of combining a glorious narrative with the benefits of modern historical research.

I add a note about names of places and people. Some similar problems have come up with other words. I found it impossible to establish a strict rule or even a reasonable consistency about when to use Italian forms and when French ones. Victorian travellers spoke and wrote to the Waldensians in French more often than in Italian. Modern Waldensian historians, without rejecting the French elements in their heritage or the Provençal dialect of the valleys, tend to emphasise the Italian traditions in their history as well as their modern commitment to the whole of Italy, from Trapani to Trieste.

I have generally followed my sources but sometimes have altered their forms, usually when they seemed at odds with the usage familiar to English-speakers or the context in which I was writing. For example I refer to Turin and not Torino but have changed some, though not all, Victorian references to La Tour to Torre Pellice. I have tried to use the forms of Christian names and surnames which the people mentioned probably used themselves. Sometimes, however,

5

they used both Italian and French forms. The difficulty arises from both the geography and the history of the Waldensians (or Valdesi, Vaudois, or Waldenses). Their old heartland is just inside the Italian frontier with France and for much of their history French was the language of their written culture and their worship.

Something similar is true of my references to British, English, Scots, and Irish, where I have my own feelings and know the nuances. Where the nations of the British Isles made distinctive or separate contributions to the evangelical cause in Italy I use the terms that differentiate. Where they had shared opinions and acted in common I generally refer to British attitudes, which often included Protestant Irish ones. If Wales is unmentioned it is because, in the conditions of the times I mainly describe, Welsh talents were directed through English channels.

I also ask forgiveness for the errors of fact which will certainly have crept into my treatment of so far-ranging a subject, as well as for any unease caused by frank expressions of opinion. Many things said in days past by Scottish and English Protestants, and by Italian ones, use words and tones that seem inappropriate today, given the changes of the last half century in the demeanour and some of the practices of the Roman Church, and the hope of further changes. I have tried to strike a mood appropriate for our own times, taking account not only of the situation in the English-speaking world but that of Italian Protestants. But I have no wish either to disown or decry the past, for often that would be to deny the truth, and I have a firm conviction that true ecumenism demands recognition of the insights of the Waldensians and the Reformation as well as of that true catholicity which Protestants sought to reform and never lost.

I rephrase the end of that sentence, to make it positive and not defensive. These insights are a vital part of that true catholicity which reformed Christianity, for all its mistakes and internal disagreements, has always expressed and affirmed, and which the whole universal or catholic Church requires, even though its future people may come to them from different traditions and by various routes. They are about the authority of tradition only under Scripture, the sole and unique mediation of Christ, the free exercise of Christian intellect and power of reason, the conciliar nature of proper Church government, the avoidance of clericalism, and the affirmation of both priesthood and ministry for all the people of God. None of our traditions has been perfect in these things, but the Waldensians have done as well as any and better than most.

Chapter 1

WHO ARE THE WALDENSIANS?

'They do not match the stereotypes of Italy....'

This is the story of mutually rewarding encounters between British enthusiasts and a small but very determined Italian minority, the Waldensians. It also links these encounters and that minority to questions which do not belong to a by-way of history but to the present needs and future condition both of a more united Europe and the universal Christian Church.

There are other mountain communities in Italy and other tenacious minorities, such as the valley people of Aosta and those admirable but involuntary and reluctant Italian citizens, the German-speaking South Tyrolese of the 'Alto Adige'. There are also signs, since the end of the post-war confrontation of ruling Christian Democrats and Communists in opposition, that Italian political and cultural trends may stimulate regional self-assertion from Sicily to Friuli. *Devoluzione* has become a familiar word in the political vocabulary of modern Italian. There has even been a protest movement claiming to speak for Northern Italy as a whole, adding colour and more confusion to the often perplexing politics of the modern Italians. But the Waldensians are, in several ways, unlike other Italians, and have been so for centuries.

They do not match the stereotypes of Italy which once suited travel-writers and visiting painters, were later adopted by Hollywood, and now provide staple fare for TV advertisements for pasta, pizza, olive oil, and sauce. The climate of their old heartland is not always gentle and their history has not been the natural source of the superficially sunny disposition associated with Naples or even Rome. Life has been no *dolce vita* for them. They are a serious people, but a reasonable one who, unlike so many Italians, were not drawn to the passionate illusions of Fascism or the Communist dogmatism which made false gods of Lenin and Stalin. They are a religious people, but not in that once-popular Italian style which blends fervent devotion, pagan survivals, and an infusion of superstition. Theirs is not the religious culture which is still eager to venerate and see canonised such very different Italian priests as the mystic Padre Pio and the authoritarian Pio Nono, Pope Pius IX. Their Waldensian biblically-based religious culture has no place for the Neapolitan liquefaction of the

7

'blood' of Saint Januarius, or (though it is near the Waldensian valleys) for the cult of the Turin Shroud and similar veneration of dubious relics. Their idea of the house of God is very different from the Holy House of Loreto, allegedly Mary's house at the time of the Annunciation but miraculously transported to Ancona in 1295. Their idea of the household of faith differs from that of the Vatican, and their recognition of Mary's role as blessed among women is a biblical one very different from the goddess-cult which Roman Catholicism and Italian popular culture often integrate with the Christian doctrines of the Trinity and the unique mediation of Christ. The Waldensians are Protestants, in the common usage of the term, but their Church was reformed long before the Reformation.

'The peculiarity of the Vaudois', wrote the notable nineteenth-century Irish-born Methodist organiser of missions William Arthur, later president of the Wesleyan Methodist Conference, 'is that they cannot properly be called Protestants'. Like many British enthusiasts of the time he saw them as a pure survival of the early Church, holding the forms and doctrines handed down from the earliest Christian times. His argument is overstated but enlightening.

The Italian Waldensians are a small minority, not just in Italy but in their original Piedmont, now best known in Britain for Fiat cars and Turin football. Even the few Alpine valleys which were for centuries their homeland have lost some of their distinctive character as farms have become uneconomic and local industries, which once included textile mills as well as quarries, have decayed. Look in the estate agents' windows of Torre Pellice, still a kind of Waldensian 'capital', and you will see upland properties which have been nicely gentrified or which are available for restoration or reconstruction. The prices seem very reasonable compared with similar places within reach of English or Scottish cities. Many ambitious and able local people have moved out, and prosperous Piedmontese lowlanders have moved into second homes or retirement retreats. It is even possible for rich Turinese who can organise their own time and business to make their main homes in the pleasant lower reaches of the valleys, just an hour away from Turin by road for those who can avoid rush-hours. As it is only thirty-five miles or so many Italian drivers probably reckon to do it in much less.

Get out of the busy centre of Turin on to the road along the River Po. It becomes a sort of inner ring road, but look for the westward exits from the city. Drive past the palatial hunting lodge of Stupinigi that once belonged to the House of Savoy and is now run as a museum by the Mauritian order. There is no need to watch out for the Alps. They are apparent soon enough, but take care to get off the main road when the signs for the Val Pellice appear or you may find yourself well on the way to France. If you are coming by rail, travel via Pinerolo, where there was once a notorious 'refuge' dedicated to catching

Waldensian children young and turning them into good Catholics.

Go on through Luserna San Giovanni, the first place in the country of the Valdesi or Waldensians, and long referred to by themselves and their visitors as St Jean. Continue over the bridge across the Angrogna river and you are in Torre Pellice, previously called La Tour, though the first building to strike you there is the Roman Catholic church, deliberately assertive in style. It was built with royal patronage when Piedmontese reactionaries and liberals like the anglophile Count Cavour were still wrangling over whether Protestants should have civil rights. Then, just as you think you are leaving the little town, you are in an enclave unlike anything else in Italy, with streets named after Protestant heroes and an assorted group of Protestant buildings - church, school, cultural centre and museum, guest house, even an elegant terrace that looks like an oddly coloured variation on a Brighton theme and testifies to the association at the crucial stage in their history between the Waldensians and English evangelicals. But you will also raise your eyes to the hills, unless the clouds have come down low or a mountain mist is lingering. These hills have sometimes been a refuge, sometimes a setting for guerrilla war.

Ahead of you then lies the Val Pellice, once known as the Val Luserna, which stretches past the large villages of Villar and Bobbio to the crest of the mountains and the French frontier. Over the shoulder of the hill to the north lies the Angrogna valley, heartland of much Waldensian history. It is a valley of venerated sites and sacred groves. Its stream flows into the main river just below Torre. Across the hills to the South lies the side valley with a winding road leading up to the hill village of Rorà, but this is accessible only by turning back towards Luserna San Giovanni. To reach the other main Waldensian valley, however, you have to go even further back, almost to the big town of Pinerolo, then branch off on the road leading north-west along the Perosa or Chisone valley which after a while splits into the Pragelato valley and the largely Waldensian San Martino or Germanasca valley which winds towards the French frontier The profusion of names and the mountain geography can both be confusing, as is the discovery that although Torre Pellice is a kind of community capital it does not have a central position.

This area, the historic country of the Waldensians, was once a kind of tribal reservation for Protestants. It was often referred to as their ghetto, for they were largely confined to these few poor Alpine valleys. They were forbidden to worship together outside these boundaries, which were drawn to make life difficult for them, limit their opportunities, and make it easier to control and overawe them, both militarily and spiritually. They were also banned from land ownership elsewhere and from commercial and professional advancement.

When British visitors first got to know this ghetto well at the start of the nineteenth century it had about 25,000 people, 20,000 of them Protestants. Today's population is a bit larger, though more concentrated in the lower reaches, and the Protestant proportion much smaller, for only about a half of to-day's Italian Waldensians live there. The calculation of Waldensian numbers varies because some statistics are uncertain and others depend on whether they include not only those Waldensians scattered across the rest of Italy but their South American settlements in Uruguay and Argentina, where there are about 20,000.

But what makes the Italian Waldensians so distinctive is not their ancestral territory but their religion. They were ahead of the Reformation from which the term 'Protestant' emerged. They are also Protestants in what is one of the world's most Roman Catholic countries, not just in the statistics of real or nominal church adherence but in the way that so much in Italian life, art, and history reflects the heritage, style, and patronage of Catholicism. There has been a Polish Pope, now there is a Bavarian German one, perhaps some day there will be an African or Latin-American one, but the concept of a Roman Catholic Church - or, as its adherents would put it, that the truly universal Church must reflect a divine authority devolved on the bishopric of Rome - inevitably creates a special relationship between Italy and Catholicism.

After a century and a half of a united Italian State, the most distinctive and significant Italian-based institution is still the one from which the Waldensians have opted out and which is not under the control of the Italian Government. Even in the days when the Austrian Chancellor Metternich regarded Italy as a 'geographical expression', the papacy was an important aspect of it.

Yet in other ways the Waldensians have opted into Italy and Italian culture, Unlike the South Tyrolese they are voluntary Italians, deliberately loosening at a crucial stage in their history their historic links with a French cultural inheritance. They continued to speak among themselves in the valleys a dialect which (so they tell visitors with some emphasis) is much more Provençal than Piedmontese, but they adopted Italian as the first language of Church as well as State. Long before its influence in the valleys was increased by the effects of television, sports journalism, and migration to and from the cities, they had also adopted it as the language of evangelisation and mission.

At first sight that evangelisation has not made any spectacular impact on the rest of Italy. The clearly identifiable Waldensian population, even counting the smaller Methodist Church which is now united with them, has no more than 30,000 members and adherents. In the whole of Italy there are only about 21,000 full communicant members. That is a tiny proportion of an Italian population of about 60 million and leaves them very much a minority even among Italian Protestants, whose federation also includes a Baptist Church scattered across Italy. But many Italian Protestants belong to Pentecostal, Brethren, or other evangelical groups outside the Federation and their numbers are hard to calculate. I have heard it said that 'the Pentecostals open three new churches a month but close two old ones'.

Total Protestant numbers are also hard to estimate. Some estimates go beyond 600,000, though even that is not much more than one per cent of the population. The English historian of the Waldensians, Prescot Stephens, says 300,000. The Waldensian theologian and historian Giorgio Bouchard gives the same figure as 'a prudent estimate', to which must be added African and other immigrants, and resident foreigners, but has only 12 per cent of this Protestant total attached to the Waldensian-Methodist Church.

There is also the phenomenon described in 1972 by Sabino Acquaviva, then professor of sociology at Padua University. After describing the current development of Italian Protestantism as confined almost exclusively to the poor areas of the South, but yielding no reliable statistics, he described what he called a 'practised' Protestantism in the North. It was 'followed by many who formally declare themselves Catholics but in practice reject the Church's rules and regulations. They have recourse to Catholicism only on major occasions such as marriage, and mainly as a tribute to custom'. In another country, he suggested, these people would probably adhere 'at least in part' to a Protestant Church. There was also the tendency, exemplified at about the same time by Ignazio Silone, a notable writer who had found the way back from Marxism, to seek 'a Christianity without churches'. More than 20 years later the Australian analyst of the Mafia, Peter Robb, found that a reforming mayor of Palermo, Leoluca Orlando, described himself in *Midnight in Sicily* as 'a Catholic Lutheran or a Lutheran Catholic' and lamented: 'We had the Counter-Reformation in the South without having had the Reformation'.

One verifiable fact is that when Italians have an opportunity to earmark a small proportion of tax to Church and charitable causes - *otto per mille* or 0.8 per cent of personal taxes - the figure for well-wishers runs much higher, as do calculations in neighbouring France for 'cultural' Protestants and sympathisers, far more numerous than active church members and adherents. However this Italian situation expresses sympathy with good works and causes and, perhaps much less than in France, a real but ill-defined religious adherence or residue of historical tradition, although there are people outside any Church who may claim to be ethnic Valdesi. The Waldensians recognise this in earmarking these funds from more than 200,000 well-wishers, with many nominal or anti-clerical Catholics and unbelievers among the contributors, only for social work.

That is a reminder that this small Reformed Christian minority of Italians has a contemporary as well as a historical importance. It continues to have a significance far beyond its numbers in Christendom, in Protestantism, and in Italy. As later parts of this book will make clear, it often seems a miracle that the Waldensians have survived at all, given the pressures on them and the persecution which they endured for much of their history. They have been great survivors; but (as they themselves are the first to recognise) survival is not enough.

They have, however, survived to be the most significant Christian presence in Italian life and history outside the Roman Catholic Church, more securely established and deeply rooted than other evangelical movements there. They are also witnesses to the truth that authority, tradition, order, and apostolic succession in the Christian Church need not take the forms prescribed and circumscribed by the Roman Church.

'Who are the Waldensians?' A simple answer might be: they are the most significant Italian Protestant tradition. But that risks over-simplification. You cannot be a Protestant without being a Christian, which implies belonging, however the term is interpreted, to the universal or catholic Church. Neither Luther nor Calvin, nor Cranmer in England nor Knox in Scotland, founded a new Church. In different ways they sought to set out principles on which the universal Church should be reformed and they tried to introduce reforms which were sound and practicable in the particular parts of the Church where they had influence. The mood and politics of their times encouraged them to seek these reforms within nation-states or smaller political units, preferably with the support of the powers that be, or what the Calvinist Confession in English calls 'the civil magistrate'.

The Waldensian experience was very different, for they practised a reformed Christian religion long before the era and circumstances we sum up as 'the Reformation'. Their gentle light was already shining before the darkness was lit up by Luther's fireworks and the brightness of Calvin's intellect. They had been persecuted long before the Czech reformer, Jan Hus, was martyred after being lured under promise of safe-conduct to the Council of Constance. They existed long before John Wycliffe survived under the shelter of powerful patronage. Perhaps even more than the scholarly Wycliffe they deserved his title, 'the morning star of the Reformation'. But the Waldensians were not created by the Reformation. They adhered to it. They opted into it, as more than three centuries later they opted for Italy and Italian culture. At the Reformation they had more than three centuries of history and persecution behind them.

Sometimes they claimed an even longer history, for example when Rodolphe Peyran, Moderator in the early nineteenth century, met the newly-styled Emperor Napoleon, then passing through Turin on his inaugural progress as 'King of Italy'.

'How long have you been an independent Church?', Napoleon asked, and got the reply: 'From the time of Claudio, bishop of Turin around 820'. The Spanish-born Claudio had been an independent-minded bishop who resisted pressures from Charlemagne and, among other matters, opposed the veneration of images, the purported intercession of saints, and the authoritarianism of the Papacy. We shall see that the Waldensians and their friends, especially their Anglican ones, were sometimes inclined to interpret history to strengthen their sense of apostolic continuity. In the 1870's Claudio was being described as 'himself almost a Protestant' in Waldensian support literature circulating in Britain.

But certainly, at the Reformation they found a place for themselves again in the structures of the Church - or at least of that part of it whose reforms they found, if not perfected, at least acceptable in good conscience. But it was to remain a precarious place, exposing them to long travail and fresh persecution.

Hus was burned in 1415. The reforming puritan friar Giacomo Savonarola, a victim of Florentine politics as well as papal excommunication, was executed in 1498. Martin Luther nailed his theses to the church door in Wittenberg, where there had once been a Waldensian presence, in 1517. Calvin first came to Geneva in 1536. But the man after whom the Waldensians were almost certainly named, Valdo or Valdes of Lyons lived around 1140-1217, though it may be argued that his ideas carried on earlier aspirations for the reform of the Church and rediscovery of a purer and more apostolic Christianity.

Valdo, later often called Peter Valdes, was a contemporary of Dante Alighieri, the greatest Italian poet, and of Francesco Bernardone, better known as Saint Francis of Assisi, the most widely popular of Italian saints in the rest of the world. In France work went on all through Valdes's lifetime on the new cathedral of Notre Dame de Paris. English and Scottish readers may find it easiest to fit him into his time if we think of him as a contemporary of Richard the Lionheart and of the reputed exploits of Robin Hood, but more than a century before the Battle of Bannockburn.

Valdes (or Valdo, or Waldo) was not an Italian but what we would call a Frenchman, though we should beware of applying the national labels of later times too freely when thinking of the Middle Ages. In the twelfth century France was not yet a well-defined political concept, far less a nation in the modern sense.

Much about the life of Valdes is still obscure - even the name Peter has been seriously questioned - but he was certainly a merchant of Lyons, generally thought of as the second city of France but not in his day yet under the rule of the French Crown. It had been Burgundian and then became a kind of city-state ruled by archbishops, nominally part of the Holy Roman Empire. He lived at a time when Latin remained the principal language of Church and State and he would have some knowledge of it. His native language was probably a Southern variety of French. Lyons was near the linguistic borderline between the group of dialects which evolved into modern French and those of the *langue d'oc* or Occitan. But, living at a cross-roads of commerce, he would be able to communicate with people speaking a variety of Latin-based languages, ranging from the French of Paris, through Provençal, to the dialects of Northern Italy and even the Tuscan Italian which Dante, Petrarch, and Boccaccio used and which became the basis of the national language of Italy, the tongue of which Byron wrote, in a poetic flight of fancy:

> I love the language, that soft bastard Latin,
> Which melts like kisses from a female mouth,
> And sounds as if it should be writ on satin,
> With syllables which breathe of the sweet South.

But Italy remains a land of dialects, as anyone knows who has tried to relate dialogue and English sub-titles in some film set in the back streets of Naples or the Sicilian countryside. In any event, even international linguistic lines were not sharply drawn in these days when Latin provided the language for record and formalities. In the sixteenth century, when the younger Latin-derived languages were taking over, the great French essayist Michel de Montaigne found communication easy in Turin and Piedmont. French was widely spoken and popular, and, he said, 'the vulgar (or common) tongue here has almost nothing of Italian except the pronunciation and is basically composed only of our own words'.

Around 1173 Valdes of Lyons, who was what the Bible calls a man 'of great possessions', sold or gave away his property for the benefit of the poor. There is no authentic account of his origins or education, if any, but he and his wife lived in a district of rich merchants. He owned houses, mills, vineyards, and ovens. He may have dealt in cloth and he may have lent out money, though medieval accusations of usury, especially against 'heretics', need to be received with reserve. But Valdes had a spiritual experience and felt called to a new way of life to find and share salvation. He took a vow of poverty, became an itinerant preacher - perhaps a medieval John Wesley - and attracted like-minded associates and a wider following, of women as well as men. They may have been in contact with the ideas of such earlier 'heretics' as Arnold of Brescia, executed in 1155 after challenging the Papacy's temporal claims and Peter de Bruys, killed about 1140 by a mob in Languedoc after his quest for salvation by faith led him to challenge popular forms of devotion. But Valdes did not set out to overthrow the Church but to purify it. We may call him the founder of the Waldensian movement but, just as the devotedly Anglican Wesley never wanted to create a new denomination, Valdes did not mean to be a founder of anything but to be an evangelist, reformer, revivalist, and follower of Christ. He did not even oppose the papal power but sought its approval. In 1179 the Pope of the day, Alexander III, who like all Popes was getting conflicting advice and subject to rival pressures, approved of the vow of poverty but prohibited Valdes and his followers, known as 'the poor men of Lyons' from preaching, except at the invitation of the clergy.

By 1184 their critics succeeded in getting them threatened with excommunication, even put in the same heretical category as the Cathars, whose name comes from a Greek word meaning 'pure'. The Cathars are better known as Albigenses, linked with the town of Albi in south-west France, the area of their greatest strength and the one where their ideas were embodied in an institutional alternative Church. It should be added that not all those persecuted as 'Albigenses' were necessarily Cathars - some were 'Vaudois' - also, distinctive Cathar doctrines were found in areas beyond the French Midi, including parts of Italy.

This is not the place to try to do justice to the Cathars or to examine in any detail the unresolved question of their influence on other allegedly heretical groups, including the Waldensians. There have even been suggestions that neo-Cathar traditions had some influence not only in some parts of the Midi's receptivity to Calvinism (although the evidence there is inconclusive) but on the austere strain of Roman Catholicism loosely described as Jansenism.

Some of the Cathar doctrines, as far as we know them with reasonable certainty, are at odds with those common to Protestant, Orthodox, and Roman Catholic Christians. They were not Trinitarians but considered themselves Christians. They had distinctive views of baptism and eucharist, and their faith was steeped in an interpretation of the Gospels, especially Saint John's. Their practice reflected the intense spirituality and devotion of a saintly elect, as well as a readiness for innovation and search for spiritual guidance which have something in common with later Protestantism in its more radical forms. They have found defenders among French Protestants, for example the Huguenot refugee scholar and Waldensian supporter Peter Allix and the nineteenth-century pastor, Napoleon Peyrat, whose passionate attack on the Inquisition was popular not only with Protestants but with secular anti-clericals, especially in South-west France. The Cathars might be roughly classed (in their relation to apostolic Christianity, not in their distinctive doctrines) as medieval equivalents of Mormons or Jehovah's Witnesses. Their doctrines appear to have contained elements akin to Manichaeism, with its notion of permanent conflict between powers of light and darkness ('cosmological dualism') and of Gnosticism, with ideas of secret knowledge of salvation shared by the elect and of the evil of material things. The Cathars certainly lacked much orthodox Christian doctrine but their faith or heresy still belongs to the Christian tradition and their lives showed many Christian virtues. They come into the Waldensian story, however, for three reasons.

The first is that they flourished in an area which had an Occitan language and some cultural identity, with affinities among peoples from Catalonia to Northern Italy. Modern French writing about the Cathars seems to emphasise the role of religious persecution in the decline and even the destruction of this culture. It would be misleading to call this an expression of Occitan nationalism, and France has no equivalent of Catalonia in Spanish life and politics, but it is a reflection of a contemporary French reaction against over-centralisation. It also shows the people of the Midi having a good and eloquent conceit of themselves, perhaps a little tired of the idea that all the greatness of France radiates from Paris and its surrounding provinces. There may also have been a greater intellectual and theological restiveness in this area than elsewhere in Europe at the time of the Cathars, with very different 'heresies' developing in this intellectual climate among peoples with significant commercial and cultural contacts. .

The second reason is that the Cathars, like the early Waldensians, demonstrate that, quite apart from any regional cultural factors, there was considerable intellectual and spiritual speculation and questioning behind the monolithic facade of the medieval Church. It would be foolish to say that Albigensians and Waldensians can never have been in contact or that all those who had some sympathy with these protest movements were clear about the difference between them, though others may have taken part in 'dialogues' to bring out their differences. Ideas circulated around the busy trade routes linking France, Italy, and Germany and even penetrated the Slav world in Bohemia. As Stephen Neill wrote in the World Council of Churches' history of the ecumenical movement, first published in 1954: 'Those who speak warmly of the unity of Western Christendom before the Reformation sometimes forget that the price for this coercive unity was paid in a gigantic movement of dissidence from the formally established Church. Much research will yet be needed before the full history of heresy in the West can be written.' That remains true in the twenty-first century.

The third reason for linking the different Cathar and Waldensian movements is that the power of the Church was mobilised against both of them at the same time and almost in the same breath, especially under the ironically titled Pope Innocent III, (Lotario dei Conti di Segni) whose empire-building in temporal as well as spiritual affairs has made historians sum up his reign (1198-1216) as 'the climax of the medieval Papacy'. Some of those critical of the way the Church was ordered may have been confused about the difference between Cathar doctrines and Valdes's example and ideas, but their persecutors encouraged and perhaps sometimes created the confusion.

The Albigensians were the more obvious target. They seemed more powerful but were easier to attack. They had territories to be subjugated, secular allies or fellow-travellers to be destroyed and despoiled, a structure to be wrecked, and large numbers of adherents to be persecuted or driven to recant if they survived the slaughter of the 'crusade' against them. Many of the more courageous or determined of them were burned or hanged. Much of what we know about them comes from the confessions forced out of the survivors, many of whom either minimised their own role or the distinctiveness of the doctrines to which they had adhered. As with the medieval Waldensians, many of whom were also martyred, much of what we know of them comes from the hostile histories and commentaries of those who sought to suppress them, and from records that demand the same scepticism as verbatim reports of show-trials under Stalin.

The Waldensians were less obviously vulnerable than the Albigenses. They did not have allies with fortresses to be besieged and such a formal 'alternative Church' structure to be destroyed. They did have elements of organisation and even synods in different countries, but they were perhaps more a network of communities, ideas, contacts, and influences. By the beginning of the fourteenth century, however, there were not only travelling Waldensian preachers or *barba* (literally 'uncles') but a system for training them.

Hardy modern visitors to the Alps scramble up a steep, rough path in the Angrogna valley to reach what from a distance looks like a decrepit steading. There they are assured, with a twinkle in the local eyes, that this is 'the oldest Protestant theological faculty in the world'. What it taught certainly had affinities with the patterns of reform which were codified later. It emphasised a personal response to the Gospel and the importance of preaching. It recognised the fallibility of Church decrees and therefore of the Papacy. It insisted, as Luther was to do later after his own voyage of spiritual discovery, that conscience is captive to the Word of God. It rejected the Church's claims to temporal authority and its spectacular accumulation and consumption of wealth. It sought a Christian ministry based on holy living with Bible teaching and not sacerdotal powers. No doubt it had also an asceticism which much of later Protestantism lacked, and may have had styles that might now be labelled Pentecostal. It meditated on the Second Coming and the creation of God's kingdom. It was visionary, perhaps both literally and metaphorically, but it also reflected impulses for social reform. Such impulses ran through medieval history (read, for example, the English Piers Plowman) and were liable to be diverted or perverted into revolutionary violence, as in the German peasant revolt which so alarmed Luther and left him sorely troubled and disturbed. However the *barba* were people of many talents. They preached, taught and, sometimes healed, both with medicine and spiritual help. Although originally they were often peasants or shepherds, they acquired trades, as a cover and a means of support. Saint Paul was not the last tent-making missionary.

Recent scholars have traced affinities between the Waldensians, who were found in Italy, Germany, and even Spain as well as France, and such apparently national movements as the English Lollards, the Hussites, and the Czech Brethren. And while some of these ideas were undoubtedly 'heretical' in the eyes of the medieval Church, other themes were within the limits of its notions of Christian freedom. As the survival in England of John Wycliffe, sometime Master of Balliol, was to show, the frontier between alleged heresy and permitted revivalism or intellectual speculation could be an ill-defined and debatable one. A lot depended on who you were, and where and when, as well as what powerful friends or venomous enemies you had. Moreover many Waldensians insisted that they rejected only those practices and doctrines of the Church which were clearly inconsistent with Scripture. They may have attended Mass and sought safety in telling inquisitors and perhaps each other that their gatherings were those of permissible private religious societies.

The Waldensian influence was widespread, but so was the persecution. What they claimed was permissible was soon not permitted. This persecution, often carried to martyrdom, was fairly effective in the centres of trade and learning, though dissent and intellectual curiosity eventually took new forms. But here and there whole communities had been touched by the new teaching and new directions of devotion. One was in Calabria, another in Apulia in the far south of Italy. These survived a couple of centuries until they succumbed. The Calabrian 'heretics' were largely wiped out by massacre and deportation. Their survivors reluctantly conformed, like the Apulian community, or became refugees, though there are claims that traces of their speech survive in local dialects. Not until recent times was a small Waldensian presence restored in these provinces of Southern Italy. Other communities were in Alpine valleys of Dauphiné, Savoy, and Piedmont, on both sides of what later became the frontier between France and Italy. Medieval life was hard in the mountains, but sometimes it was safer.

There were still large Waldensian communities in the mountains there and smaller groups in northern Italian cities when the name of Martin Luther was heard in the land. Good news came through of the turbulence that spread from the Church in Germany into France and across the Alps, and most particularly of the reforming of the Church in various parts of what we now call Switzerland. First came this encouraging and dramatic news. Then came the formal contacts, accompanied by much heart-searching and debate, and finally the acceptance of Reformed Church doctrine and order, including a settled ministry with the freedom to marry. This last point seems to have posed difficulties for some of the older *barba*, set in their celibate ways, but it was one fairly easily resolved (as it can be today) by reference to the Bible and the customs of the first-century Christians, as well as the need to tackle the abuses that compulsory celibacy imposed on the wider Church.

This Waldensian acceptance of the Reformation and reconciliation with the institutional Church in the Protestant style is traditionally associated with a site at Chanforan in the Angrogna valley, over the hill from Torre Pellice. A pillar of stone, a simple but noble monument, marks the reputed place of this general assembly. The detail has been argued over by modern historians - but the evidence for a decision, probably with some hesitation, reservation, and minority dissent, is clear enough. So too is the association of this act of decision or ratification with the Angrogna Valley in 1532, in the presence of 'all the ministers and also of the people'. They had accepted a place in the Reformed family and can henceforth be called 'Protestants', though that word did not emerge in Germany until after 1529 and would not be used in the valleys until rather later. It is of course a name which does not merely or mainly mean to raise an objection., though that has often to be done, but to take a stand for truth and to bear witness to it.

The most powerful persuader of the Waldensians had been Guillaume Farel, best known for his role in the Swiss Reformation at Geneva and Neuchatel but originally from Gap in the French Alps of Dauphiné, a province where there was a 'Vaudois' tradition that made its contribution to French Protestantism. Powerful persuasion was clearly one of Farel's talents, for Calvin, whom he later earmarked for the chief ministry in Geneva, testified that it was not so much exhortation as the creation of a feeling as if 'God himself from on high had stretched out his hand to hold me there.'

At least part of the debate among the Waldensians had been conducted in Italian, for some of those involved were from Lombardy and even Calabria. There is also evidence that they consulted with the Czech Brethren. But one result of the Reformation settlement was to be the pre-eminence for more than three centuries of French in the worship and written proceedings of the Waldensians, although the political attachment of the main part of the Waldensian valleys to the French Crown was very brief (1536-59), and despite some preaching in Italian in Reformation times and into the seventeenth century. There was nothing of modern national feeling in this situation any more than there was any rejection of nationality in the Scots decision a generation later to use the Bible in English as the basis of Reformed worship, preaching, and teaching. The reason and reasoning was the same. A Reformed Church based itself on Scripture and put the Bible into the hands of the people. It had to be the best translation of the Bible available in a speech which they could understand: English used in a very Scots style, French in the accents of the Alps. There had been some earlier Waldensian rendering of the Bible (from the Latin Vulgate version) into the Occitan language of the Alpine valleys but it would not have been easy in the sixteenth century to deploy the scholarship and authoritative literary skills needed to sustain the Bible's necessary place in the newly reformed Church. Even as late as the early twentieth century there were reckoned to be 15 varieties of patois in the valleys. Instead of insisting on a new Reformation translation of their own, the Waldensians, like their Occitan-speaking French neighbours, shared possession of the French translation by Pierre Robert Olivetan, whose cousin Jean had supplied a Latin introduction to the 1535 edition and revised the text after Olivetan's death. We know this Jean Cauvin as John Calvin. The translation developed into the French 'Geneva Bible', the approximate French equivalent of the Authorised Version or King James Bible in the English-speaking world and Luther's translation in Germany, though the chronological equivalent is the English Geneva Bible. In the preface to the first edition, written in the Alps and possibly in the Angrogna valley, Olivetan had dedicated his work to the Waldensians, who put up all or some of the money to finance the project.

An unknown hand added a postscript to Olivetan's work, testifying to the Waldensian (or 'Vaudois') role in publishing this treasure:

> *Les Vaudois, peuple évangelique,*
> *Ont mis ce trésor en publique.*

But enough of history for the moment, though there is more to come. One of the criticisms of the Waldensians - which a friendly outsider can repeat, because he knows it has also been a theme of self-criticism - is that 'they live too much on their past history'. I pick the phrase from an analysis of the nineteenth-century Italian situation given by a Bible Society agent in Rome to Jacob Primmer, the celebrated Scots Victorian Protestant propagandist. Similar words had been heard before, often discreetly muffled in flattery, and are still heard.

The Victorian woman novelist George Eliot (Mary Ann Cross) said that 'the happiest women, like the happiest nations, have no history'. The Waldensians might wish that they had been allowed some of that happiness. The trouble is that they have such a lot of history, most of it a fight to survive as well as a proclamation of faith. You cannot understand who they are without their history, including the part of their history - one of their happier interludes - when they were most closely associated with the British evangelical revival.

Chapter 2

THE GLORIOUS RETURN

'One of the defining seasons in Waldensian history'

This author does not claim sufficient specialist expertise to pronounce with any authority on the many uncertainties and disputed circumstances in Waldensian history. They have proved a rich field for research, scholarship, and argument. However some more history is unavoidable, and also an encounter with one of the defining seasons of Waldensian history, 'The Glorious Return'.

The story is told (or soon will be, for I have just thought of it) of the Waldensian visitor to Belfast's Shankill Road who admired the local murals invoking the memory of 1690 and all that. 'But you're a year out', he said.

The return that is so well remembered and seemed so glorious was in 1689, a year before the Irish battle in the same European conflict, when the Waldensians contrived a successful fighting reappearance in their native valleys where a long time of persecution had culminated in slaughter and expulsion. The event made an emotional and historical impact on their community which survives today. To try to understand this one might think of the emotional scars left in parts of Scotland by the Clearances, of the Orange Irish enthusiasm for the deliverance of the Boyne, of the rebel Irish songs for the men of 1798, of the old Lowland Scots veneration of the memory of the Covenanters, of the American tales of Washington at Valley Forge, and - the closest case - the French Protestant folk-memory of the last stand of the Huguenots in the Cévennes, when peasants fought on after the Protestant middle classes and intelligentsia had sadly submitted or fled abroad. Mix these memories, distil the purest spirit from them, and you have something of the flavour of The Glorious Return, as it seems to the Waldensians.

Near the head of the Val Pellice my colleagues on a trip induced me to climb up the hill above Bobbio, last big village before France, to find one of the monuments commemorating 1689, the Sibaud obelisk. They either didn't know or didn't let on how high up the hillside it was. It seemed a long way up but it was worth it. One of our next engagements was a visit to a Waldensian-run old people's home down the valley in Villar. We did our best to make conversation with the Protestant residents, who had been occupying the sitting-room for their weekly service while the Catholics relaxed elsewhere. Conversation did not come too easily, for most of us had limited fluency in French and less in Italian, while the locals didn't have English. But I managed to tell two old ladies that we were just back from an exhausting climb to the Sibaud monument. At that they burst brightly into song in praise of the Glorious Return. It was not just a first few lines and then a faltering la-la-la but the complete piece, with style and flourish. Consider the improbable prospect in a Scottish Kirk eventide home these days of being welcomed by a musical denunciation of Bloody Claverhouse and it is easier to grasp the continuing power of history in the Waldensian community.

This is not the place to tell the story of all that led up to the events of 1689, far less to disentangle the ways in which religious belief, power politics, and shifting alliances were fankled together. Also, these Alpine frontier regions had some of the turbulence that once marked the Scottish Highlands and even the Anglo-Scottish borderland. The Waldensians did not find that accepting the Reformation brought peace and security and no doubt some of them made their own contribution to turbulence and insecurity. A number of them certainly shared the aversion to customs and excise duties which was long evident, without distinction of nationality or creed, on France's Alpine and Pyrenean frontiers.

But the whole Waldensian community suffered much for the sake of conscience. It had endured many troubles before the cruel and shattering blow came in 1685. Then Catholic Savoy, at that time in alliance with Louis XIV of France, agreed to apply in Piedmont the same policy which devastated the French Huguenots, drove so many of them into exile, and had already harried the Waldensians of the Val Pragelato and Pinerolo, at that time part of France.

This may be the point at which to slip in a note about the names of States and provinces. To-day's Savoy is part of France, but the possessions of the Dukes of Savoy included much else, including the Italian lowlands and frontier Alps of Piedmont, where they made Turin their capital. Dauphiné (to which Pinerolo was temporarily attached) is on the French side of the Alps. But the House of Savoy eventually took the regal title which went with the island of Sardinia, not acquired till 1718. Although ruling from Turin they were kings of Sardinia until in the nineteenth century they gained the throne of the newly united kingdom of Italy, holding it till Italy became a Republic after the Second World War. It was as Dukes of Savoy that they dealt so harshly with their Waldensian subjects.

Although the initial intellectual impact of the Reformation on the Latin countries had been considerable, the Protestants struggled to survive in face of a reorganised Roman Catholic power in which Church and State were usually allied. Only in some parts of Switzerland and France, and in what was then the city-state of Geneva, did Protestantism hold its own among peoples speaking the 'Romance' languages. Only in areas of the Grisons, the most linguistically mixed part of Switzerland, were 'Romansch' and Italian Protestant communities to survive. And even in France the Reformed faith was eventually forced back on the defensive and gradually worn down until Louis XIV, grandson of the Protestant Bourbon Henry IV who decided that 'Paris was worth a Mass', felt strong enough to declare it extinct and revoke the Edict of Nantes which secured Protestant rights and worship.

In most of Italy Protestants had much earlier to choose between recantation and exile or worse. There had been considerable initial Italian response, both spiritual and intellectual, to the Reformation beyond the Alps, and to the intellectual ferment in France. In 1536, for example, the young Calvin (at that point a scholar on the run rather than a leading Reformer) was able to linger for a while at Ferrara, whose French-born duchess welcomed dangerous thinkers. He had also stopped off at Aosta. But the main rulers of Italy, unlike many German princes, remained securely allied to the Roman Church, except perhaps in Venice, which tolerated free thought and private Protestantism and even provoked a papal interdict as late as 1606. Throughout Italy the screw was turned on the Protestants - sometimes literally. There were martyrdoms to encourage conformity and even to suppress intellectual speculation which might wander off in a potentially Protestant direction. Galileo survived but the philosopher-scholar Giordano Bruno, an exile who returned home, did not. Nineteenth-century Rome gave him a monument on the Campo dei Fiori, where heretics once suffered. Modern Italian Protestants still remember such Roman martyrs as G.L. Pascale and Aonio Paleario. Waldensians have distinctive heroes to continue their earlier roll of martyrs, such as Giafredo Varaglia, a former Franciscan who became a pastor in the Angrogna and missionary to lowland Piedmont. He was apparently allowed to preach a fifteen-minute sermon on Grace and Love before being burned in the main square of Turin.

Some of the Italian Protestants who were forced into exile made their mark elsewhere, including Pietro Martire Vermigli, brought to England by Thomas Cranmer and remembered, from his time as an Oxford professor and canon of Christ Church, as Peter Martyr - a Florentine who had been prior of Neapolitan and Tuscan monasteries but ended his days as a professor at Strasbourg and then Zurich. Among his friends was Bernardino Ochino, a Siena-born former vicar-general of the Capuchins who is recorded as preaching to Italian congregations in London, Zurich, Augsburg, and Geneva before moving to Cracow and dying in Moravia. Another notable Protestant exile was Alberico Gentili from near Ancona, who became a leading English jurist and held the Oxford chair of civil law.

The Italians in Geneva even had their own version of the famous Genevan Psalter, the inspiration for Scottish metrical psalmody. Although their complete version did not appear till 1603, dedicated to the Italian-speaking Queen Elizabeth of England, a partial version had been printed in 1560 by a Piedmontese refugee who may have had Waldensian connections. He was Jean-Baptiste Pinereul to the French but in his Italian imprint Giovan Battista Pinerolio.

In the seventeenth century Italian-speaking exiles and refugees were still a part of Protestant life. When, for example the Scottish traveller William Lithgow visited Geneva in 1615 and was hospitably entertained by its seven ministers they presented him with 'a Bible newly translated into the Italian tongue by one of themselves'. When the English diarist John Evelyn visited Geneva in 1646 after his long tour of Italian classical antiquities and artistic treasures he had a letter of introduction to the Genevan-born Giovanni Diodati, whose translation of the Bible into Italian had appeared in 1607, was promptly smuggled into Venice by the English Ambassador, Sir Henry Wotton, and reached its definitive edition in 1641. This is the nearest equivalent Italian has to a version matching the literary authority of the 'King James Bible', though modern scholars suggest that its fine Italian was already slightly old-fashioned in its time, thanks to the Diodati family's long exile from Italy.

It was probably Diodati's first Bible with which Lithgow had been 'complimented', although he was not (as the Scot stated of the author) a native of Milan. Evelyn and Diodati had a long talk about the sadness of the English civil war and, if the Cavalier-minded Evelyn is a sound witness, the virtues of episcopacy as a form of Protestant Church government. The interview was not conducted in the most auspicious circumstances, for Evelyn was sickening for smallpox. It was several weeks later that he heard Diodati preach on a Thursday morning in Italian and noted that many of the Genevan Italians, like the great translator, were Tuscans with origins in Lucca, where Peter Martyr had once been prior.

Even the well-connected Evelyn had to watch himself in Italy. He mixed with scholars, churchmen, and English Roman Catholics but as his party approached Milan, then under Spanish control, they remembered that the Inquisition was 'severer here than in all Spain'. Perhaps they had heard of the sad case of John Molle, a nobleman's tutor and captive of the Roman Inquisition who died after 30 years in prison, or the more complicated case in Bologna of Lord Wentworth's tutor, who got out of jail by recantation and joining the Jesuits. Evelyn's party thought of throwing away Protestant books and papers. However the customs men were less doctrinaire: they, 'finding we were only gentlemen travellers, dismissed us for a small reward'. Small rewards from English gentlemen were almost part of the conditions of service in the customs and excise departments of Italian States until the mid-nineteenth century.

Life was not so easy for local dissidents, not just in Milan or Rome but in the valleys and Alps of the Dukes of Savoy. There was guerrilla warfare, sometimes savage, and the defence of one religion and the persecution of another often became tangled in the power politics of Europe. But the Waldensians had in the main group of their valleys a heartland which was easier to defend than to attack and which, even when invaded, was difficult to subdue permanently. A nineteenth-century Scottish visitor, the minister and Free Kirk editor J.A. Wylie, wrote of it:

'Each valley is a fortress, having its own gate of ingress and egress with caves and rocks and mighty chestnut trees, forming places of retreat and shelter so that the highest engineering skill could not have better adapted each several valley to its end. It is not less remarkable that, taking all these valleys together, each is so related to each, and the one opens so into the other, that they may be said to form one fortress of amazing and matchless strength - wholly impregnable in fact.'

God, said one of the Waldensian leaders, Jean Léger, had destined this land 'to be the theatre of his marvels and the bulwark of his ark'.

Wylie and Léger, who devoted his exile in Holland to preparing and publishing a major history of the Waldensians, may have over-stated the case a bit, militarily and theologically, but their analysis helps explain why the Waldensians survived when so much Protestantism in and beyond the Alps was crushed into submission or exile, and why it suited the Dukes of Savoy to allow them a limited and grudging toleration.

The Waldensians' equivalent of the Edict of Nantes, earlier in date and a much more restrictive, provisional, and precarious document, was drafted in Italian, and signed in 1561 at Cavour in Piedmont by the Duke of Savoy's representative and the Waldensian leaders. To the Waldensians it was an agreement, to the ducal government an act of grace and favour by which their subjects were absolved from the consequences of the most recent mountain wars and allowed rights to worship in a limited area, including the Angrogna valley and much of the Luserna one.

The modern Waldensian historian Giorgio Tourn recognises that the Cavour agreement was in some ways a Waldensian acceptance that the high hopes for the evangelisation of Piedmont had to give way to a stubborn insistence on survival. But he has also claimed it as a significant historical statement, recording 'for the first time in European religious history the fact that subjects who practised a religion different from that of the ruling power possessed officially recognised rights', with a Roman Catholic prince tolerating 'heresy' and renouncing its destruction.

Unfortunately the renunciation was neither sustained not wholly sincere. The Cavour agreement was somewhere between a treaty of truce and a point of reference for the future. It was also a tactical move in the frontier politics and conflicts of Savoy and France. But the tension continued. Summarised history might omit even the main episodes in the conflicts of the mid-seventeenth century, which created folk-heroes like Josué Janavel, but for the intervention of one of the great rulers of England, Oliver Cromwell, and the involvement of someone more significant in English literature than even the elegant Mr Evelyn. This was the future author of *Paradise Lost*. John Milton's vast erudition had given him some knowledge of the Waldensians even before the civil war, at a time when Cromwell was still more interested in farming than soldiering. He was also, in the job description of the time, 'Latin secretary' to the Council of State in Cromwell's Protectorate. We might call him a special adviser, political civil servant, or very high-class spin-doctor, though after the early years of the Protectorate he was already affected by oncoming blindness and took a less active part in conducting and defending foreign policy. But in 1655, after a brutal attack on the Waldensians around Torre Pellice by Savoyard troops, he contrived to spin one of the greatest English sonnets, 'On the late massacre in Piedmont'. It can hardly fail to come into anything written since about the British and the Waldensians. I have omitted most of the apostrophes (e.g. scattered and not scatter'd) to make the poem more easily read, but I have kept his style of Piedmont but Piemontese:

> Avenge, O Lord, thy slaughtered saints, whose bones
> Lie scattered on the Alpine mountains cold;
> Even them who kept thy truth so pure of old,
> When all our fathers worshipped stocks and stones,
> Forget not: in thy book record their groans
> Who were thy sheep, and in their ancient fold
> Slain by the bloody Piemontese, that rolled
> Mother and infant down the rocks. Their moans
> The vales redoubled to the hills, and they
> To Heaven. Their martyred blood and ashes sow
> O'er all the Italian fields, where still doth sway
> The triple Tyrant: that from these may grow
> A hundred-fold, who having learned thy way
> Early may fly the Babylonian woe.

The occasion which turned hideous atrocity into an artistic triumph came in the turbulence which followed an attempt to squeeze the Waldensians into their inner valleys, driving them out of farms, property, and even their towns of Torre and San Giovanni. There were gestures of defiance. Someone killed a priest. There was a punitive expedition, in which Piedmontese troops and militia were accompanied by exiled Irish mercenaries. There was pillaging, burning, and killing, some of it said to have been on the Castelluzzo, the prominent height which soars above the far end of Torre Pellice, where the old Protestant church of Coppieri was permitted beyond the town itself. The expedition was strong enough to pursue those who had fled with their families to the higher mountains, where they were already suffering in a cold, late spring.

T.S. Eliot called April 'the cruel month': it was certainly cruel in 1655 in the valleys and their rampart of mountains. This was the time that Waldensians have ever since remembered as 'the Piedmont Easter'.

Cromwell's Government did more than inspire the famous sonnet, though its attempt to mix publicity and diplomacy could be criticised as more spin than substance. It collected money for the Waldensians and exerted what diplomatic pressure it could on their behalf, some of it expressed with great Miltonian eloquence. Its best equipped diplomat, supplied with a script by Milton and well briefed by Huguenot and local sources was Samuel Morland, sent to confront the rulers of Savoy in Turin. He also wrote a history of the Waldensians, invented calculating machines, and suggested the application of steam-power to navigation. One of the less successful diplomats was the devious George Downing, whose name is commemorated in a street off Whitehall where he built some property.

Cromwell's initiative, which tried to exploit the French desire of the time for English good will, won some grudging concessions. It also gave the Waldensians their first British heroes, and is usually regarded as marking the beginning of a special but never exclusive relationship, though the 'Vaudois' had earlier advocates in the British Isles, among them not only Continental refugees but the Irish scholar, Archbishop Ussher of Armagh. It is a relationship which survives to the present day, undamaged by the vicissitudes of politics and diplomacy. It always also had an ecumenical dimension in that it was unconfined and relatively (perhaps one should repeat, relatively!) unaffected by the sometimes vigorous denominational differences among British Protestants and by the Waldensian insistence on their own traditions and independence.

It is also a cause which has, on the British side, overcome the suspicions and rivalries which have sometimes made for uneasy ecclesiastical relations abroad between English and Scots. Among Cromwell's sources, at a time when

Scotland and its Kirk had little reason to love him, was John Durie, son of the Scots minister of the English Reformed church at Leyden in Holland. Durie, who was ordained both by a Dutch Presbytery and in the Church of England, was a pioneer of ecumenism among Protestants and, through his friendly contact with European rabbis, played a part in securing the return of the Jews to England after several centuries of exclusion. In the 1650's he was Cromwell's 'messenger' to the Continent and at one stage even lived in what had once been Calvin's house in Geneva. He was the channel through which Cromwell and Milton learned not only of the massacres of Waldensians but of the threat of total destruction which loomed over them.

But let's move on 30 years or so from Cromwell and Milton. It takes us to a great crisis in the Waldensians' history which coincides with a European crisis, one whose outcome settled the future pattern of European affairs and even the shape of the British constitution.

In 1686 Geneva was even fuller of refugees than it had been in Evelyn's time, many of them Waldensians. The Cromwellian intervention had not led to a real settlement. There was only a limited religious freedom in a very limited area. There continued to be clashes, accusations of banditry, and military repression. The final blow had been a decree from Duke Victor Amadeus of Savoy, under pressure from Louis XIV after complaints that the Waldensians were helping the harassed French Protestants of Dauphiné. No doubt they were. It banned Waldensian worship immediately and forever, on pain or death and confiscation of goods. It revoked ancient privileges, ordered the expulsion of pastors and schoolmasters within 15 days, and announced that all Waldensian churches were to be demolished. Most devastating of all, it declared that their children were to be baptised and educated as Roman Catholics The simple aim of the policy was extermination - if not of all the heretics, at least of their 'heresy'.

The Waldensians resisted and were broken by French and Savoyard troops. There followed in a small area the kind of ethnic cleansing which in more modern times Stalin practised on large scale and which later reappeared in what had been Yugoslavia. Of 14,000 people involved more than half were rounded up and imprisoned. Two thousand had conformed to Catholicism to save their lives and property. About 1500 had been killed in the fighting or put to death afterwards. Another thousand or so of the prisoners submitted in despair and the rest, drastically reduced in number by disease, were allowed to go to Switzerland and Geneva. Most were peasants who had become landless refugees and were often expected - for the Swiss had a dispersal policy for asylum seekers - to settle in German-speaking areas where they felt utterly foreign.

But the peasants had leaders, the most notable of whom was Henri Arnaud, educated as a pastor at Basle and Geneva but also an experienced soldier who had served William of Orange and embodied the Church militant at its most belligerent. He was a French subject, born in Dauphiné of a Huguenot father and Waldensian mother, and is remembered today in Waldensian folklore and commemorated in Torre Pellice by a statue which bristles with defiance. He has also left his name to the street that leads from 'downtown' Torre Pellice to the main group of Waldensian institutions. Under his leadership an expedition, risky to the point of foolhardiness, returned to the valleys, crossing Lake Geneva and achieving a remarkable march across the Alps. It endured great hardship, some internal wrangling, and fierce fighting before achieving a political success rather than military triumph, for the Duke of Savoy changed sides with the fate of the war-torn and depopulated valleys still undecided. At that crucial point Arnaud's Waldensians were there to stake their claim and their community eventually survived the convulsion, partly because Catholic powers had needed Protestant alliances and the House of Savoy had to make grudging concessions. It was, says a modern Waldensian historian, the policy of William III of Great Britain, the Dutch William of Orange, which really allowed the Waldensians to survive. The point was also made with rhetorical splendour by the great English historian of Scots descent, Thomas Macaulay, when he wrote of the Waldensian shepherds being surprised by glad tidings: 'Those simple mountaineers probably never knew that their fate had been a subject of discussion at the Hague and that they owed the happiness of their firesides and the security of their humble temples to the ascendancy which William exercised over the Duke of Savoy.'

In fact the Waldensians, and especially their leaders and contacts in exile, were probably shrewder and better informed than Macaulay allowed. As the grandson of a Scots Highland minister he should not have underestimated 'simple mountaineers', though his view of King William, the hero of his history, is basically sound. However, the mountaineers were also less secure in their firesides, and especially their temples, than he claimed. They were largely confined to the reservation and kept under sustained pressure as well as restrictions. They were allowed and even expected to serve the Dukes of Savoy, soon to be Kings of Sardinia. But they had neither civil rights nor any but a circumscribed and very local religious freedom within Piedmont. They had also to accept the loss of territory and temples (as their churches were called) in one area, the now Piedmontese Pragelato Valley, which they thought their efforts and their alliances had secured for them.

They were a changed community in some ways from that which Cromwell and Milton supported. Many refugees never came back and many like Arnaud (on the grounds that he was French) were not allowed back and had to stay in Swiss or German exile. But some less eminent displaced French subjects may have managed to move in or stay on and some Protestants from elsewhere in Piedmont came to where they could survive. But there was continuity in this survival under pressure. The light still shone, reflecting the Light of the World in Jesus Christ, only Head of the Church. And after the fires of war and persecution the community was not wholly consumed. The biblically based metaphor of the Burning Bush, dear to Huguenots and Scots Presbyterians, had also its power in these Alpine valleys.

The Waldensians were not entirely without moral and practical support. British diplomats in Turin retained links with them, whether in the line of duty or from personal sympathy. The files which were the eighteenth-century equivalent of today's Foreign Office web-sites and Ceefax pages with information for travellers would also record that Protestants unfortunate enough to die in Piedmont could obtain decent and dignified Christian burial in the valleys, along with diplomats who did not survive their Turin posting. As in Spain, heretics were unwelcome in Roman Catholic 'consecrated ground'. There are monuments which still testify to this melancholy connection, most notably in the country church of Ciabas, built in 1555, in the Angrogna valley. Among the mainly British ones is that of Baron Leutrum, a doughty German fighter for the House of Savoy who held out both against his king's enemies and against offers to have him converted on advantageous terms. There were also contacts with the Swiss Churches which made it possible to provide higher education for prospective pastors and there was Dutch help with the Latin or secondary school. Other useful contacts and even means of influence were provided when the House of Savoy continued to hire German Protestants for its army and other service.

In addition there was also some British financial support, distantly derived from Cromwell's special collections, the cause of much wrangling after the Restoration and sometimes alleged to have been diverted to the mistresses of Charles II. A formal 'royal subsidy', paid in 1692 from the purse of Queen Mary, wife of William III and joint sovereign with him, survived into Queen Anne's reign and, after a few years' interval, was resumed under the Hanoverians and paid until Napoleon's Italian campaigns and conquests.

There were also occasional collections and in 1768 a new appeal, launched by the Waldensians by favour of George III, raised enough to create a 'national subsidy', paid through the United Society for the Propagation of the Gospel, to supplement the royal subsidy. The subsidies hardly provided gracious living for the Waldensian pastors, whose stipends at the time seem to have been around £40 a year, but they were a life-line for a small and beleaguered community. They ensured that there was a settled ministry, though its theology and potential for evangelism may have been unsettled, especially in the latter part of the century. This was caused not only by the need to avoid provoking the Piedmontese Government but by the influence of the 'Enlightenment' on Swiss, French, and German Protestants and through them on the pastors who came back to the valleys.

In its milder and sometimes beneficial forms the 'Enlightenment' stimulated Protestant ministers' interest in philosophy, literature, and the natural sciences. It may even have deepened their knowledge of their own and other religions and no Scots Presbyterian, conscious of the best in the Moderate tradition, should disparage it. But some trends in the movement encouraged a cold formalism and ethical discourse rather than preaching of the Word, distrusting enthusiasm and even discouraging personal piety. These trends also encouraged submission to the State, even when it put the Church under pressure. They also sometimes strayed from a Reformed to a Socinian or Unitarian position in the way in which they interpreted and sometimes virtually abandoned the doctrines of the divinity, uniqueness, sacrifice, and lordship of Christ. It has been said that Waldensian pastors of this time tended to preach from Proverbs rather than about Christ's Passion. There is of course no finality in these arguments: some of them are heard in most Protestant Churches today. But they were to unsettle the Waldensians, not only during the French revolutionary years but for decades afterwards. Their difficulties were similar to those experienced in the French Reformed Church and several Swiss Churches, notably in Geneva and Vaud.

In this age of 'Enlightenment' and a cool spiritual temperature the Protestant world was no longer greatly concerned about the Waldensians, but it was not unaware of them. Like the far more numerous French Huguenot emigrants, their exiles in Germany, mainly in Württemberg and Hesse-Darmstadt, tried to retain a sense of identity, though the task became difficult as generations passed away. There was continuing contact with the Swiss and Dutch Reformed Churches. A few foreign visitors to the valleys, as well as diplomats in Turin, learned something of their ways and their plight. Occasionally they even got a favourable mention from freethinking or sceptical Roman Catholics, like the 'prince of infidels', Voltaire, who found it remarkable that this obscure people had 'preserved from time immemorial usages that the rest of the world had altered'. Inevitably however most foreign interest and sympathy came from Protestants.

In 1753, for example, a London publisher brought out an anonymous pamphlet giving 'a brief account of the Vaudois, his Sardinian majesty's

Protestant subjects in the valleys of Piedmont'. It was a mixture of undependable history going back beyond Bishop Claudio, reporting of the state of the valleys, and comment on controversies of the time, including a rebuttal of accusations that Sardinia's Waldensian troops had not fought hard enough in recent wars. The author was 'a gentleman on his travels to Italy' whose name may have been Goldwin, but even this hypothesis depends on a note written on a surviving copy. Like all journalists reporting after fairly brief visits, he got some things wrong, such as his assertion that Italian, the language of the State and of the Counter-Reformation, had to be used in the pulpit. But his reporting ranged from an account of silk-worm cultivation, despite the economic discrimination against Protestants, to an impression of the dialects of the valleys. He said they differed little from Piedmontese, used even in the court, but seemed to regard them as a barbarous patois, claiming that it was difficult to give an impression of them in print because they had unusual sounds which it was difficult to express by letters or combinations of letters in the alphabet.

But relatively few British travellers made a diversion from the Grand Tour to visit the valleys and there was not much business travel there. Not all Grand Tourists visited Turin, which lacked the appeal of Florence, Venice, or Rome. Even the many who did were inclined to be in a hurry, either recovering from an arduous Alpine crossing or brooding over a homeward one. Those for whom Turin was their first great city of Italy were eager to get on to the even greater cities of art and antiquity. In a century which found mountains abhorrent rather than picturesque, and which had not developed the tastes later to be labelled 'romantic', those who had emerged from the Alps were ill-inclined to make a foray back into them. For although the valleys were not far from Turin, they lay off the main access routes to it.

The renewal and strengthening of the British connection lay in the future. It awaited a time when there were more travellers, improved facilities for travel, a more 'romantic' view of rugged mountain landscape and, most important of all, an evangelical revival and a greater readiness to identify with a community despised, rejected, and severely restricted by its temporal rulers in Turin and their Roman Catholic spiritual advisers.

Chapter 3

REPRESSION, REVOLUTION, AND REACTION

When Italy was still a 'geographical expression'

I told an eminent British churchman of the modern ecumenical and liberal Establishment about my enthusiasm for the Waldensians. His reactions seemed to vary from surprise to amusement, though it turned out that he shared my admiration. 'But they're not on your side', he said, meaning that their modern political consensus is probably centre-left, like his, and not any Italian equivalent of traditional British Conservatism. That might have worried me a little if there were such an equivalent. There probably isn't. But in any case such political alignments are on the margins of the faith and not of its substance. They are shaped by context, tradition, and a community's experience as well as by exercise of personal inclination in areas where Christians may legitimately differ.

But my eminent churchman had a point. The Waldensian approach, and probably that of other Italian Protestants, is conditioned by their long history of persecution and by their experience of what has been historically the most conservative force in Italy, the Roman Catholic Church. Often it has also been the most dynamic one, for good and ill. For centuries it tried to destroy the Waldensians. Then it resisted the extension of their limited religious freedom to equal rights under the law.

Even when that battle was lost by the reactionaries and Italy was united, in face of papal resistance, the new State's reluctance to extend its quarrel with the Roman Church while the Pope pretended to be 'a prisoner in the Vatican' meant that religious freedom did not extend to equal opportunity to preach the Gospel and serve the community. Mussolini's Fascist régime consolidated this situation when it reached a concordat with the Papacy and the Vatican enclave was allowed to be a symbolic remnant of the old temporal power. Even after the fall of Fascism and the subsequent fall of the House of Savoy, which broke with Mussolini too late to save itself, the new Italian democracy was dominated by political Catholicism. In the post-war years it may have been the only alternative to a turbulent Communist experiment and it was a marked improvement on what had preceded it, though it eventually became a mere political machine for holding power and sharing out the proceeds. But even in its best years, under Alcide de Gasperi (briefly secretary of the pre-Fascist People's Party), the Italian style of 'Christian Democracy' could hardly appeal to Italian Protestants. Otherwise moderate Waldensians still speak of it with extreme dislike.

I offer that little leap forward into modern history and politics in case readers may share my culture-shock at discovering that the Waldensian interpretation of history tends to approve of the French Revolution, more akin to the first reactions of Robert Burns than the profounder reflections of Edmund Burke or the British folk-myths embodied in Dickens's *Tale of Two Cities*. It even inclines to a mildly favourable view of the Revolution's brilliant but appalling Corsican step-child, Napoleon Bonaparte, whose personal ambitions and taste for war ravaged Europe, caused far more slaughter and misery than the Jacobin Reign of Terror and revolutionary wars, and ensured that the eventual reconstruction of Continental Europe after his defeat was attempted on reactionary principles and not conservative reforming ones.

But it is not hard to see why the Waldensian historical perspectives are so different from the British ones, and even perhaps from those of French Protestants. The Huguenots rejoiced in the liberation of 1789 but soon had mixed feelings about the course of the Revolution. Among the Girondin victims of the guillotine was Rabaut Saint-Etienne, a pasteur from Nimes, the Constituent Assembly's most eloquent advocate of religious equality and the son of the most notable French Protestant leader among the 'ministers in the wilderness' of the eighteenth century. When Napoleon brought France civil peace and internal stability, the legal recognition he provided for Protestants was within a framework of State control. It was at odds with Reformed principles but recognised by French Protestants as part of a new order which gave them much more security and liberty than the old one.

The Waldensians were spared the French Revolution's episodes of terror and direct assault on Christianity, though not the consequences of the wars which accompanied them and continued more fiercely than ever after the fall of Robespierre and the Jacobins. But they were inevitably affected by the hopes, fears, aspirations, and reactions which the Revolution provoked throughout Europe. The monarchies of Europe took fright as the militant Republic which challenged them both with force of arms and force of ideas, inspired by a new and passionate kind of French nationalism but preaching liberty, equality, and fraternity. The Waldensians had little liberty, no equality, an open mind about fraternity, and no national prejudices against the French of the kind which contributed mightily to the long, difficult, and ultimately successful British war

34

effort. The only leaders they were allowed, the pastors educated abroad, mainly in Switzerland, had been touched and in some cases carried away by the ideas of reason and enlightenment which partly inspired the Revolution. They were a simple and suppressed people, without the complex interests and ideas which inspired Burke's *Reflections* and even modified Burns's opinions once French idealism turned to arrogance and oppression.

Long before the Revolution lurched into a European war which was bound to cause trouble for frontier peoples, the Sardinian Government worried about its impact on Piedmont and Savoy. When at the end of 1789 the great touring economist and English authority on agriculture, Arthur Young, set out from Turin on his journey home via Paris, taking the main route north of the Waldensian valleys and crossing the Mont Cenis pass on the shortest day of the year, he found that even the local gentry were grumbling. He thought them an irresponsible lot but noted the effect of the turbulence in France. 'These idle people are this Christmas disappointed by the court having refused admission to the usual company of French comedians - the Government fears importing among the rough mountaineers the present spirit of French liberty.'

In the next few years the Franco-Italian Alps were to see more armies than strolling players. Some of those who commanded them, like the Russian Suvarov, were to make a vivid but brief impression, but the Corsican-born French general who made his name reviving the Republic's 'Army of Italy' had a profound impact.

Napoleone Buonaparte was to become Emperor of the French but his Corsican birth ensured he was always a Franco-Italian. When his empire was at its greatest extent he controlled Italy as well as France, through annexations, the creation of a dependent kingdom under his rule, and the control of satellite States. He called his infant son 'King of Rome'. Historians debate the extent to which he sponsored, inspired, or provoked the Italian nationalism which was to triumph long after his death. Aspirations for Italian unity went back as far as Machiavelli, even Dante, but the French Revolution created a new kind of Europe and Napoleon helped create what came to be called nationalism. He exploited it in France, he provoked it in Germany, and he stimulated it in Italy.

The Waldensians were also Franco-Italians, of a very different kind but with no prejudice against someone else belonging to two cultures and owing his advancement to talents and good fortune and not to royal patronage or family connections. And, compared to the *ancien régime* in France and the traditional powers in Italy, Napoleon had relatively little prejudice against Protestants. He knew almost nothing about them but recognised their abilities and opened careers to their talents. They could believe what they liked and practise their religion, provided he knew what was going on and detected no whiff of subversion. And by Napoleon's standards most Protestants were good citizens, even more trustworthy ones than old Jacobins like his Police Minister Fouché or old aristocrats like his Foreign Minister, the ex-bishop Talleyrand. Few Protestants were in league with emigré royalists and eager for a Bourbon restoration.

Political and diplomatic expediency also encouraged Napoleon to avoid antagonising Protestants. There were substantial Protestant populations in his client or satellite States in West Germany, the Netherlands and Switzerland. Within France, as he defined it and expanded its frontiers, there was not only the reviving Huguenot remnant to conciliate. There were also Protestant communities in its borderlands, not just in Alsace (which had not been covered by the revocation of the Edict of Nantes) and adjacent parts of Germany but in his French-speaking annexations on the Swiss and Italian frontiers. When 27 Protestant ministers attended his coronation in 1804, for example, the most senior was Pastor Martin of Geneva, to whom it fell to present a loyal address. Also present was the youngest of the Rabaut family, contrasting the new freedom with the sufferings and martyrdoms of the past. They all probably enjoyed the proceedings much more than the most eminent but unhappy guest at the coronation, Pope Pius VII, who was both bullied and humiliated by Napoleon.

And within the boundaries of Napoleon's Greater France, and among its Protestant population, were the Waldensians.

Their valleys were annexed to France after Napoleon's victory at Marengo in 1800, when Citizen Buonaparte was still First Consul, during the campaign whose political implications provide the background for the French play, written by Victorien Sardou for Sarah Bernhardt, which was the basis for Puccini's opera *Tosca*. But for the previous decade the valleys had been much involved both in war and revolution, most spectacularly in 1799 when the King of Sardinia retired to the island from which he derived his title and left Piedmont to a provisional Republican Government of which the Waldensian Moderator, Pierre Geymet, became a member. This Government was, said the great conservative French Protestant historian-statesman, Guizot, 'moderate and prudent, of necessity under French influence and soon demanding union with France, despite popular revolts and the patriotic repugnance of the nation.' But the new régime crumbled when Suvarov and his Russians crossed the Alps to assist the Austrians and their Italian. allies. Only after Bonaparte returned from his Egyptian adventure and reasserted French military supremacy did the plans for incorporation in France become effective. The Waldensian valleys then became part of the 'Department of Pinerolo' and Pierre Geymet exchanged his moderatorial and ministerial role for the dignity of sub-prefect. And what had hitherto been known as the Val Luserna took the name of Val Pellice

For the Waldensians this turbulence, followed by the deceptive stability of Napoleon's empire, brought a brief but vivid emancipation which was also a false dawn. They had freedom of worship and civil rights within the imperial system, though they found difficulty in securing formal autonomy for their Church, thanks to the bureaucratic rules which were part of the Napoleonic system of control. Some of them moved from the valleys to Turin. Others built a new church at Luserna San Giovanni, just along the Turin road from Torre Pellice but the first visible symbol of release from the ghetto in the valleys.

It may have seemed to some Waldensians too good to be true, and it was. Prescot Stephens has summed up the irony of their situation: 'The cause for which thousands down the years had been martyred was won by the military triumphs of a revolutionary régime.' When that military power over-reached itself and was broken there was to be a reaction. The old régime returned, though without the old rigour. The San Giovanni church was closed for a time but eventually survived, as did ex-sub-prefect, ex-moderator Geymet, who became a head master, though he felt in his own family the pain caused when Waldensians sought the professional careers, other than the ministry, for which their education fitted them. His son did well as a Sardinian army doctor but at the enforced cost of conforming to Roman Catholicism, along with his wife and children. The Waldensian community was always under pressure of this kind, felt most acutely (a modern Waldensian authority told me) at both ends of its social and economic scale. Some of the very poor could be tempted by the knowledge that conforming could bring what could be called either a bribe or a resettlement grant, probably access to a menial but secure job. Those who had acquired a good education had few professional opportunities unless they felt called to the ministry, and knew that conversion, even if only in form, vastly improved their prospects.

The migrants to Turin could not have a church or freedom of worship, though an arrangement was made from 1827 by which the Protestant ambassadors appointed a Waldensian chaplain, who was able to provide embassy chapel services for valley people working in the city. Many of these Waldensians were in the service of leading families, even the royal house. A Presbyterian who visited Turin in 1837 and 1843, Dr Robert Baird of New York, estimated this unofficial Waldensian congregation of Pastor Bert at well over 300. It then met in the 'spacious residence' of the Prussian Ambassador.

These valley people working in Turin were honest, diligent, literate and (as even modern Waldensians assure me) had one other priceless advantage in domestic service. They did not go to confession and spill the family secrets. They did well and were well thought of by the more liberally-minded part of the Roman Catholic Turinese. But the Sardinian State continued to restrict their freedom and support attempts at their conversion. The Roman Catholics not only built new churches in the valleys and sponsored missions there but recovered the hated 'Hospice for Catechumens' in Pinerolo which Waldensians regarded as a headquarters for child-snatching - as that other persecuted minority, the Jews, did elsewhere in Italy when faced with similar institutions. For the Jews, anxieties remained acute until the unification of Italy, most evidently in the Mortara case, where a Jewish child was secretly baptised by a maidservant and claimed by the ecclesiastical authorities.

The concession to the Protestants through the embassy in Turin was mainly due to the Prussian Ambassador, Count Friedrich Waldburg-Truchsess, accredited to the Sardinian court for more than 30 years. He was a devoted friend of the Waldensians, died at Turin, and was buried in Torre Pellice. In addition to this concession he used his influence to overcome resistance to the rebuilding of the *tempio* (as Waldensian churches were and are called) at Pomaretto, gateway to the Waldensian country from the Val Perosa, and the establishment of the first school for girls, at San Giovanni, and the Waldensian hospital at Torre Pellice.

However the laws about owning property in Piedmont outside the valleys and access to professions were only slightly relaxed, even though British and Prussian diplomats tried to win greater concessions The Waldensians were, in terms of the law, almost back where they were before the French Revolution, though they had the advantage of a different intellectual and spiritual climate.

It would, of course, be a grotesque distortion of social history to imply that the Waldensians spent all their time lamenting their condition, looking for external help, praying for deliverance, or singing about the Glorious Return. They had a living to earn, whether on the rough higher pastures or the better ground at the foot of the valleys. Some found a market even for the chestnuts that fall in such profusion each autumn on the wooded slopes and sometimes seemed manna for fugitives and guerrillas. Many went furth of the valleys to work and save; some ventured successfully into commerce. Many whose homes remained in the valleys went outside them as seasonal or occasional workers. It would be wrong to think of them as cut off from the rest of Piedmontese society or always at odds in their daily lives with the Roman Catholics beside them, not numerous in the upper Waldensian valleys but an overwhelming majority in the neighbouring foothills and the plains of Piedmont.

In 1825 James Jackson, a visiting Dorsetshire clergyman, discovered the happier side of the unequal and unfair relationship in which the Waldensians were forced to live with their Roman Catholic neighbours. His book *Remarks on the Vaudois of Piemont*, highly valued by modern Waldensians, followed the pattern of numerous British travellers' reports. They visited the pastors, they were briefed on glorious history and contemporary injustices, and they praised the Hotel de l'Ours at Torre Pellice, which Jackson found cleaner and more comfortable than the bigger hotels he had visited on his travels. Then Jackson went to the rugged frontier of the Waldensian territory, up a branch of the Germanasca valley on the way to Henri Arnaud's 'Glorious Return' battlefield of Balziglia, to visit the pastor at Massello, Pierre Monastier, who had written a history of the Waldensians. He was surprised after an inspection of the church when his host suggested that they drop in on the local priest. This was Canon Balcet, a small elderly man of rather rosy complexion. Jackson had been assured his new host was agreeable and reasonable but also found him generous. The wine came out and then the brandy, with insistence that an English visitor had to be served a particular way - half a large glass of brandy filled up with the lighter stuff - an Italian version of the destructive Scots 'hauf and hauf'. There appears to have followed a warm, but not heated conversation.

But despite these sociable moments and encounters the years after Waterloo were to be a testing-time for the Waldensians. They needed leadership which would not be diverted, as Moderator Geymet had been, up a political cul-de-sac. They needed more connections with the rest of the Protestant world than were provided by their traditional links with the Swiss Churches, which faced internal troubles of their own. And though they could profit from foreign help, indeed still needed it to survive, it would have to be in some more modern and relevant form than an ancient subsidy, half-heartedly resumed after Waterloo.

But by the grace of God this kind of help was to come. The surviving remnant was to become a reviving Church, not as a British or German satellite but with the benefit of some remarkable voluntary management and theological consultancy and with a generous helping of what later ages would call the oxygen of publicity.

There was another even more pressing need that had to be met, and which eventually was met. The French revolutionary and Napoleonic years had demonstrated the limitations of attempted emancipation through dependence on an alien secular ideology and a foreign Power which pursued its own ends and made enemies of countries which wanted to be the Waldensians' allies.

Although the people of the valleys were a frontier tribe, it was clear they were necessarily involved with the rest of Piedmont and, as a result, with the rest of Italy. Full emancipation was likely to come and to become permanent only as part of a wider Italian movement in which the people of Italy sought and secured civil and religious liberty, and in which they regulated the relation of their State to the country's most powerful and historic institution, the Roman Catholic Church.

These conditions were also to be met in the decades ahead, though not without delay and frustration - and perhaps not fully met until the 1980's. But in the years of peace and stability after Waterloo it was hard to foresee this, and even those who thought that dramatic change was coming in Italy could not predict when or how. These were the years when Europe, and especially Germany and Italy, remained dominated by ultra-conservative and often repressive systems which made all British Tory Governments appear on the liberal side - not just in the times of Canning and. later of Peel but even in a mild way from the days of Castlereagh, target for so much invective from Shelley and Byron. They were the systems especially associated with the Rhenish-born Austrian Chancellor Metternich, who still insisted in 1848-49, when the system first showed signs of breaking up, that 'Italy is a geographical expression'.

That phrase can be overdone and taken from context. Metternich himself was far less reactionary than some of his Italian allies and was a product of the 'Enlightenment'. He was neither a very spiritual Catholic nor a bigot. For example he was ready to remonstrate with the Pope against the barbarous treatment of the Jews in the Rome ghetto. It has also been argued that Austrian direct rule, especially in Venetia, provided a synthesis of Habsburg bureaucracy and Napoleonic innovation which provided the 'most effective and responsive Government in Restoration Italy'.

Language, culture, and the distinctive style of the Roman Catholic Church in Italy created affinities strong enough to be called unity of a sort. The Metternich system maintained a kind of Italian political community allied to Austria and dependent on it. Lombardy and Venetia were Austrian provinces. Family connections as well as reactionary politics linked the duchies of Tuscany, Modena, Parma, and Lucca to the Hapsburgs. There were similar links with the two 'kingdoms' in Italy - with Sardinia, whose core was Piedmont though it then included Savoy and Nice, and the kingdom of the 'Two Sicilies', which was much more Neapolitan than Sicilian in outlook. There was also the profound entente with the Papacy: the Pope not only claimed authority in the Church but exercised a temporal power which made him in effect a king in Central Italy. He ruled Rome and its surrounding province and was monarch of great areas of Italy in Umbria, the Marches, Emilia, and the Romagna. These were the 'States of the Church', where any restriction on papal absolutism came from local tradition and ancient privileges, not from modern constitutional ideas. The Pope's government was patriarchal but bigoted and backward.

The first crack in the system was to come in Piedmont, the land in which the Waldensians had been uncomfortable subjects of the House of Savoy, often fighting for them against foreign enemies, yet always under pressure.

Chapter 4

THE ENGLISH LEND A HAND

Pilgrimage and consultancy in the 'Israel of the Alps'

The Grand Tour never quite recovered from more than two decades of war, political convulsion, and social change in Europe. But if the leisurely Grand Tour was almost extinct, new forms of tourism were vigorous and developing. The revolutionary and Napoleonic wars had created a pent-up British demand to see classical antiquities and the new Europe. The romantic movement also encouraged new kinds of pursuit of the picturesque, not least in the Alps. The industrial and commercial development which the wars had sometimes obscured but never stifled had widened the market for foreign travel, and were soon vastly to increase both demand and opportunities.

But at the time of Waterloo and the Congress of Vienna, Thomas Cook was a child of seven and steamboats were also in their infancy. Although horse-drawn industrial railways were common, the potential of the locomotive was still uncertain. The rapid development of passenger trains still lay a decade or more ahead. For the moment passenger travel still depended on sailing-ships, coaches, post-horse teams, and diligences, though wheels rumbled more quickly and evenly along the roads which Napoleon had improved.

The new British interest in world travel and European tourism was not caused by the coming of steamboats and trains, though it was soon to take advantage of them. The same is true of the new British Protestant enthusiasm for missions, including a mission to show practical solidarity with fellow-Protestants in difficulty. They were part a of great surge of ambitious national self-confidence, sometimes tempered with self-criticism and soon expressing itself in movements for reform.

There was also a renewed vigour in British Christianity, inspired by the evangelical revival but not confined to it. At its best it tried to respond to changes in society and movements of population. It also took an unprecedented interest in the wider world. There was denominational rivalry and sectarianism but there was also a trans-denominational missionary enthusiasm never before apparent. It was mainly expressed in the Protestant missions to Africa, India,

41

and sundry other parts of the world, and in the longing to see a Hebrew Christian Church centred in Jerusalem, but it also had European dimensions. One was encouragement of evangelicalism in European Protestant Churches, another the nurture of Protestant communities in countries where the Inquisition had once been dominant but was now in retreat. It was the age of George Borrow's great tours as a literary colporteur for the Bible Society in Spain, of the emergence of tiny Protestant communities in Portugal and Madeira, and of the rediscovery of the Waldensians by British Protestant public opinion.

This poor, struggling, confined, and still harassed community even eventually found itself flattered as 'the Israel of the Alps'. That popular phrase, however, was not of Anglo-Saxon origin. It came from of a history of the Waldensians, published in Paris in 1851 and later translated into English, by Alexis Muston, a Waldensian pastor, scholar, and propagandist who got into trouble with Piedmont's religious and political censorship and found asylum and new opportunities in France. Yet it is Muston's phrase which best sums up the attitudes and emotions of the Waldensians' British friends.

This was the age in which the great English missionary societies flourished. Several of them had been founded during the long wars. But it was an older society, not one of the new 'foreign missions', which created the occasion from which there developed a new and significant contact between Britain and the Waldensians. The Society for Promoting Christian Knowledge dated from 1698 and was English and Anglican, though a similarly named Scottish society had played a major part in the eighteenth-century evangelisation of the Scottish Highlands, with results still evident in the twenty-first century. The society was involved in promoting charity schools and publishing Christian literature. But it was through the SPCK, who received a request for help from Pastor Peyran of Pramollo, that William Stephen Gilly's interest was aroused.

Gilly (1789-1855) was a son of an East Anglian parsonage, a Cambridge graduate who had recently become rector of North Fambridge in Essex. Later he moved North and became vicar of Norham, where he took up the cause of what he called 'the peasantry of the border', exhorting landlords to improve country housing conditions. In his last years he was a canon of Durham Cathedral. But the real achievement of his life was the creation of a London committee, and soon a support network, to promote the Waldensian cause. He was also one of those responsible for making the character of the Genevan-born evangelist Felix Neff and his work in the French High Alps well known among British Evangelicals, although it has been suggested that Gilly himself was more of an old-style, pre-Tractarian, Protestant High Churchman. Nevertheless it was mainly through Gilly's devotion to the Waldensians' cause that British and Irish Evangelicals overcame a suspicion, still lingering into the 1840's, that (as the Religious Tract Society put it) Waldensians had generally avoided false doctrines but 'yielded to their admission of many worldly practices', and that 'till within the last generation few indications of real spirituality were seen in them'.

Gilly, according to his own account, knew very little about the Waldensians when Dr Gaskin, the secretary, read Peyran's moving letter to an SPCK meeting. But Ferdinand Peyran, although minister for 31 years in the mountains beyond the Angrogna valley, had studied at Basle before the French Revolution and knew a good deal about the outside world. His family already had English as well as Swiss and French contacts. They are also said to have had dealings with the Russian general Suvarov. Ferdinand was also the brother of the Moderator Rodolphe Peyran who had tried to initiate Napoleon into the history and character of the Waldensians and who also greatly impressed one of the first British visitors to the valleys after Emperor's fall, the Church of England clergyman Thomas Sims. Sims wrote a book about a visit to the Waldensians in the autumn of 1814 and aroused enough interest to run to a second edition and to follow up his personal account with a translation of Rodolphe Peyran's defence of the Waldensians against the verbal assaults of the Bishop of Pinerolo. In 1821 the Oxford Clarendon Press also brought out a new edition of the late seventeenth-century account of the 'ecclesiastical history of the ancient Churches of Piedmont' by Peter Allix, a Huguenot refugee who founded a French church in London and became treasurer of Salisbury Cathedral.

Peyran's appeal for help with money and books was not a hopeless shot in the dark. It was written at a time of post-war reconstruction in Europe, when the latest political changes had an adverse effect on the Waldensians, and when the old British support, suspended during the wars, had not yet been restored. It is not surprising that it occurred to Waldensians that they might obtain much-needed help by tapping into new interest and reviving old associations.

Although Peyran's momentous letter was in 1818, Gilly's interest in learning more about them from Sims' and other books was not followed up by a visit until January 1823, following a winter crossing of the Alps. His own influential books on the Waldensians appeared in 1824 and, after a second visit, in 1831. The London committee, of which he was secretary, was formed in 1825, with the immediate aims of securing the reinstatement of the royal subsidy, interrupted by the Napoleonic conquests, and support for the new Waldensian hospital. It was chaired by Dr William Howley, the Bishop of London who became Archbishop of Canterbury in 1828 and is best remembered in general British history as one of the two messengers who brought the eighteen-year-old Princess Victoria the news of her accession to the throne. Originally the

London Vaudois Committee, it later became the English Committee in Aid of Waldensian Church Missions. It drew support and contributions from the great and the good (and from King George IV who was neither) but it provided the framework within which Gilly could deploy his considerable talents as organiser, lobbyist, and publicist. Although others later revived and reorganised fund-raising in Britain, notably the Scottish evangelical philanthropist Dr Thomas Guthrie, Gilly had laid the foundations and helped make the cause popular and fashionable. Those who responded came from a wide range of opinions, and included the political philosopher Sir James Mackintosh, the historian Henry Hallam, and Jane Austen's rather dilettante brother Henry. Mr Austen, who had been soldier and unsuccessful banker as well as clergyman, now turned his hand to a sermon and fund-raising pamphlet in aid of the 'Vaudois'. A more important and popular literary memorial of the movement is *The Hymn of the Vaudois Mountaineers* by the then popular poet ('poetess' in the idiom of the time), Felicia Hemans.

> For the strength of the hills we bless Thee,
> Our God, our fathers' God.

If the cadences of this hymn are surprisingly familar (See Appendix 2) it is because it was later borrowed by C.A. Horne as the basis for the less specific praise of 'For the might of Thine arm we bless Thee'.

Support and enthusiasm also came from the greatest English poet of the time. For one of the truly great and really good to be attracted to the Waldensian cause was William Wordsworth who, for all the intensity of his Englishness, had long shown an affection for foreign as well as British mountains and an interest in French culture. He had also studied Italian, starting in his Cambridge undergraduate days, and translated epitaphs by the Ligurian-born poet Gabriello Chiabrera and sonnets by Michael Angelo. The impetuous young Wordsworth had welcomed the French Revolution, as the Waldensians did - 'Bliss was it in that dawn to be alive, but to be young was very heaven' - and had fathered a child in the Loire valley. The mature Wordsworth, given over to plain living and high thinking in the Lake District and settled now in his Christian faith, was still eager for foreign excursions and interests. He was one of those whose enthusiasm was roused by the interest in the Waldensians stimulated by Gilly and others. He wrote three sonnets on the Vaudois or Waldenses, published in 1835 though the date of their composition is uncertain. He preceded them in his 'ecclesiastical' sequence with perhaps a better one on transubstantiation. In this he contrasts the style and ethos of the Mass and the claims of the medieval priest with the heroic role he confers on Valdo of Lyons, whose followers stood apart 'from rites that trample upon soul and sense':

...This Valdo brooks not. On the banks of Rhone
He taught, till persecution chased him thence,
To adore the Invisible, and Him alone.

The four sonnets, among hundreds found now only in full Wordsworth collections, would hold up this narrative but they appear in Appendix 2.

However the most influential of all Englishmen in the British connection with the Waldensians and the one with the closest connection to the life of the valleys, did not visit them until 1827, directly influenced by the first of Gilly's books, the *Narrative of an Excursion to the Valleys of Piedmont.* The new recruit to the cause, back in London after a visit to Canada, encountered the book in the library of the Duke of Wellington's London home, Apsley House, while waiting to see the great man (shortly to have a brief and troubled term as Prime Minister).

The guest who browsed to such purpose was John Charles Beckwith (known by his second Christian name), an old subordinate of Wellington's. Beckwith (1789-1862) came from a military family and was a professional soldier with character and managerial qualities as well as powerful army connections. His uncle, Sir George Beckwith, made a reputation in the American Revolutionary campaigns and did well in the Napoleonic wars, when he captured the French West Indian islands, then of considerable economic importance. His father, however, had stayed in North America to marry into a Nova Scotian family, so that Charles Beckwith (if a slightly anachronistic use of the phrase is permissible) was Canadian-born. However he was destined for the British army and also did well, serving with Sir John Moore in a rifle regiment on the retreat to Corunna and then with Wellington in Portugal and Spain. He emerged with credit from the ill-fated Walcheren expedition, and had become a divisional deputy assistant quartermaster-general and brevet major in 1814 when the Peninsular campaign ended deep in South-West France at Toulouse. At Waterloo he was on the staff of Picton's Light Division and severely wounded. He lost his left leg to a cannon shot in the final phase of the battle, but recovered considerable mobility and even agility with the help of will power and a wooden leg. The former was to do great things for the Waldensians; the latter is honoured in their historical museum at Torre Pellice. Less than a mile along the road he is buried in the local cemetery, beside his wife, the Waldensian Caroline Vola, and their daughter Charlotte (1862-1927), born six months after his death.

Lieutenant-Colonel Beckwith's disability had not formally closed the file on his army career, though it ended his prospects of further active service and rising to high command. He went on half-pay in 1820 but got a full colonelcy in 1837. More than 30 years after Waterloo, on formal and final retirement in 1846, he was allowed the dignity of major-general. But Charles Beckwith had become increasingly involved with the Protestant community in the Alps after that first visit in 1827, settling among it in Torre Pellice and marrying into it twelve years before his death. He fell out with the Waldensian Synod for a time but came back and died in the valleys. In the words of the original Dictionary of National Biography, whose contributor H.M. Stephens had a military rather than theological inclination: 'Of all the officers of the Light Division none found such a strange mode of employing his unexhausted energies.'

But Beckwith's involvement can be seen from a different perspective and his involvement as more than coincidence. It is not a pious Victorian but the contemporary Waldensian historian Giorgio Bouchard who describes the phenomenon as one 'in which it is difficult to see only the hand of man'.

Beckwith was a great English personality. He was not unique in his later vocation, as the DNB implied, for at least two retired Royal Navy officers, Captain Pakenham and Lieutenant Graydon, were enthusiastic distributors of Italian-language Bibles. But Beckwith had a touch of the grand eccentric about him. He was a practical man and an 'ideas' man, with a gift for public and human relations; he had considerable influence on the history of the valleys, but his role is hard to define in modern terms. He stumped about the valleys and up the mountainsides, with dog and telescope, as adviser, enabler, candid friend, consultant, even a kind of director of education. He was also an important link with the London Anglican evangelicals and at times a conciliator in Waldensian disagreements. The Waldensians did not take all his advice any more than they accepted all Gilly's ideas. If they had, their Church would have moved closer to Anglicanism than Presbyterianism, both in liturgical style and concepts of episcopacy. But they rightly respected and honoured him, and retain his memory in their treasury of history. Not surprisingly, Torre Pellice's Via Arnaud leads up to the Via Beckwith, with its church, synod hall, cultural institutions, and slightly English air to its fine residential terrace. And down the road in San Giovanni, where the fate of the new church hung in the balance after Napoleon's fall, there is today the Protestant Radio Beckwith which broadcasts to the Valleys and adjacent parts of Piedmont. He is certainly one of the saints who from their labours rest, with his work continued and his name honoured.

Gilly and Beckwith are sometimes praised by friends of the Waldensians almost as if the clergyman saved the community from extinction and the soldier founded their system of education. These are false impressions, like any suggestion that it was only the British who showed solidarity with this isolated Protestant community. It had also significant support from Germans, especially Count Waldburg-Truchsess and other Prussians, and from the Netherlands as well as from France and Switzerland, where Waldensian pastors were trained.

A good-will donation of 4000 francs for the Waldensian hospital even came from Tsar Alexander I of Russia, apparently as the result of lobbying by William Allen, an English Quaker scientist and philanthropist who, when not lecturing at Guy's Hospital, devoted himself to a wider range of good causes, including prison reform in Contintental Europe. He was also an anti-slavery associate of Wilberforce and Clarkson. Allen had lobbied the Tsar and the Duke of Wellington at the Congress of Verona in 1822, a year before the visit to the valleys of the hospital's British benefactor, William Prenderleath.

There was also renewed interest in the valleys from their traditional areas of contact in France and among Swiss Protestants. Some of it reflected the theological turbulence there which accompanied the revival or 'awakening' among Evangelicals, which was assisted by such Scots as Robert Haldane and Thomas Erskine of Linlathen, the one in Geneva and the other in Lausanne. Both these lairds and their Swiss associates clashed with the prevailing 'rationalist' tone of the Protestant leadership, with the dispute in the Canton of Vaud by far the more embittered and lasting. Neither of these Scots had a direct influence on the Waldensians but the movement with which they were associated in Switzerland and France did have its impact. In Italy *le Réveil* became *il Risveglio*.

In July 1825, for example, Felix Neff visited the valleys, crossing on foot into the upper Pellice valley over the Col de la Croix. The Genevan-born Neff was a saintly but austere puritan, with an intensity and power of example not unlike that of Robert Murray McCheyne in Scotland. He had already made his name as evangelist and revivalist in the French-speaking cantons of Switzerland and in the French High Alps, just across the border from Piedmont and with a 'Vaudois' tradition which in a few remote places had survived the long persecution under the Bourbon kings. Neff's account of the visit reveals something of the problems of the Waldensians at the time, as well as of the deep division then between evangelicals and moderates, whom their critics called rationalists, in all French-speaking Protestantism. He was distressed to find that the services at San Giovanni (St Jean in his account) were kept short because of a Sunday shooting festival and what he called a ball in the evening, though the word today may convey a more elaborate and formal kind of dancing than the valleys offered. Of the pastor there he wrote: 'I never saw a more ingenious apologist for luxury and dancing and all worldly pleasures. He is quite to the taste of the Vaudois and is adored at St Jean.' This was David Mondon, the leading Waldensian 'rationalist', an elderly man who had lived through Enlightenment, revolution, Napoleon, and reaction. Neff also met several pastors who 'to say the least were neither hot not cold', though he found the Waldensian Moderator, Pastor Pierre Bert, lived up to his reputation as a faithful pastor.

Yet it was not just the Moderator but the other pastors too who invited him to preach. The following Sunday at San Giovanni they even made sure there was no ball, sent the musicians away out of consideration for Neff (so at least he thought), and gave him the freedom of the pulpit in their church with notoriously bad acoustics. Neff left Piedmont 'deeply grieved by the degenerate state of this once interesting people', though making two admissions, one personal and one political which help in assessing the weight of his severe judgment.

The personal one was that he was out of sorts during his visit. He found the summer climate at the foot of the valleys stifling and longed to breathe the High Alpine air. He was a sick man and, like McCheyne, was to die young. The political one is that is that he discovered his visit had been followed by 'a thundering letter' to the Waldensian pastors from King of Sardinia, with an order that it should read from pulpits. 'I was not surprised at this, for I knew that the preaching of foreigners in Piedmont was prohibited by an ancient law, and I wondered that the pulpits should be offered to me, as they constantly were.' In the circumstances, he seems a bit harsh on the Waldensians.

Neff's experience reveals some of the pressures on the Waldensian Church, as well as the theological cross-currents influencing it and causing divisions within it. Although he himself never returned to Piedmont, his colleague and convert Antoine Blanc led a protest or renewal movement against 'rationalist' pastors, something between a secession movement and a loyal opposition. Neff's visit also records the way in which its pastors perhaps mixed courage, discretion, and some modest pleasures. It also emphasises how important it was that British Protestants could and would help. The Waldensians needed help to adapt to coming social and political changes. That was easier when the assistance was available from a country influential and confident enough to force the Turin Government to restrain its irritation and persuasive enough to encourage a new liberalism among its people.

Things didn't depend on Britain, or on the other foreign friends of the Waldensians. Without Gilly and Beckwith the Waldensians would have survived, as they had done in the centuries of active persecution and the more recent times of severe restriction and sustained pressure. There was much in their way of life which enabled them not only to resist but to prepare for opportunities. Beckwith was able to do what he did in education because there already existed a respect for learning, with an understanding that a people of the Word must be able to read the Bible, a Latin or secondary school, and a poverty-stricken rudimentary village school system that responded to new leadership and ideas. The Waldensians were a literate people at a time when the great majority of Italians were not. In 1861, a decisive date in the reshaping of

Italy, 68 per cent of Italian males and 81 per cent of females were illiterate, though these figures reflect the abject state of the South and Sicily. Rome, for example, had a Church-run elementary school system in the early nineteenth century which was good enough for its day to win some Protestant praise, for example from the Scottish traveller, Samuel Laing. But Gilly and Beckwith were organisers and modernisers. They were also ready to encourage experiment, for example in their co-operation with Waldensians exploring the possibilities of making the valleys' dialect or *patouà* a language of devotion. To an extent, for they had to be cautious and diplomatic, they were even conciliators in the internal disputes of the Waldensian community, though they could also be heavy-handed in their attempt to persuade the Waldensians that they should move closer to Anglicanism and away from their three centuries of Calvinist tradition.

That was not an entirely implausible proposition. Nor was it a wholly unreasonable view, though Gilly underestimated the importance of the Waldensian ties with French-speaking and Swiss Reformed religion. Waldensians did, and do, have a sense of historic continuity that has much in common with Protestant Anglicanism in Britain and Ireland. They had a simple liturgy or Common Order and their Moderators, serving for several years, had some of the standing and influence of a good Anglican bishop, though they also had a democratic element in the local government of the Church quite alien to the Anglicanism of the day. For them, as Giorgio Tourn has argued, the importance of the Reformation was that it seemed to be a search for a primitive purity of the Church. The role of their Moderator also seemed to Gilly to lend itself to a transition to formal episcopacy, while he and other nineteenth century Anglican visitors seem genuinely to have felt an affinity with the forms of Waldensian worship which they did not have for the Scottish and other Presbyterian services of the time.

Gilly, Beckwith, and their Anglican collaborators also ensured that some of the most significant outside support for the Waldensians came from a country which, though it nourished many kinds of emotional attachment to Italy, was relatively disinterested in the power-political implications of the national and liberal movements there.

Gilly organised support which was far more relevant to Waldensian needs than the old British subsidy, resumed eventually for a time after the lobbying but on a reduced basis, which provided £21 a year towards the stipend of each Waldensian pastor. Most important of all, he established a support system for the Waldensians and a bridgehead for Protestantism in Italy, before Scots Presbyterianism, Methodism, or Americans were much involved, which allowed them to take advantage of the first great crack in the Italian alliance which after 1815 had united repressive Roman Catholicism, ultra-reactionary politics, and the Austrian alliance.

The pro-Waldensian movement also had its failures, in Britain and well as Italy. One was to be with the most significant British politician of the century to feel real interest in Italy, speak its language, and show commitment to its freedom. He was an Englishman, of Scottish descent on both sides of his family, whose father had moved from Leith and Presbyterianism to become a successful Liverpool merchant and pillar of the Church of England. William Ewart Gladstone was to become the greatest Victorian Liberal but when he toured Italy in 1832 he was a Tory, soon to make a name as a very able but rather headstrong admirer of Sir Robert Peel. It was in Milan that he heard of the Duke of Newcastle's offer of patronage, and a passport to Parliament, for the borough of Newark. Indeed Gladstone was to become a zealous and outspoken supporter of Italian liberalism before he was firmly settled as a British Liberal. It may even have been Italy which defined his political position for him once Peel had gone and 'Peelites' had to think about their future.

Italy did not define his religious position but it certainly influenced it. Gladstone was a pious young man who had thought at one stage of taking holy orders and who moved in the circles much influenced by Gilly and his Waldensian committee. When he and his brother set out for Italy, shortly after the publication of Gilly's second book, the Waldensian valleys were on their agenda. They had been given what William called a 'lofty conception' of the valley people as ideal Christians. But that part of the Italian trip was not a success. Gladstone confessed to 'a chill of disappointment at finding them much like other men.' The pastor he met seemed to lack what Gladstone called 'vital religion' - a reaction very similar to that of Felix Neff.

Although Gladstone gave what money he could spare he hustled on towards Rome - in the geographical, not the spiritual sense. Gladstone was moving towards the distinctive religious position which was to influence not only his personal theology (and he was a formidable lay theologian) but his thinking about Italy. He was already on the way to a characteristically individualist style of Christianity, very high Anglican but not at all pro-Roman. That stance was to influence his later approach to Italian problems and to the crisis in the Roman Catholic Church which coincided with the completion of Italian unity.

He returned from Italy, as he told the Duke of Newcastle a few months later, thinking that 'the Roman Catholic religion is so bad, and yet the prospect after its overthrow is so very dreary that one scarcely knows whether to wish for its continuation or destruction'. Others have felt the same way since.

Chapter 5

THE LAST YEARS OF CAPTIVITY

A new world invades the old order

Between the 1820's and 1848, the year of Waldensian liberation, the Protestant Alpine community so valiantly and effectively assisted by Gilly and Beckwith attracted support, funds, attention, and a scholarly interest which continued for most of the Victorian era and reached far beyond committees of the well-connected. When, for example, the Hawick lad o' pairts, James Murray, later to be a great lexicographer and principal creator of the Oxford English Dictionary, set out his C.V. in seeking entry to the world of learning he listed a knowledge of 'Vaudois' among his linguistic qualifications.

There was also a continuing flow of British visitors. Unlike Gladstone, most of them were sympathetic and several wrote books. Two of the most significant, William Beattie and Ebenezer Henderson, were Scots working in England who broadened the base of Waldensian support in Britain far beyond the Evangelical and Broad Church sections of the Church of England. Another, Robert Stewart, was a Scot whose Presbyterian ministry began at home but moved to Italy. In 1838 the valleys also found their first significant place in a guide-book, John Murray's *Handbook for Travellers in Switzerland and the Alps of Savoy and Piedmont.*

This volume is one of the classics of the genre, bearing out the claim by Aldous Huxley that 'an early Murray is a real treasure'. It appeared a year before the first of the superb line of guide-books from the German Karl Baedeker, whose development of Murray's pattern and acknowledged debt to him bear out the old saying about imitation being the best form of flattery. Collectors' market prices today for early Baedekers run ahead of those for Murrays but that merely reflects a fashion. The great merits of both may be weighed and argued, but Murray was first in the field.

The John Murray (1808-92) who produced the Swiss handbook with Piedmont added was the third of the great publishing line. The family retained a Scots connection despite its long involvement in London publishing, sending John III to Edinburgh University after Charterhouse, and something of a

Scottish outlook remained in this young Anglo-Scot's view of Europe. It was as determinedly Protestant as the prevailing English outlook of the day but perhaps readier to identify with the Continental Reformed tradition, as his father had done in 1827 when he published a new edition of Henri Arnaud's account of the Glorious Return. The Murray tradition was also severe in its warnings (notably in the handbooks for France) about the ungentlemanly ways 'which render the English so unpopular on the Continent.'. The offences listed in various editions included resorting to fisticuffs in disputes, name-calling, levity during Roman Catholic Masses, and 'caprice, extravagant squandering, or ill-timed niggardliness' which built up problems for subsequent travellers.

Some of Murray's other practical advice for travellers in the first of his nineteen Swiss editions (from which Piedmont was soon transferred to Italian volumes) gives an impression of the kind of journeys which visitors to the valleys in his time had to undertake. Like us, but unlike the later Victorians, they had to worry about passports. They needed one to get through countries on the way to Switzerland, could expect to have it demanded at the gates of Geneva, and once there had to get the signature of the Sardinian consul before crossing the Alps. It was obligatory, said Murray, 'in order to secure that official a fee of four francs'.

When Murray compiled his guide the steamship had displaced sail for passenger traffic on short sea routes and was coming in on rivers and the Swiss lakes. Travellers to Italy who wanted to avoid the arduous Alpine passes were using steamboats on the Rhone as well as on the Mediterranean. But there were as yet no trans-European railways, and only a few inter-city ones to follow up the pioneer Manchester-Liverpool route. Even Edinburgh and Glasgow were not connected by rail till 1842 and it was another few years before Scotland was linked to England. Italy's first stretch of railway, from Naples to Portici, beside Herculaneum on the way to Pompei, dates from 1839, though the main early progress was soon to come in Piedmont. Travel information in Murray's guide was therefore about post-coaches and the *voiturier* or *vetturino* for longer journeys, with a heavy emphasis on the need to check the reliability of horses, carriages, and those who had them for hire. There were stern warnings never to let hotel waiters make the arrangements and to get everything down in writing

For shorter and middle-distance journeys, however, there were diligences, literally, if sometimes inappropriately, 'coaches of speed'. They were only fast in the mechanical sense when compared with country carts and wagons, but they provided rather basic public transport services.

They looked like a cross between a horse-bus and our traditional idea of a Christmas-card stage-coach. Their 'speed' came largely from their organisation and determination to push on at the expense of passenger discomfort at a time when hired vehicles usually involved overnight stays and leisurely meals for drivers and horses. In Italy, for example, the English barrister and Member of Parliament, T.N. Talfourd (later a judge but more notable for a Copyright Bill and Browning's dedication to him of *Pippa Passes*) found them 'the most fatiguing but surest method of conveyance'. That was in the late 1840's, when they linked Rome to Florence in 48 hours as against four or five days by a *vetturino* hire. Long spells of hunger sustained by Protestant meditations on the condition of Rome seem to have alternated with bouts of heartburn caused by hasty draughts of sour acidic wine. One of Anthony Trollope's complaints about the routes to Italy was that on the French part of the route the operators deliberately overbooked - a tradition reputedly maintained by modern airlines - but as the diligences gave way to railways he became quite nostalgic and sighed for 'the dear old continental coaches'.

Shorter diligence routes in Northern Italy included one from Turin to the foot of the Waldensian valleys. There was a daily service between Torre Pellice and Pinerolo, which had two connections a day with Turin along a good road, by the standards of the time. William Gilly recorded that it took him six hours, presumably in a fairly fast local vehicle, to get from Turin to the foot of the Val Pellice. But in the era after the Napoleonic wars, contemporaries thought of the standards of the time as unprecedentedly high. Murray was among those who had one good thing to say about Napoleon: he had built good roads across Europe to link his dominions and move his divisions. In particular he had greatly eased the journey across the Alps from France, previously much more difficult than the Brenner route which linked Italy to the German lands of the Holy Roman Empire. The Mont Cenis route to Turin was still arduous enough, but not as dangerous for man and beast as it had been in the eighteenth century when that stage of the Grand Tour was spoiled for the essayist Horace Walpole. He let his King Charles spaniel 'out of the chaise for the air' and saw it carried off by a wolf .

But things were much harder for those who ventured off the main routes of commercial, diplomatic, and tourist travel. The Waldensian valleys had not greatly benefited. Napoleon had ordered construction of a road from Cesana down to the Italian plains via Pinerolo, gateway to the valleys, but Murray complained that 'the miserable policy of the Sardinian Government has allowed it to fall into decay and thus almost compelled travellers to pass by Susa and Turin' on their way to the foothills and the valleys.

The detailed descriptions of the valleys, however, were not the work of the already much-travelled young John Murray himself. They had been delegated, along with the rest of Piedmont and Savoy, to William Brockedon (1787-1854) a man of modest origins, many talents, and diverse achievements. He came from Totnes in Devonshire and had been a watchmaker but he became artist, author, inventor, Fellow of the Royal Society, founding member of the Royal Geographical Society, and member of the academies of art in Rome and Florence. One of his patents was for a vulcanised rubber substitute for bottle-corks, possibly better than modern plastic ones. He was also an alpinist, interested in mountains, passes, and people rather than peaks for their own sake. His most celebrated works were a twelve-part series of *Illustrations of the Passes of the Alps* and an Alpine journal.

The mountain landscapes Brockedon loved best were mainly off roads suitable for 'diligences' and his preference was for rambling on foot, with a mule when a load had to be carried, though he also had advice on frontier formalities for horses, carriages and *chars* as well as mules, as well as avoiding vexatious delays in a land of smuggling. 'The French can rarely be bribed - the Piedmontese easily - to facilitate the passage from one country to another.'

But he had a good opinion of the mountain Piedmontese, Catholic as well as Protestant. 'Crowds might find provisions short and want of room, but parties of two or three would fare well, be received with civility without obsequiousness, and meet with less extortionate hosts than in Switzerland.' He was one of many Victorian travellers who reported well of the inns at Torre Pellice, as well as of the Waldensians. 'The civility of all classes to strangers, especially English, ought to be a recommendation to ramblers in the country... They are from ancient habit honest, civil and quiet, and from their situation and necessity simple and laborious.'

Here and there things may have gone wrong. He praised in rather awkward terms the syndic or mayor of 'Marcel' (properly Massello or Masselle) in a branch of the Upper Germanasca valley. 'He is a man remarkable for his hospitality; but this virtue does not extend to his wife and family, and the stranger who expects to receive it will fare ill in his absence.' Unlike most Protestants drawn to the Waldensian valleys, however, Brockedon had a thorough knowledge of the whole of this Alpine region and objective standards to decide when inns were good, tolerable, bad, and miserable, where trout were good and even ptarmigan was sometimes available to travellers 'for which however they will pay handsomely'. He noted where wines were good and poor, where a hundred Alpine flowers bloomed amid apparent sterility, where sledges were used in winter, where on the French side the memory of Felix Neff was venerated. And like Neff he complained of the acoustics in the church at San Giovanni. He also noted how in the decade since

Neff's visit Gilly and Beckwith had done great things for the Protestant community.

Brockedon was able to use his notebooks to enrich Murray's Handbook, the main practical source-book for British visitors to the valleys until almost the end of the century. Baedeker carried only a much briefer note, and even that seems missing from German editions. Brockedon's sketchpad, however, not only provided the basis for his own Alpine book but contributed, along with that of another outstanding English artist, to the first significant record of a Scottish enthusiast for the Waldensians, the literary physician Dr William Beattie (1793-1875).

Beattie's main niche in literary history is probably as the biographer of his friend, the poet Thomas Campbell. He was an Annandale-born Edinburgh medical graduate with a taste for travel as well as literature, studying in Paris and attending the future King William IV on three visits to Germany. In 1835-36 he travelled in Switzerland, France, and Piedmont and in 1838 his account was published in London as *The Waldenses or the Protestant Valleys of Piedmont, Dauphiny, and the Ban de la Roche*.

The two main illustrators were Brockedon and Beattie's friend and companion in the Alps, W.H. Bartlett, best known for his later works on Palestine, *Walks around Jerusalem* and *Jerusalem Revisited*. William Bartlett was an Anglican of evangelical leanings, strongly attached to the project for an Anglican bishopric and cathedral in Jerusalem. He was sympathetic to the Waldensians with an eye for their landscape and churches and an imaginative professional readiness to illustrate their history. In that relatively peaceful age, long before the violence of cinema and TV, artists found the market responsive to battle-scenes. And no-one had more battles long ago than the Waldensians.

Beattie too was receptive to Waldensian history - for example to the story that as French and other troops harried and despoiled the valleys even Roman Catholics from the area entrusted their daughters for safety to the Protestant guardians of such remote retreats as the caves of Ghieisa d'la Tana in the Angrogna Valley. He also had the obligatory account of The Glorious Return. But his strength lay in contemporary observation, enhanced perhaps by less enthusiasm than some clerical visitors (Gilly among them) to select or interpret evidence to suit their views on liturgy, theology, and apostolic succession.

The other expatriate Scot to leave a vivid impression of the valleys in these last years of the captivity was Ebenezer Henderson (1784-58), a Fifer with a rare gift of tongues (and uncle of the Ebenezer Henderson once famous for his astronomical clock and the Annals of Dunfermline). The elder Henderson was a Congregational minister who eventually settled down to teach at a missionary institution in Hoxton and then at his denomination's theological college in Highbury. But earlier in life he had shown his zeal for languages and travel as well as missions. The East India Company thwarted his original hopes of mission to India but he became involved in starting Bible Societies in Scandinavia, Russia, and Iceland, introduced Congregationalism in Sweden, and disagreed with the Bible Society over the Turkish text of the New Testament. He translated from several languages and also wrote his own Old Testament commentaries as well as accounts of his travels, among them *The Vaudois*. This also bore the splendidly elongated sub-title: *Observations made during a tour of the valleys of Piedmont in the summer of 1844, together with remarks introductory and interspersed respecting the origin, history, and present conditions of that interesting people.*

Henderson could be long-winded but his diary was a plain but lively narrative and the 'interspersed' comments brought a useful new perspective. Being a Congregationalist, he was neither conditioned like Gilly to seek signs of a pure, apostolic Church which only needed to formalise its episcopacy nor, like many Scots, to emphasise the Presbyterianism in the Waldensian system. But the fact that he was neither English nor Anglican adds force to his reporting of the status and personal popularity Beckwith had achieved in the valleys, not least when he quotes the Roman Catholic complaint to their Protestant neighbours. 'You don't want to venerate the Virgin but you've no scruples about adoring a colonel.'

Depending on the tone used, that could have been a good-natured remonstrance, but Henderson encountered more difficult and provocative situations. One Sunday he went to San Lorenzo in the Angrogna Valley for the afternoon service. In the middle of the sermon a noisy Catholic procession approached the church. The local Protestant dogs, apparently trained to keep silence during the sermon when stowed away under the benches, started up and joined in the noise. The doors, which had been left open to let fresh air circulate, were closed but the procession was determined to march round the immediate surroundings of the church. It became impossible to hear the sermon, and an elder rose to suggest a pause. The congregation then waited in silence till the noise died away. Not surprisingly Henderson reflected on the fortitude with the Waldensians had borne their afflictions over the centuries. This particular demonstrative attitude of Roman Catholicism during Waldensian worship, which was not confined to the Angrogna valley, is said by Waldensians to have lingered on until the end of the 1950's.

The more serious of the afflictions had not to be borne much longer. Henderson visited the valleys at a lively time when there were apparently contradictory trends in Piedmont. The new vigour stimulated by Gilly and

Beckwith had provoked alarm and reaction on the Catholic side, supported and even sponsored by the Sardinian King, Charles Albert, who had moved from a vaguely liberal to a clerical and reactionary position. He had also appointed a former tutor to his children, Andrea Charvaz, as Bishop of Pinerolo. Charvaz, of Savoyard origin, was able and energetic and was later to be promoted to the archbishopric of Genoa. As a controversialist he challenged the historical and apostolic credentials which the Waldensians and their foreign supporters had claimed for their Church, exploiting some of the weak points where they had allowed leaps of faith to bridge gaps in real historical knowledge. He was also noted for his personal courtesy and developed a more-in-sorrow-than-in-anger vocabulary, reputedly inventing that ambiguous expression 'separated brethren'. But he also took a hard line and sought to revive the force of the Piedmontese law against the Waldensians. He challenged their right to property they had acquired outside the reservation and, even more emotively, sought enforcement of the laws which Waldensians saw as a threat to their community, including those which regarded children of mixed marriages as illegitimate and demanded Catholic upbringing for illegitimate children. He also encouraged a missionary Catholic presence in the valleys and got the King to sponsor and open a large new church at Torre Pellice.

But there were other currents flowing through Italian life, and flowing far more freely in Piedmont than in the Austrian dependencies, never mind the Papal States. There was a liberal party there among the professional classes and even the nobility, including an anglophile ex-soldier and agrarian expert, Count Camillo Cavour, whose mother was a Swiss Protestant. He was also editing a journal called *Risorgimento*.

Liberal politics in the Italy of the 1840's meant nationalist inclinations, even though there was no clear notion of when and how Italy might be united, and in what form. The most vocal school of nationalism was that of Giuseppe Mazzini, an ardent Republican exiled in Switzerland and (after 1837) in London, but Mazzini and Cavour did not have the field to themselves. The election in 1846 of Giovanni Mastai-Ferretti as Pope Pius IX, at a time when he seemed a very liberal conservative, revived the ancient notion that the Pope might preside in some form over an Italian confederation. There were also murmurs about confederation even within the Austrian sphere of influence, though Metternich remained hostile. This notion had its last flutter as late as the 1850's when the Archduke Maximilian, later to perish in Mexico, was governor-general of Lombardy and Venetia, but at odds with his brother, the Emperor Franz-Joseph.

That was the background against which Italy and Piedmont found themselves drawn into the European turbulence of 1848. This became most conspicuous with a new French revolution and quickly gathered momentum, though some significant changes had already begun in Piedmont's internal politics and Italian risings had preceded the French one.

In almost all Continental European history 1848 is The Year that Might Have Been: a year of revolutions which failed. Much of Italy rose against the Austrians and was crushed. Garibaldi failed to hold Rome for the Republic. Mazzini, who had been made 'triumvir', was soon back in exile. A supposedly liberal Pope became a frightened reactionary. Sicily lost the home rule it had briefly won from Naples. In France the revolution which overthrew the moderate Orleans monarchy of Louis Philippe was soon to be taken over by a new autocracy of Louis Napoleon, later Napoleon III. Germany sought unity but failed. Hungary fought for independence and was ground down. Even in Britain there was a brief threat of attempted revolution from the Chartist movement.

But the Waldensians remember 1848 with joy and thanksgiving. The improvement in their position (and that of the Jews) was one of the reforms which survived when the Italian revolutions failed and Charles Albert of Sardinia abdicated after his attempt to lead a war of liberation against Austria foundered at the battles of Custozza and Novara. (The victor was an aged Austrian general of Slav extraction, Field-Marshal Josef Radetzsky, to whom the elder Johann Strauss dedicated the march that still sets Viennese feet tapping and hands clapping.).

The pressures for liberal constitutions had been building up in several parts of Italy, especially after the election of Pius IX. By the time the new French revolution toppled the monarchy on February 24 Piedmont already had a new constitution, with a narrow franchise and Roman Catholicism as the State religion, but with religious toleration and the removal of the civil disabilities of Protestants. The law now allowed Waldensians all civil rights and access to university degrees, with entry to professions and Government service. Abolition of censorship meant that they could now publish and print in Piedmont and no longer depended on imports. The news reached the valleys on February 25, when there were celebrations, a thanksgiving service, and bonfires on the hilltops. The bonfires still burn annually above the valleys, and there are annual services followed by a communal festival meal but the date settled on February 17, the anniversary of the promulgation of the decree of Waldensian liberation.

It was not a law for religious equality, far from it. It left the Roman Church as the established Church, entrenched and privileged in a style that was already obsolete not only in Protestant countries with national Churches but even in French and German-speaking Catholicism. It declared that nothing was changed in the exercise of Waldensian worship - a provision which could be construed to mean that although the Protestants now had full civil rights their worship was still restricted and their missionary work prohibited. In the immediate aftermath of the new toleration the Piedmontese Government showed itself hostile to Waldensian and other Protestant evangelism. It was the determination of the Waldensians and others, not official encouragement, which extended mere toleration to considerable liberty. But the law was later interpreted in a more liberal spirit, not only by Count Cavour and the enlightened part of the Piedmontese aristocracy but by the middle-class public opinion which was shaping the new constitutional monarchy in Savoy, soon to be the basis for the Kingdom of Italy. There were to be problems many years later when a very different kind of Italian régime took a narrower view of the law, at least in respect of public evangelism.

But, for all that, things were never to be the same in and around the valleys again. There had been a spirit as well as a legal act of liberation. Many more of the former things were also passing away all over Italy.

In just over a decade between the emancipation of the Waldensians and the creation of the almost completely united Italian kingdom the pressures of the *Risorgimento* increased, despite the apparently immovable political barriers maintained with Austrian help. In exile Mazzini remained both a disruptive force and an intellectual influence, though Waldensians distrusted his republicanism and secularism. Verdi continued to have trouble with the censors, and the Italians rendered his older hit tune of 1842, the *Va Pensiero* chorus in *Nabucco*, as if it applied to the banks of the Tiber and not the Waters of Babylon. There was widespread and powerful sympathy from abroad, especially from Britain, and the demagogue who now called himself Napoleon III wondered about a cheap war in the cause of Italian freedom and personal glory.

In Tuscany, always the Anglo-Saxons' favourite part of Italy, the political pressure had a parallel campaign for religious freedom. Meanwhile in Piedmont the Waldensians and their British friends, with growing Scottish interest to supplement the legacy of Gilly and the work of Beckwith, tackled two rather different problems of expansion. They had to reorganise their ministry to serve adherents in Turin and places like Pinerolo close to the valleys. With Beckwith's encouragement and involvement, supplemented by large personal donations from him and the first Waldensian in Parliament, Giuseppe Malan, they acquired a fine central site in Turin and built an imposing Gothic church. They also looked beyond Turin and even Piedmont to the rest of Italy.

In Britain Gilly still led the campaign for support, though it was about to gain new strength from Scotland and he himself had only four years to live.

Writing from Norham vicarage - his letter of September 9, 1851 became a pamphlet - he still glowed with enthusiasm, despite the reluctance of the Waldensians to adopt an episcopal system. He reported on his fourth visit to the valleys, where he had found more prosperity, less poverty, and less sickness. Gilly claimed that he had never heard Christianity better expounded than in Waldensian schools, and argued that 'two-thirds' of the Waldensian pastors were distinguished in preaching and theological debate - though he implies that this was an unusually high proportion in any church.

But his campaigning zeal focussed on the new Turin church for the Waldensians, 'which should be visible to the world and be a monument to the toleration enjoyed by them'. He also wanted it to be in keeping with the architectural merits of central Turin, emphasising the Sardinian government had made this what we would now call a condition for planning permission.

Beckwith was probably even more enthusiastic about the style and quality of the new building than either Gilly or the Sardinian Government. During the building work he seems to have moved dangerously close - the phrase is not inapt - to adding a role as master of works to his other functions. In the summer of 1852 the Edinburgh Episcopalian evangelical minister, D.T.K. Drummond, called on him in Turin, where Beckwith was living at the time, and was redirected to the building site. Here the wooden-legged veteran was found on the highest scaffolding, surrounded by building materials and workmen, and greeting his visitors with what they regarded as a real military salute. Drummond, who was allowed to get his hands dirty with a token contribution to the work, professed himself unable to imagine how Beckwith managed to get up there or down again. But get down he did in time to entertain his visitors to tea in the evening. Although he could speak his mind forcefully - giving the Waldensians a telling-off for being too Calvinist, for example - he seems to have been as rich in public relations talents as in leadership qualities.

But the Waldensians also planned to be missionaries, supported by British and other Protestants, seeking to attract Piedmontese with no Waldensian or valley connections as the first step in a wider contribution to the evangelisation of Italy. Much was to be achieved, but much was not to go smoothly.

Chapter 6

THE SCOTTISH CONNECTION

Expatriates, missionaries, and Italian unity

It is hard to quarrel with the modern Fodor guide to Italy which sums up Leghorn as 'an important port but of minor interest for tourists'. Oil refineries and chemicals don't attract casual visitors, though some cruise ships stop there to allow passengers a quick coach trip to Florence and Pisa. There is even a modern tendency to refer to it in English by its Italian name of Livorno, under which reference books list two Baptist churches and the Waldensian one.

But in the eighteenth and nineteenth centuries Leghorn had important British connections. Its far-ranging commerce made it, even in the age of sail, the maritime equivalent of a 'hub airport' today. About 300 British ships a year called there in the 1840's. It was also the gateway to Tuscany generally and to Florence. It attracted many British visitors, particularly those who preferred the risk of a squally Mediterranean voyage to the certainties of a bumpy coach journey or arduous crossing of the Alps. There were around 200 permanent British residents, possibly with a Scottish majority, and there had been preliminary discussions in a sub-committee of the Church of Scotland Colonial Committee about a Presbyterian chaplaincy there even before the division of the Kirk at the 1843 Disruption. The Scottish firm of Henderson Brothers had an especially important role in its trade and for three generations served the Scots Kirk in Italy, with one of the family leaving Tuscany only on the eve of the Second World War.

Leghorn had also that hard-won but necessary convenience for the Grand and lesser tours, a Protestant cemetery. The one there provided the last resting place for many travellers, among them the first great Scottish novelist, Tobias Smollett, and the Edinburgh-born parliamentarian Francis Horner. Leghorn was also the last port of call in the tempestuous life of the poet Shelley, who set sail from it 'in a frail boat unskilfully handled'.

In the nineteenth century the port developed a Scots connection of a very different kind. In 1839 visitors included the Scottish 'mission of inquiry to the Jews' whose work was chronicled by Andrew Bonar and Robert Murray

McCheyne. They stopped off there because the city was a major Jewish centre - they reckoned the Jewish population at more than 10 per cent - and had, by the standards of the time, convenient connections for Palestine and Syria via Malta and Egypt.

This preliminary encampment of the Scottish reconnaissance of the Jewish world also turned into a reconnaissance of prospects for evangelising Italy. Even before reaching Leghorn, Bonar and McCheyne had signed up an Ulster-born ship's engineer to distribute tracts on board and 'among the other engineers along this coast, all of whom are Englishmen and Protestants'. On landing they decided that at a free port they should be free to spread the Gospel and gave more tracts to the eight porters who carried the deputation's luggage and to bystanders. An hour later all their books and tracts, along with their Hebrew literature, had been seized and sealed up, for despatch to the Tuscan Government censor in Florence. Yet by contemporary Italian standards Tuscany had a relatively liberal régime. One can even feel a little sympathy for policemen and censors who were encountering the evangelical revival for the first time and at first hand.

Most of the Scots' dealings in Leghorn were with the Jews, but they gathered such news as they could, as they had done earlier in Genoa, of the religious condition of Italy. They expected it to be in a low spiritual and moral state and rather enjoyed having their best fears realised. When they left a week later they were annoyed to discover that some of their books had been confiscated and rather less upset to hear that they had been banished from Tuscany in perpetuity. Their brief visit did, however, yield one flash of real insight among the rather conventional lamentations about Popery and the reluctance of Italians to brave the legal penalties for apostasy. For, with a mixture of Scots thrawnness and some tactlessness, they also attributed the lack of Protestant conversions to a different cause. 'Another reason, no less powerful, is to be found in the licentiousness of Protestants in Italy. The English in that country are generally gay and dissolute, regardless of all religion, One of the most profligate Italian towns is Florence, and the English residents take the lead in dissipation. Hence it has become an almost universal impression that Protestantism is the way to infidelity.'

It was a wild judgment based on hearsay and only a week's research, and in some ways a better summing-up of an age that was passing than the one that lay ahead. It fitted Byron and Shelley's time rather than that of Robert Browning, who had first visited Italy six years before. But it had two elements of truth within it. One was that, even when Victorian religious culture was most vigorous, a proportion of British visitors and residents in Italy were largely indifferent both to their own religion and to the one prevailing around them. Even many of those who attended and sustained the numerous expatriate churches and English, Scottish, and American chaplaincies that flourished in later Victorian times adapted the eighteenth century's live-and-let-live approach to the new age. In most of Italy and especially in Tuscany foreign Protestants were personally welcome and there was a wide range of provision across the peninsula for their religious needs, ranging from a Hungarian congregation with German services in Venice, mainly military and official, to chaplains for the 2000 Protestant mercenaries said to be in the army of the Neapolitan Bourbons. Leghorn had religious provision for German and Dutch Protestant traders as well as its English chaplaincy. The Protestants who were personally acceptable were also economically appreciated, and were left alone provided they did not offend Roman Catholic susceptibilities or encourage indigenous Protestantism. A grudging Piedmontese exception to this important proviso had been made only for the British and other Protestant diplomats in Turin who, with varying degrees of enthusiasm or reluctance, kept in touch with the Waldensians.

The other element of truth was that any British Protestant impact on a rapidly changing Italy depended on character, commitment, and an unpatronising sympathy with many sorts and conditions of Italians. Such was not always the prevailing tone of those attracted to Italy by its cultural inheritance, artistic treasures, attractive climate, and low cost of living. Some of those most enthusiastic about classical antiquities and the Roman heritage tended to look down on contemporary Italians and their language.

Gilly and Beckwith, whose approach was very different, had already made their impact on the Waldensian 'ghetto' in the Alps, though they looked to much wider Italian horizons. Now, in the aftermath of the brief visit by Bonar and McCheyne, a new outpost of British commitment to Italian Protestantism was to be established at Leghorn, with important lines of communication to the valleys and the Waldensians. It was to be the channel for a Scottish interest in things Italian which, though stimulated by the work of Gilly and Beckwith, had its own roots in the surge of missionary activity after the end of the Napoleonic wars. Only three years after Gilly's first account of the Waldensians appeared, Thomas McCrie, biographer of John Knox and Andrew Melville and critic of Sir Walter Scott's handling of the Covenanters, brought out a history of the Reformation in Italy.

The next reconnaissance to Leghorn after Bonar and McCheyne was undertaken by one of the most remarkable Scottish scholars of the nineteenth century, John Duncan, best remembered as 'Rabbi Duncan'. The nickname hints not only at his Hebrew scholarship but at his manner and style of devotion, which also reflected a life-changing experience and encounter with the notable Genevan leader, César Malan. Both had moved from a philosophical and almost sceptical Christian liberalism to a biblical and evangelical faith. In Malan's case this distanced him from the Genevan Church leadership of the day, which influenced the Waldensians through Geneva's role in the education of pastors. In Duncan's it helped to carry him into the Free Church at the Disruption in 1843 and set the tone for his 20 years as professor of Hebrew at New College, Edinburgh.

As the Disruption approached, Duncan was developing the Kirk's mission to the Jews in Budapest, established under cover of a chaplaincy to Scots building the Danube bridge, and developing links between Scots Presbyterianism and the Hungarian Reformed Church. But in 1842 anxieties about his health and the onset of the Hungarian winter saw Duncan moved to Leghorn, where he established a temporary preaching station in a Scots hotelier's annexe and an informal chaplaincy, even though only ships' captains and mates were allowed ashore to join land-based expatriates. Crews were confined on ship. Duncan also provided an alternative to the English chaplaincy, which was said to be too High Church for the prevailing taste. When he left to return to Budapest, to be diverted almost at once to New College by the Disruption, he had stimulated the demand for a Scots-led Protestant chaplaincy. By 1845 the Free Church was sufficiently organised not only to maintain the work in Budapest but to seek a man for Leghorn.

They found one in an East Lothian-born minister and son of the manse, a Glasgow graduate who succeeded his father at Erskine in Renfrewshire but was 'ordered south' for his health's sake. This was Robert Walter Stewart (1812-87), who had hurried back from Constantinople to be in time for the Disruption. He just made it, richly deserving his place in that neglected polemical classic, *The Annals of the Disruption*, by arriving in Edinburgh at four in the morning of the sad and glorious day in Scottish history. Stewart, who was grandson of a Scottish peer and son-in-law of the celebrated judge, Lord Cockburn, had high standing and good connections in Scotland and London. His cousin was the twelfth and last Lord Blantyre, once his patron in pre-Disruption times and a Scottish representative peer. It was said of Blantyre that he 'was nominally a Liberal but generally voted with the Conservatives on important occasions.' However he was also a leading lay supporter of Italian causes.

Stewart, who had spent a session of his divinity studies at Geneva, had also got to know Italy long before his ordination. A family stay of nine months in Rome in 1829 had given him a good grounding in Italian language, life, and culture, part of a wider knowledge of continental Europe. It is said, for example, that he first joined in the Lord's Supper at a Communion service in Geneva taken by César Malan. Even before he was settled in Leghorn he had already raised money to buy books for the college at Torre Pellice, with a scheme for a 'Scottish Library' for those who read English. This *Bibliotèque Écossaise des Pasteurs Vaudois* was still gratefully remembered nearly half a century later when virtually the entire Waldensian ministry sent Stewart individual messages of congratulation (kept in bound volumes in the Torre Pellice archives) to mark his ministerial jubilee.

Stewart remained based at Leghorn for more than 40 years and was the driving and guiding force in the Italian Presbytery formed by the Free Kirk's chaplaincies and missions. He and his wife raised a large family there but lost two sons in infancy. His letters show that he struggled to cope with the volume and diversity of work he created for himself, especially during the long energy-sapping summer heat in Leghorn. The letters, which at his death filled fifteen volumes of 500 letters each, suggest that he was not really fit for strenuous work then. But he established such a reputation from such an unlikely place that he was the Free Church's Moderator in 1874, though his earliest recognition seems to have been a doctorate of divinity from the American Presbyterians of Princeton. His ministry quickly developed from a sailors' and commercial chaplaincy in the Bethel and Harbour Mission into a kind of Scots agency for the assistance of Protestantism in Tuscany when it was still being persecuted there. Some of his correspondence with Scotland shows him privately suggesting that some converts could be too impatient and ready to act in ways which were likely to provoke the Grand Duchy's Government (e.g. on July 11, 1857), though this emphasises that the Tuscan evangelicals had strong wills of their own and were neither opportunist nor feeble-minded. This caution, however, was only occasional and tactical. Stewart was utterly committed to the Protestant cause in Italy and probably the most important influence on Italian matters in Scotland, not only through the Free Church but in his 30 years of contact with the Italian Evangelisation Society (which developed from an Edinburgh committee set up in 1850) and the Scottish Waldensian Missions Aid Society.

The Scottish-Waldensian archives also show that he and other Britons in Italy, notably Robert Maxwell Hanna in Florence, played a major part in the research and information which went into a campaign to put pressure on the British Government to help the Tuscan Protestants, of whom there were a few thousand. The Ulster-born Hanna had been a minister in Galloway, went to Italy for his health's sake, gathered the nucleus of a congregation in Florence, and supported the local Protestants, but died in 1857 before the revolution which opened the way for Italian Protestant churches there. His work had been done from 'his own hired house'.

The Tuscan Protestants had worshipped and evangelised openly for a brief period after 1848 but were harshly persecuted in the subsequent years of reaction. The memorial of 1856 to the Foreign Secretary, Lord Clarendon, was presented by a group of well-disposed peers and financed by London and Edinburgh Italian evangelisation committees, with the great reformer Lord Shaftesbury among the moving spirits. The detailed appendix of injustices - including the harsh treatment of the expelled Waldensian Pastor Geymonat as well as of native Tuscans - was prepared by Hanna. Stewart had been adviser and consultant, though some of the ideas he contributed (such as suggestions that Tuscan Protestants might have some of the rights conceded to Christians in Turkey) quickly became obsolete when Italy won political freedom. But one of Stewart's virtues was a readiness to adapt to changing circumstances and to persuade others, such as the Waldensians, to do the same.

He was also a zealous promoter of Protestant literature, with strong views on its quality as well as quantity. Eventually, after the great political changes, his Leghorn ministry was really the base for a Presbyterian embassy to Italy, as well as for presbyterial administration of the Free Kirk's network of stations and congregations in Italy and the Riviera. He was also to have a significant role broadening the British connection with the Waldensians and helping them, as Beckwith did, to adjust to the opportunities and difficulties of a new freedom and a new Italy. More than anyone else he established a new kind of Scottish connection, with a broader view of Italian needs and Waldensian mission than travellers like Beattie. It was not so much a change of Scottish opinion as, in the case of Beckwith at Torre Pellice and Gilly in his last years, a developing response to the changes which had put a more liberal Piedmont and the Kingdom of Sardinia in the forefront of the Italian national movement.

Even before the first territorial changes on the way to Italian unity, but after the internal liberalisation in Piedmont, Stewart was already weighing up the opportunities created by the Waldensian move out from the valleys and the difficulties which arose when the only continuous Protestant tradition in Italy was found on the French frontier. Moreover it was found among a people whose main languages, written or spoken, differed from those of other Italians and whose ways of life and thought had been conditioned by enforced isolation and a struggle for survival. Like Beckwith he was an enthusiast for modernising Waldensian education, developing its links with Italy, and increasing the emphasis on Italian. He too had a great but far from uncritical admiration for the Waldensians.

For example he wrote to the secretary of the Edinburgh committee (October 15, 1855): 'You know how anxious I am to get Italian students (not Vaudois by birth) who might be educated in the Valleys and then return to Italy to evangelise instead of *snooving* among the Alps as the native Vaudois are prone to do.' The emphasis on the Scots word used by Burns - meaning glide or twirl - is Stewart's own. But no-one was a stronger supporter of those Waldensians who in the next two or three decades overcame any tendency to 'snoove' and not only moved themselves but at times risked over-reaching themselves in their response to the opportunities in the new united Italy.

'The name of Dr Robert Walter Stewart is almost forgotten in modern Scotland. His achievements deserve commemoration in an adequate biography written by one who knows and loves Italy'. So wrote the Church historian A.L. Drummond in *The Kirk and the Continent*, published by the Saint Andrew Press half a century ago, though it should be said that Stewart himself had 'interdicted' the biography which missionary enthusiasm might have rushed into print soon after his death. He had also ordered the destruction of his personal correspondence, posssibly - so it has been suggested to me in Italy - because it contained Masonic confidences. But a manuscript collection of sermons survives in Torre Pellice and a large number of letters can be traced in Scottish and Italian archives. As a public literary memorial, however, there was only the 1890 account of *An Italian Campaign*, written by Stewart's son-in-law Wood Brown and published at a time when the Waldensians' supporters in Scotland had been stimulated by the bicentenary celebrations of 'The Glorious Return'. Alas, in a Scotland which undervalues its Victorian past Stewart does not even make an entry in the monumental and excellent Dictionary of Scottish Church History and Theology (1993).

At least the Waldensian Claudiana publishing house in Turin has not forgotten him, though its modern summary of his career does not repeat Drummond's statement that Stewart was its 'founder'. Claudiana dates back to an Italian religious tract society set up by the Waldensians in Turin in 1855, along with a book depot, and directed by a triumvirate of Pastors J.P. Meille and Peyrot and the leading layman, Giuseppe Malan. Even the outside help was by no means all Scottish. Its printing press is variously recorded as having been paid for by two Dublin Presbyterian ladies, the Misses Lyster, and by 'the Anglican gentlewomen of Dublin'.

Stewart was certainly much involved as a driving force and guiding force in Claudiana's early days, especially when it moved from Turin to Florence in 1862. Historical Italian notes written in 2004 call him its *anima* and 'lifeblood'. He consistently encouraged Scottish help for it, which included a large donation from the leading Free Church layman, George Freeland Barbour, a Liberal enthusiast for Italian unity who was proud to have attended the first Waldensian synod after the 1848 emancipation. Stewart also secured for it two other Scots who built it up in its early decades - John McDougall (1831-1900), who was minister in Florence but later disagreed with Stewart on mission strategy, and James Will, yet another Free Church man who went to Italy for his health. At first he acted as tutor in Stewart's family and as private secretary but then was for 23 years secretary of the Italian Evangelical Publication Society and director of the Claudiana Press till his death in 1889.

Claudiana's modern team deserve credit for extracting some of Stewart's views on Italy from an 1845 reprint of a lecture delivered in Scotland after he had visited the valleys for the inauguration. But he seems to have been, like Beckwith, a doer and facilitator more than a writer of purple prose. He was, however, the author of Gospel commentaries in Italian which were to have a long and lasting influence as well as a forty-year flow of long, purposeful, but cramped letters home, squeezed into limited space to ease the postage bill. The modern Italian historian Giorgio Spini, from the Methodist side of the Church, says that his commentaries made him 'a kind of spiritual father' for the Waldensians. Giorgio Bouchard calls him 'a second Beckwith'. As presbytery clerk Stewart also produced the terse minutes but copious correspondence of what began as the Presbytery of Leghorn but became the Presbytery of Northern Italy.

However, Stewart was not the first Scot to respond to the evangelical enthusiasm for the Waldensians stimulated by Gilly. In 1833 the Rev Adam Blair of Ferryport-on-Tay wrote a history of them which has been summed up as two portly volumes 'well documented but uncritical in the use of sources'. Stewart was also to be only one of several significant Scottish Victorian visitors to the valleys, among them the splendidly florid ministerial editor of the Free Kirk's Record, .James A. Wylie, and the Edinburgh evangelical social reformer, Thomas Guthrie. But Stewart committed himself to Italy and worked to get things done there in ways that demanded tact and diplomacy as well as will-power, together with an ability to respond to dramatic political and cultural changes. In his early days at Leghorn one of his extra-curricular chaplaincy duties was to assist in smuggling Italian Bibles into Tuscany at a time when (to put it very mildly) the Roman Catholic Church had little enthusiasm for widespread distribution of the Scriptures and such Italian translations as it had were mainly dominated by the Vulgate tradition. Stewart later shared a more formal and legal responsibility for Bible distribution as agent of the National Bible Society of Scotland, and co-operated with another Scot, T.H. Bruce, representative in Tuscany of the more important British and Foreign Bible Society. By the end of Stewart's long ministry Italy was united with Rome as its capital and with the liberal and anti-clerical strains dominant in its politics, thanks to the obstinacy of the Papacy in refusing to co-operate with the new régime.

The modern Waldensians recognise Stewart's role in what was for them an awkward and uncomfortable adjustment. They had been a persecuted local minority, but their grievances were largely met when Piedmont recognised religious freedom, though with some restrictions and ambiguities, and gave them full civil rights. They had then to decide in what way to become a Protestant presence in Italy. As a local Piedmontese phenomenon? As a proud historic survival? As a francophone minority? Or, as the most vigorous of the Waldensian leaders believed, supported by Stewart and Beckwith from their different points of Protestant view, as the nucleus of an evangelical Church for people everywhere in Italy?

On that at least the English Anglicans and the Scots Presbyterians agreed, despite the disappointment with which Gilly and Beckwith received the Waldensians' preference for the Reformed structure which they had adopted at the Reformation. By Victorian standards this denominational rivalry was relatively restrained and well conducted, though Stewart on occasion spoke of 'specious promises' when Beckwith, following Gilly, urged the Waldensians to become Episcopalians, and he complained (for example in a speech in Aberdeen on July 23, 1866) that 'Episcopalians had not been slow to say that the Waldensians had submitted themselves to the Free Church'.

Although the mission policy was based on Waldensian convictions and decisions, Beckwith had a leading role in its first stage after emancipation, the move out of the valleys of which the city-centre church and halls in Turin were the very visible symbol. But it is Stewart who is credited with a decisive role in securing the move of the Waldensian theological faculty to Florence, and in the acquisition of the Palazzo Salviati on the Via dei Serragli south of the Arno, one of several Florentine palazzi bearing that famous Tuscan name. His successful scheme to buy the palazzo, with funds provided by Scottish benefactors and by the Presbyterian Church in Ireland, is commemorated by a memorial tablet in the building, still in Waldensian hands as the Instituto Gould, though some explanatory material mistakenly suggests that Stewart was an Irish Presbyterian.

Though it was later to move to Rome, the faculty demonstrated in this first flitting another symbolic affirmation of the Waldensians' commitment to Italy as a whole, and of their increasing use of the Italian language. Stewart also played a major part in raising the money for the first Waldensian church in Rome, where he is commemorated. When he was Moderator of the Free Church's Assembly the visiting Waldensian Moderator claimed him as a citizen of the valleys and said his name was 'indelibly written in 20,000 hearts'. He had also 'taught Roman Catholics to respect Scotland'. He deserves to be a prophet with more honour in his own country.

There were of course both hostile and sceptical voices as the Waldensians moved beyond their valleys, Mrs Gretton, an English Protestant who lived for ten years in Italy, tells a story which brings out both the hostility and the scepticism. She was a lady of strong convictions, good manners, and social graces as well as many Italian connections in the upper as well as middle classes and she spoke good Italian. At a reception in one of the most elegant of Turin's palaces she noted that the reactionary element of the old nobility talked either French or Piedmontese, though the new liberal régime encouraged Italian. Of the old guard she said: 'Peevish regrets for the past, bitter allusions to the present, and Cassandra-like forebodings for the future furnished the staple of conversation.'

She knew when to keep silence but noted the reverence extended to a bishop in violet stockings and the trend of the conversation around him. It was about the opening of the Waldensian church in Genoa, which in this circle was regarded as 'an act of sacrilege' and opposed even more than the other Waldensian churches already built outside the valleys, at Turin and Pinerolo. This dispute had been especially bitter because, although Mrs Gretton does not mention it, the Waldensians had planned to use a deconsecrated former Roman Catholic church, though they eventually built their own. She added:

'I had a specimen of the bitterness of their feelings in the stories which were mingled with their invectives. It was inexpressibly diverting to one who knew the straitened circumstances of the Valdesi pastors, and the difficulties they had encountered in raising subscriptions for the building of this church, to hear of the immense bribes they employed to gain converts to their Communion. Three, four, nay five thousand francs was no uncommon largesse to a hopeful catechumen.' But she also quoted a rather sceptical Roman Catholic from Genoa, 'more just than flattering to his townspeople,' to rebut the absurd charge. 'I do not believe these charges of bribery', he said, 'not from partiality to the Valdesi but because if they paid people for going to their church half Genoa would be with them.'

The bishop's circle also lamented the 'impiety and atheistical toleration of Cavour' (who remained within the Roman Church) and denounced the distribution of Bibles as a national calamity. But it is worth quoting another sceptical voice, that of the Baltic German, Victor Hehn, whose father and grandfather were Lutheran pastors in Estonia. Hehn wrote a remarkable book on Italy which showed him to be no admirer of the papacy and a brutally candid friend of the Italian people. Some of his comments on dull food, bad wine, and lack of winter heating sometimes still occasionally apply, even if the coffee has improved. But he was equally candid about 'pious Englishmen', among whom he doubtless included pious Scotsmen.

He noted their complaints about the sensuality of Italian religion and their eagerness to import shiploads of Bibles, formerly under threat of perpetual imprisonment. 'Now it is permitted and this permission is diligently used by the eager missionaries. But one may doubt whether the result will be very spectacular. For in fact to sit in undecorated churches on wooden benches, to sing long hymns to three-centuries old tunes, to walk around dressed in black with an air of humble presumption, to give loud voice to biblical texts, to hold family prayers, to celebrate silent fast days, to honour only the disembodied Word - all this would taste like Swedish oat-bread to the Italian.'

The Italians, Hehn said, did not share the Northern Europeans' separation of the spiritual and the sensual (*Geist und Sinnlichkeit*). 'They do not know any devotion without display (*ohne Darstellung keine Andacht*) for they must transform their innermost being into some sensual presence.'

It is worth quoting Hehn's argument and pungent rhetoric, sometimes also deployed at the expense of the Vatican and the Catholic opponents of Bismarck, because they express feelings which, rather differently expressed, worried many English and some Scottish Protestants. It was a problem which also created perplexities for Waldensians, and led many Italian critics of the Roman Church, including converts to Protestantism, into experiments and down cul-de-sacs. Even today there may still be echoes of the argument in discussions of the greater apparent receptivity of Italians, like Latin Americans, to Pentecostalism rather than mainstream Protestantism.

The argument which was to perplex, divide, and weaken the Evangelical mission to Italy had begun even before the country was united and before the opportunities opened to the Waldensians in Piedmont after 1848 had yet been extended to Florence, never mind Rome or Naples. It was apparent as soon as the Waldensians encountered Italian dissenters from the Roman Church who wanted to exercise the new Piedmontese freedoms, and was encouraged by the expectation that these freedoms were bound to spread to other parts of the peninsula.

In 1855, for example, Gilly already felt a need to urge Presbyterians as well as Anglican Evangelicals to commit themselves wholeheartedly to the

Waldensian alliance, in these words: 'It is manifest that unless the Waldensian Church be strengthened and put in the front of the battle, all the Reformed Churches in Europe and America will be without a pivot to turn upon in Italy. This has been my constant and invariable strain and it will be a shame upon the Presbyterian Churches, if a prelatist, as I am, should be the most unshaken of all the advocates of the poor little Presbyterian Missionary of Piedmont.'

Gilly also wrote to Sir George Rose: after the formation of an Italian Evangelical Society, forerunner of the later *Chiesa Libera*. 'Many after having united themselves to the Waldensian Church became restless and unwilling to submit to any ecclesiastical discipline whatever.' He suggested that these converts were dissatisfied politically as well as religiously and ill at ease with the way the Waldensians stood for Church order 'with the discretion which their well known loyalty and their position require of them'.

'We cannot abandon the venerable remnant of the primitive Christians of Italy, tried as they have been in the fire, for the sake of a new society, Italian and Evangelical though it proclaims itself to be.'

Dr Stewart, who had a better acquaintance with Italy's new Protestants and knew the situation on the ground, shared the same worries and encountered day-to-day frustrations with converts. He told the Scottish Italian Evangelisation Society in a letter from Leghorn (November 12, 1855) that they often took a very 'low' view of the Lord's Supper and saw it as 'as little more than a sign and pledge of their initiation into Protestantism.'

For the moment Protestants of various styles in Tuscany still felt a sense of solidarity with each other and with the various chaplaincies and expatriate ministries which supported them. But the anxieties expressed by Gilly and the practical difficulties reported by Stewart pointed to a cloud, as a yet still no bigger than a man's hand, that was to gather over Protestant prospects and Protestant unity in Italy.

Perhaps it was too rashly assumed, possibly more by enthusiasts in Britain than by expatriates like Stewart, that political liberation would bring religious revolution and that Protestant opportunity would sustain Protestant harmony. But it was easy in the 1850's to be carried away by enthusiasm, both religious and political. It was not clear how change would be brought about in the Austrian and Austrian-dominated parts of Italy, never mind in the temporal realm of the Pope, but there was no mistaking the power of the reform movement and the probability of revolution in some form. It was very difficult even for people of sober judgment and balanced outlook to look ahead. We who claim the omniscience of hindsight 150 years later must recognise that the pace of change also depended on the hazards of battle, first at Novara and Custozza, then at Magenta and Solferino in 1859.

But these years of uncertainty probably mark the high point of British interest in Italy and enthusiasm for things Italian. It is not surprising that Victorian religious enthusiasm and political liberalism were both important in that relationship, or that political and evangelical expectations were confused and sometimes rather naive. It was easier to greet a new dawn and denounce forces of darkness than to guess what the bright new Italian day would bring.

These were the years in which the great rising power of British politics, W.E. Gladstone, moved from merely protesting against tyranny and misgovernment to supporting Italian liberalism and then Italian unity. At the beginning of the 1850's he spent three months in Naples. It was partly for the sake of an ailing daughter, but his restless energies involved him in translating an anti-papal history of recent government in Rome and assessing the sermons and liturgy in Roman Catholic churches. He was rather taken by the office for the dead but appalled by the sermons, especially on Purgatory. It was this Neapolitan visit which provoked his famous denunciation of the Bourbon government in Naples as 'the negation of God erected into a system of government', a translation of a resonant Italian phrase he had heard in Naples: *la negazione di Dio eretta a sistema di governo.*

At the time he was trying to persuade his fellow-Conservatives to take a strong line against abuses of power in the Italian States, and still unpersuaded of the feasibility of Italian unity, which he regarded as 'an abstract proposition'. But in the next few years, when British opinion, including many pro-Italian evangelicals, was increasingly enthusiastic about the *Risorgimento*, Gladstone committed himself to a united Italy. Like many evangelicals, he was influenced by the arguments of exiles in London. But he also had the benefit of a long conversation in February 1859 with Count Cavour when he stopped briefly at Turin on the journey home from a political mission to the Ionian Islands.

There were still sceptical spirits, even in Britain, and among some political friends of Austria, which had been seen since 1815 as a stabilising conservative force in Europe. Lord Palmerston, the great Whig survivor in British politics who went along with the trends of the times and favoured 'leaving Italy free for the Italians, also professed himself as 'very Austrian north of the Alps'. And by an irony of history the most distinguished of the sceptics, Benjamin Disraeli, was of Italian descent, grandson of a Sephardic Jew who left his native town near Ferrara to seek his fortune in Venice and then London.

Disraeli had a romantic steak which made him more receptive to the ageless charms of Venice than the contemporary state of Neapolitan prisons, but even the sceptics in Britain were soon carried along with the tide. In just over a decade Italian unity had moved from an impossible dream or unrealistic proposition to a rapidly accomplished fact. There was a revolutionary situation which was to excite those whose main interest in Italy was religious and not political. For some Protestant enthusiasts it was to induce ideas of a religious as well as political Utopia. And even the most sober and realistic of the Waldensians and their British friends had to adjust to the sudden and dramatic changes of Italian politics.

Chapter 7

IN THE KINGDOM OF ITALY

Great expectations in a brave new world

The Kingdom of Italy under the Sardinian Crown, in which the Waldensian Church established a modest network of congregations outside the valleys, was very different in political and social outlook from the Italian States and provinces of Metternich's 'geographical expression'.

By the late 1860's Italy's boundaries were almost those of today, as defined in the peace settlement after the Second World War. Only Trieste, Gorizia, the Trentino, and the German-speaking South Tyrol, all added after the First World War and retained in 1946, remained Austrian.

The first stage had been the Sardinian alliance with France which brought war with Austria in 1859, though Napoleon III's price was to include Savoy and Nice, the first conceded by Cavour with a good grace, the latter more reluctantly. By the time the Austrians gave up Lombardy, after the battles of Solferino and Magenta, the Austrian satellite régimes had also been swept away, including those of the Papal States, apart from Rome and its surroundings. The expedition of 'The Thousand', the red-shirted volunteers led by the rumbustious anti-clerical Giuseppe Garibaldi, born in Nice, then brought down the Bourbon Kingdom of Naples (or the 'two Sicilies'), opening the way for it to adhere to the enlarged kingdom of Victor Emmanuel II.

Garibaldi had been involved in South American guerrilla warfare as well as various revolutionary enterprises in Italy before a mixture of luck, judgment, and timing made him not only 'the Liberator' of much of Italy but one of the heroes of the century, not least in Victorian Britain. His revolutionary tactics and Mazzinian radicalism were far removed from the policies of Cavour and the mood of the Piedmontese Waldensian leaders and their main British supporters, but Scots and English enthusiasts for Italian causes did not neatly separate politics and religion.

The Leghorn-based Scots firm of Henderson at Leghorn, for example, did not separate them from each other or from business. One of its bright young men, a nephew of the original partners, was Donald Miller, then only 22 and later to become the influential Scots minister in Genoa for 35 years. After six years in Italy he was already a pillar of Dr Stewart's Leghorn congregation. When news came through of Garibaldi's first success in Sicily he abandoned a scheme to sell surplus French army stores in Genoa to Newfoundland and decided to offer them to the Italian expedition instead, following 'The Thousand' to Sicily in the Scots-manned paddle-steamer City of Aberdeen which had been chartered to carry revolutionary reinforcements. He caught up with Garilbaldi in Palermo and made the sale, although he had to pursue him to Caserta near Naples to get the accounts settled.

Miller recalled that the bill was paid at the Neapolitan treasury's expense by the future Italian Prime Minister, Francesco Crispi. But his memory of Garilbaldi himself, as recorded in his family papers, was far more striking. 'There was such a wonderful combination of majesty and meekness in his countenance that it came nearer to my ideal of Christ's face than any picture I had ever seen.' Even a reprimand from Garilbaldi to a subaltern made Miller 'think of Christ when he used the whip of cords... But that was the only time I saw him angry. As a rule his look had that mixture of majesty and gentleness which I imagine Christ must have had when he took little children into his arms.'

When such an impression was made on so firm and orthodox a Victorian Presbyterian, one who declined to deal with Garibaldi's commissariat on the Sabbath and may already have had the first hint of a call to the ministry, it is not surprising to discover that one of the many causes of scandal which the great revolutionary gave to Rome was that he allowed some admirers to bring their children to him for baptism. But he was to have more honour than influence after the union of Italy which he had so dramatically accelerated.

The revolutionary triumph in 1860-61 which created the new Italian Kingdom was not quite what even Cavour had expected, for his plan was the extension of Piedmont into the Kingdom of Northern Italy, and it was not at all what Napoleon III had intended, for it created a major new Power on France's frontiers. This irritation was to make the Emperor of the French insist on his claim to Nice as well as Savoy, though both cessions were ratified by plebiscites, and did not endear him to politically conscious Italians. The new State was no grateful satellite, for Napoleon III was blamed for the failure to incorporate Venetia and the delay in moving into Rome. The new State also thought itself stronger militarily, diplomatically, politically, and economically than it really was and for the next half century was to play some devious international roles before the ultimate recklessness and misjudgment of the Mussolini era.

Perhaps too much had happened too quickly for the good of Italy. The swiftness of the change, the contagious effect of revolution, and the weakness of satellite régimes in face of their protector's reversal of policy and loss of confidence had a modern parallel in east-central Europe after 1989. The Italians too had a velvet revolution, at least in the north and centre of the peninsula. The South had wanted to overthrow the régime there but not necessarily to unite with the North or accept the House of Savoy. The Bourbon collapse and the accession of the southern provinces and Sicily to the united Italy was followed there by what according to taste one may call guerrilla warfare or widespread banditry, accompanied by some corruption and much inefficiency - at least in the eyes of Northern Europeans and even Northern Italians.

Austria's next defeat, by Prussia in 1866, brought Venetia into the new Italy. The Italians joined the war and had setbacks on land and a disaster at sea, but they secured Venice when peace was made. Rome itself followed in 1870 when the French garrison that sustained the Pope's remaining temporal power was called home by the Franco-Prussian war which destroyed the régime of Napoleon III and opened the way for the Third Republic.

Italian national feeling was triumphant and to an extent consolidated, though the new kingdom was handicapped by the backwardness of the South and by the alienation of those 'good Catholics' who followed the papal line and distanced themselves from political life. Other Roman Catholics, either liberal in their views or nominal in their allegiance, heartily supported the new Italy and accepted the idea of religious freedom, in some cases even sympathising with the Waldensians and romanticising their history. This was most evident in the case of the Ligurian-born Edmondo De Amicis (1846-1908), a novelist, poet, and travel-writer notable for his descriptive powers. He was the author of *Alle Porte d'Italia* (written, according to a memorial tablet, in the Hotel de l'Ours at Torre Pellice) and the idea of 'the Waldensian Thermopylae', though he could be much less romantic in pen-portraits of Turinese tram-conductors or emigrants taking ship at Genoa. Modern Waldensians say that his secular enthusiasm for their tradition of resistance went with some misunderstanding, for example in a tendency to exaggerate the role of pastors - it was a pastor who assured me of that - and underestimate the importance of the community of faith and 'lay' leadership.

With hindsight it is easy to see that new Italy was far less unified than it seemed after the Republicans of the Mazzini and Garibaldi traditions accepted the House of Savoy, with varying degrees of reluctance. But there was an Italian State, and many of the former things had passed away. Bibles circulated freely and were on public sale, both in the streets and through the travels of colporteurs. Passports were only wanted to secure delivery of registered letters and prove nationality if requiring consular help. 'Passports, though not required in Italy, are occasionally useful', said Baedeker's nineteenth-century guides. One of his rivals added: 'The traveller who possesses one should certainly not leave it behind.' There were now numerous expatriate Protestant churches in Italy. An evangelical guide published in Paris listed 23 Anglican churches or stations in Italy along with two English-speaking Methodist churches and six Scots Presbyterian ones, supplemented by seasonal arrangements elsewhere, for example in Venice. Most of the outposts of the Scottish empire were garrisoned by the Free Kirk, but there was a gentleman's agreement that the different Presbyterian denominations would not compete and would provide a common fold for the divided flock.

In Rome Protestants at first still exercised their new freedom outside the inner city beyond the Porta del Popolo. There had been a Church of England chapel from 1818 and the first church had been improvised by buying a large house and knocking four rooms together. But soon after 1870 there were several Protestant churches, with a Scots one in the heart of the city from 1885. Previously *Murray's Guide* directed Presbyterians to 'the first entrance on the left after the Episcopal Church'. The new Scots one was (and still is) in the Via Venti Settembre, whose name commemorates the raising of the Italian tricolour in Rome just over a fortnight after the fall of the French Empire at Sedan.

The market for these churches was created by the large number of permanent British residents - Florence probably had the most and Rome relatively few - together with tourists and winter residents on the Riviera. This reflected the increasing ease of communication. Italy was being united not only by politics but by the railways which coped, among other things, with the move of the country's capital from Turin to Florence in 1865 and then to Rome after 1870. But local lines as well as trunk lines were changing the patterns of Italian life.

Access from the Waldensian valleys to Turin now meant getting to Pinerolo and catching a train. It was a leisurely journey, as all trains were slow trains. They still are. The agnostic novelist Samuel Butler had time enough between Turin and Pinerolo to hear a vigorous and detailed exposition of Waldensian mission-work from a fellow-passenger and to be put off going on to Torre Pellice by diligence because he feared that tracts would be as common there as in Victorian England. This notable iconoclast decided Waldensians were 'malcontents'. By the end of the century an extension of the line (out of commission for several years due to flood damage but scheduled to reopen in December 2004) had been opened to Torre itself, with trains taking two and half hours. It was slow going, but it was a link to the main networks of Italy and Europe. There was also a steam tramway from Pinerolo to Perosa, near the entry to the more northerly valleys at Pomaretto.

Italian travel was also relatively cheap, even though British travellers usually travelled first or second class - the assumption was that travelling third meant sharing a wooden bench with a goat and more than a whiff of garlic. In the higher classes there were only the problems, still considerable for Victorians, about smoking in non-smoking compartments, opening or closing the windows, and overcoming Italian insistence on drawing down the blinds when the tourists wanted to enjoy the views. Towards the end of the century a second-class single ticket from Turin to Torre Pellice cost 3 lire 75 cents, roughly three shillings in British money of the time.

One incidental result for the Waldensians of the new unity of Italy and of the ease of movement within it was a change from a French-speaking religious culture to an Italian one. The pastors were now trained in Florence, with a further move to Rome coming later. They might still go abroad for further theological education, but there were now opportunities in the British Isles and Germany as well as Switzerland and France, although some influences from French-speaking Protestantism remained strong, among them the legacy of Alexandre Vinet in the Canton of Vaud. His emphasis on separation of Church and State strengthened instincts and convictions of Waldensianism which remain apparent today.

But the move away from French was gradual, as a walk round the late nineteenth-century gravestones in Torre Pellice cemetery makes clear. Even in the schools there was a change in balance and emphasis rather than the kind of pressure exerted on linguistic minorities elsewhere in Europe, though this was partly because Beckwith and his colleagues had recognised the importance of teaching the Italian 'language of State' even before the unification of Italy. They also recognised that with emancipation formal Italian and the Piedmontese dialect of Turin would both play a greater part in Waldensian life. Indeed the Waldensians were probably more polyglot in the late nineteenth century than at any time in their history, for much thought and effort had gone into biblical and literary and religious experiment with the Valdese or Vaudois dialect. In the later decades of the century British visitors were even grumbling a little about the way Italian was coming into the Waldensian Synod as well as French, which more of them understood. The Glasgow Herald also recorded a complaint in September 1892 that speakers were inclined 'to glide from one language into the other', but with Italian becoming ascendant because of the 'politics and alliances' of the day.

Thanks largely to the new links with British and German universities and colleges, English and German were becoming widely spoken among pastors. In Edinburgh, for example, there began the long and still surviving tradition of Waldensian bursars at New College, originally the Free Church college and now seat of the university divinity faculty. As early as the 1850's one of the Waldensian visitors was assuring the Free Kirk editor-minister James Wylie that Edinburgh was the most beautiful city in the world. Wylie returned such compliments by declaring that he found the valleys a second homeland.

One of the powerful influences in making the Waldensians more familiar with Italian was not the school, whose playground language would be the local dialect, but the Italian Army. Vaudois men usually became really proficient when they served their then obligatory military service. Girls often learned Italian working in factories or domestic service and some Waldensians who worked in Turin spoke Piedmontese dialect, as the House of Savoy itself had done. It was even said that the only King of Italy who really thought in Italian and not Piedmontese was the last one, Umberto II, titular monarch for a few weeks in 1946.

There was a transitional period when Waldensian Church life was bilingual (trilingual if one includes the dialect to which the congregation reverted when the kirks skailed in the valleys) with French as the language for traditional Waldensian worship but Italian as the language of mission and Church extension. Perhaps it was also already the language of innovation, for an Italian version of psalms and hymns was coming into use from the 1870's.

A passage in the rather extended Continental memoirs of William Miller brings out this bilingualism. Miller was an Edinburgh lawyer prosperous enough to take long trips abroad in the 1870's for the sake of his wife's health, covering a lot of country between Pau and Naples. He was a Scots Presbyterian, though his wife was English, and the considerable detail in his book of 'practical hints to travellers' includes a good deal of valuable source-material about Scots and English expatriate religion as well as on hotel customs, medical matters, and travelling conditions. But on their way home from the Riviera in 1878, via the Mont Cenis line and the new tunnel - the first route there had depended on an awkward, nerve-wracking, twisting system of drags and Fell rails - they stopped off at Turin. They admired the Cavour monument but not the cathedral, which they found the dirtiest church they had seen in Italy, 'which is saying a great deal'. On Sunday, however they got into a tangle. They found an English service on Sunday morning in a room off the yard behind the Waldensian church and returned to the main building in the afternoon expecting a French one. But their hotel had got the information wrong and in the afternoon they found an Italian service going on.

'The church, which is a large one, was scantily attended by a shifting congregation of the poorer classes of Italians. Many, apparently Roman

Catholics, just entered to see what was doing and after a few minutes went out again to be replaced by others.' The Millers left but back at their hotel met a lady who told them that the morning service had been in French and that then 'the church was crowded by a most respectable congregation'. In fact there had been difficulties in Turin, from the early years of emancipation, in providing for the co-existence of 'Old Waldensians' and new converts. Some were deeper than the problems of linguistic adjustment.

There is also a graphic description of linguistic co-existence and transition in the letters home of the notable Scottish social and temperance reformer Thomas Guthrie, the 'apostle of ragged Schools' and driving force in the successful efforts to provide manses for the ministers who 'came out' of the Establishment at the 1843 Disruption. It was said of him that 'from homeless ministers his exertions turned to houseless children'. They also turned to the Waldensian missions in Italy.

Guthrie was Moderator of the Free Kirk's Assembly in 1862. Three years later, when his main European enthusiasm was the formation of the Evangelical Alliance, he also attended the Waldensian Synod and on his return became the first chairman of a missions aid society in Scotland and the driving force in the creation of a similar type of fund-raising body in England. In 1869 he went back to the Italy and the valleys, this time with a party of more than a dozen family and friends which also included the daughter of Hugh Miller, the Free Kirk editor and stonemason-turned-geologist.

His letters home record how they stayed in Torre Pellice, and on their first Sunday went to the Waldensian church where they found the 'regent or schoolmaster' reading from the Bible while the congregation assembled. There followed a service which that day included both sacraments, Baptism and the Lord's Supper. Guthrie found the sermon preached by a visiting minister, previously in Naples, a little hard to follow. The following Sunday, however, the sermon was 'in most intelligible French'.

On each Sunday however Guthrie hurried away from the church down to the market place near his hotel to hear proceedings, in front of the town house, which appear to have been wholly in Italian and very different from the stately worship of the Waldensians, who in those days stood for prayer and for repetition of the 'law' or Commandments, but sang seated. Torre had a more diverse local culture than was suggested in some descriptions by Waldensian supporters, such as the New York minister Robert Baird who called it (in the 1840's) 'the Lacedaemon of the valleys'. The open-air events round the town-house now provided a Sunday afternoon treat for Protestant visitors, who had chairs fetched out from the Hotel de l'Ours to watch in comfort. The new religious freedom of Italy, however circumscribed it might be in some ways, was being exercised. The Pope was being denounced in public and in Italian, even on occasion by those who were still within the Roman Church, and priests at that. 'A man can preach Jesus Christ with more safety in Italy than in many parts of Ireland', wrote Guthrie.

On both Sundays an English evangelist and minister called James Wall was preaching in fluent Italian. Wall, honoured today as a founding father of the Italian Baptist Union, had come to Italy in 1863 under the auspices of a 'Gospel Mission to the Italians'. By 1869 he had established a congregation in Bologna and extended his work to Modena, though he was soon to move to Rome. He had come to Torre Pellice as a friendly observer at the Waldensian Synod.

On the first Sunday, however, there was an even more exciting attraction than the Wiltshire pastor who had mastered open-air evangelism in Italian. This was Don Ambrogio Giuseppe, a priest who, Guthrie was told, had been one of Garibaldi's chaplains and 'whose throat the priests of Rome at La Tour and elsewhere would be glad to cut.' He had 'not renounced all the errors of Popery; but his aim as he said was to restore purity to the Church and liberty to the country.' His hour-long sermon 'was a curious melange - a compound of politics and an imperfect Gospel', delivered with energy, fire, and occasional impassioned vehemence . He wore a high crowned and broad-brimmed beaver hat, a cross between a Tyrolean and Quaker style, decorated for additional effect with the red, white, and green colours of the Italian flag.

The second Sunday the evangelist Wall preached on his own. Don Ambrogio, for whom the visiting Protestants had a whip-round at their Sunday-night English service, was presumably playing to an audience elsewhere. But this time there was a rival attraction across the square: a cart turned into a stall for a travelling healer and medicine man, selling powders wrapped in silver or gilt paper and purporting to heal all manner of diseases. His promotional and publicity props and aids included a trumpet, drum, set of cymbals, tortoise, and four-foot spotted snake. Local Protestants muttered that the rival show had been arranged by the priests but nearly a century and a half later what probably strikes the reader is neither the devious ingenuity of Rome nor the possibility of Jesuit snake-farming but the resemblance to Donizetti's *L'Elisir d'Amore*.

The Guthrie family visit to the valleys and other parts of Italy, however, was not entirely a solemn affair, enlivened only by these Sunday treats of rebel priests, evangelists, and a quack healer with snakes and tortoise. It also had some objective social observation, and even praise for some aspects of contemporary Roman Catholicism. The temperance-minded Guthrie, like most

British evangelicals in Europe, was struck by the absence of drunkenness in Italy despite the abundance and cheapness of wine. He also noted the large Saturday night attendance at the Roman Catholic church of a congregation that seemed to be mainly mill-girls and day-labourers, lamenting the rather different Saturday-night customs of Victorian Scotland.

The Guthries and their party also displayed that Victorian enthusiasm for getting out and about on the mountainside which had made Switzerland so fashionable, expensive, and crowded. Part of the success of Switzerland had been in making mountain excursions socially acceptable and eminently practicable for both sexes, a reflection in part of the high standards of hotels which even the most fastidious Victorian guide-book could recommend for ladies.

The Val Pellice did not have hotels in the Interlaken manner - it still doesn't - but British travellers spoke well of the Lion d'Or as well as the Hotel de l'Ours where the Guthries put up and where end of century photographs show that the Italian version of the name had been added to the older French one.

When the Guthrie party set out for the historic village of Rorà, high up in the next valley to the Pellice but accessible only by a very rough scramble over the hills or by a detour downriver followed by a long, slow climb, they left Mrs Guthrie behind. She said she had 'no predilections for a mule's back'. But the other women shared in the procession of assorted horses, mules and donkeys, with Hugh Miller's daughter Bessie on a small pretty donkey and 'looking with her auburn hair and rosy face fresh as the morning'.

It was a long way round and then a stiff ascent by a winding road to get to Rorà. The Waldensian folk-hero Janavel had once held off vastly superior numbers there and in 1704 Duke Victor Amadeus of Savoy had been driven by French invasion to seek a mountain refuge among the Waldensian subjects he had persecuted. As the Guthrie party at last approached it they heard the local Roman Catholics (not more than twenty) firing a salute in honour of the Corpus Christi festival. When they arrived they found that hospitality had been laid on by the previous year's mayor or syndic in a house marked out by 'excellent cooking and unusual tidiness' and a hearth that reminded him of his grandfather's kitchen. The lunch was eggs, omelette, and *polenta* with coffee but it came in a style which Dr Guthrie attributed to his hostess's time as a domestic servant in Florence.

There was more evidence at Rorà of the way Waldensians sometimes managed to see the world and still return home, as well as a much more immediate reminder of Scotland. In that 'eagle's nest' at Rorà there was a 'bright, blooming Scotch lass' with blue eyes and golden hair, so recently arrived that she hardly spoke the language yet. She came from Inverness but while working in the big house at Muirton in Stracathro had married the Waldensian valet of the owner, a doctor who encountered the valleys on his way home from India and decided that he wanted a Protestant Figaro. The couple had moved to Italy on the doctor's death, where the bride had found her husband's family kind enough and seemed happy. But 'how happy she was to see us, and sorry when the time came for us to leave.'

The day's outing had a less placid final phase, as one of the Guthrie girls on a donkey got separated from the main party on the long descent. The men got alarmed and Guthrie was stricken by fears that his daughter Nell had fallen from a rock into a mountain torrent, and only partly reassured by thoughts that the donkey was likely to be more sure-footed than either horse or human. In fact the 'unprotected female' was becoming rather an exasperated one, waiting for the men to catch up when they had managed to move on ahead. When finally traced she had just negotiated with a peasant to guide her back to Torre Pellice and her escort had to cancel the contract for a fee of one franc.

Guthrie is a good example of the genuine sympathy and admiration which Gilly, Beckwith, and Stewart had stimulated and encouraged back in Britain. Curiously he also reveals in his family letters a weak spot, an inclination to persuade the Waldensians to conform to British evangelical ways of the time. Gilly and Beckwith had shown a similar fallibility in a quite different area of doctrine and order. They would have liked to make the Waldensians good Episcopal Protestants. Guthrie wished they could be induced to keep the Scottish Sabbath - not the Calvinist one but the Puritan one. The distinction is worth drawing because Guthrie drew it himself

Guthrie seems to have worried more than other British Victorians about the Waldensian Sunday, though of course Felix Neff had been grieved by the evening dancing and Stewart aired similar views in a more restrained way when he delivered lectures on the Waldensians in Edinburgh and Glasgow in 1845. The Religious Tract Society had also worried about Sunday habits as well as an inclination in some Waldensian quarters to cards and dice, though it allowed that 'even now the Waldenses may be reckoned the most moral people in Europe'.

Gilly found the mood in the Waldensian country reminded him of Sundays in his native Suffolk. Beattie, the Scots doctor, also felt very much at home . He emphasised the contrast between the Waldensian country and other parts of the province and was moved to quote extensively from Gray's *Elegy in a Country Churchyard*. Even Guthrie's Free Kirk colleague James Wylie seemed happy enough. He worked into one of his purple passages something about the contrast on Sundays between the Catholic Perosa valley and the Waldensians in Pomaretto across the Chisone at the foot of the Germanasca valley. On one side noisy celebrations seemed to get louder as the day wore on. On the other side there was peace and calm that seemed to grow sweeter in contrast to the revelry across the river. It reminded him of Sir Walter Scott's epigram that there wasn't much of a Sunday in the Pass of Killiecrankie, once the border between Presbyterian Scotland and the then wild Highlands.

From Torre Pellice, however, Guthrie grumbled in his letters home (May 24, 1869) about the market under the windows of the Hotel de l'Ours, card-playing by Germans in his hotel, and dancing in the evening. Although he blamed much of it on the Roman Catholic half of the population, 'the ideas of many of the Waldensians in regard to it were, like those of almost all Continental Protestants, much too low'. He put the blame on the way the pastors had been educated in such lax environments as Montauban, Berlin, and Geneva!

Guthrie reached Torre Pellice with a bit of a bee in his bonnet about the Continental Sunday. At Florence he had been distressed to discover that the Protestants, mostly converts, tended to come to evening services after a day's recreation. Like other British Victorian sabbatarians he made a point of wandering through stalls and markets to see just how bad things were. Unlike others, he took his criticism of Continental Protestantism to the highest level, with an audacity which may be admired and a judgment which may be questioned. 'Calvin's, and especially Luther's views of the sabbath day', he wrote home on May 19, 1869, 'have wrought much evil. Let us speak tenderly of the faults of these great and good men: their views were probably more correct than were the terms in which they expressed them.'

Nothing can readily surpass this very Scots Presbyterian and sabbatarian readiness to put even the great Reformers to rights as a dramatic demonstration of the self-assurance of mid-Victorian Britain. But it is perhaps equalled by the determination with which one of the greatest of all Victorians, William Ewart Gladstone pontificated on Italian matters, theological as well as political.

The two men had very different opinions on Italian religion. It is perhaps as well they did not exchange them when they met, on Guthrie's outward journey, at the dinner-table of the Duke of Argyll in London. Gladstone had become Prime Minister for the first time a few months earlier. and Guthrie was an enthusiastic supporter of his Bill to disestablish the Anglican Church in Ireland. The conversation had been about Ireland and the future of the Church of England, with Guthrie having the self-restraint to hold his tongue about his notion for disestablishment all round. Gladstone waxed eloquent after dinner about the way the English Establishment was rooted in the soil and institutions of the country, demonstrating the High Churchmanship which kept him apart from the evangelical Waldensian enthusiasm and the Roman Church whether in Italy or England. 'I thought it best to leave providence to be his teacher', said Guthrie.

Chapter 8

INTERLUDE IN FLORENCE

Literary lions and Italian enthusiasts

Guthrie's Italian visit also took in the Waldensian theological college at Florence, then at the climax of its brief reign as the capital of Italy.

The Parliament of the new Italy had promptly declared in 1861 that Rome would be its capital, but Rome was still out of bounds. The elegant city on the Arno with its dazzling literary and artistic heritage had been favoured as the provisional capital of the new Kingdom of Italy after the union of the northern and southern parts of the peninsula, though the move was not formally made till 1865. The move was encouraged by pressure from Napoleon III of France, anxious to pose both as friend of the new Italy and defender of the Papacy.

Turin had been ruled out as capital, despite the reluctance of King Victor Emmanuel II to move to his new quarters in the Pitti Palace. He still fancied the hunting, and the women, of his native country. But Turin was set almost at one extremity of the kingdom. To have stayed there would have made the united Italy seem only an engorged Piedmont. But the largest cities of Italy were also ruled out. Rome was still the last refuge of the temporal power of the Pope as an Italian sovereign, and under French protection. Naples was for a long time Italy's biggest city but it was too backward and unruly as well as too far south. Milan, though a great commercial and cultural city and a centre of Italian nationalism under the Austrian occupation, was too far north. Turin, which saw riots in protest against the effect of the move to Florence, would have been even more affronted if the capital had just moved along the road to the bigger city in Lombardy.

Then as now, Florence was in some ways the most attractive of Italian cities, the special case of island Venice excepted. The main Victorian drawbacks were occasional inundations from an overflowing Arno and some health hazards which included an unexpected late bout of epidemic cholera in 1884. In the nineteenth century it was not the centre of Italian culture in the way it had been in medieval times but the relatively enlightened rule of the Grand Dukes had already made it a centre of intellectual life and had modernised the city, demolishing the notorious Stinche prison. Florence had railways when the Vatican still opposed them, and it had gas lamps which allowed the relatively mildly censored newspapers to be read in the streets after dark. It also had a number of Italian Protestants, some of whom had unhappy experiences with informers and the authorities. Among them were the Madiai, a husband and wife - she had been converted while in domestic service in Britain - who ran a guest-house in Florence but got long prison sentences in 1851 for 'impiety by means of proselytism' after hosting a Bible study group. Their sufferings became the subject of a skilful lobbying campaign from London involving Lord Shaftesbury and other Evangelicals and they figured again in the memorial to Lord Clarendon of 1856. While Turin's Protestants were still mainly Waldensians from the valleys who had come to work there, the Protestants of Florence were not a church of tradition and community but a much looser group, mainly of political liberals, inclined to innovation, exploration, and sometimes individualism - a situation which was to bring some problems in its train. However one of the places where they gathered - if they could get past the police watching the doors - was the Swiss church from which the Waldensian Pastor Malan had been expelled in 1851, because Florentines were attending the Italian services, ostensibly held only for Swiss from the Grisons and Ticino.

But even before Florence became the capital of Italy it was already an international city. In the 1850's the French Goncourt brothers, the celebrated literary partnership, noted that it seemed to have become *une ville toute anglaise*. The exaggeration was pardonable, especially as a French view was unlikely to note the differences among English, Scots, and Anglo-Irish and between all of them and Americans.

The rent-rolls and hotel registers of nineteenth century Florence certainly incorporate a roll of honour from the English and American literature of the time: not only Robert and Elizabeth Browning, Walter Savage Landor, Charles Lever, Frances Trollope, Algernon Charles Swinburne, George Eliot, and Henry James as long or short-term residents but a host of visitors from Thackeray and Dickens downwards. Anthony Trollope dutifully visited his mother, but had the tact to make Lake Como and Milan, not Florence, the habitat of the appalling Anglo-Italian Stanhopes in *Barchester Towers*. His elder brother Thomas wrote the city's history in four volumes, but was criticised by Evangelicals for making the old grand-ducal régime appear more tolerant than it was. Thomas later moved to Rome with his second wife, sister of Dickens's enigmatic companion, Ellen Ternan. Florence also had a long line of eminent visiting Americans, among them Fenimore Cooper, Mark Twain, Nathaniel

Hawthorne, Harriet Beecher Stowe (whose attendance was a boost for the Scots church), and Henry Wadsworth Longfellow, the author of *Hiawatha*.

Many of the passing visitors joined in the social life of the English-speaking community and its churches, though if they came in high summer they might find that the permanent residents were away and that in some years, the Scots church had closed till September. When, for example, Dr Guthrie visited Florence in May 1869, staying at the pension of an English-born Signora Jandrelli who kept her Cockney aspirates after 24 years in Italy, he was more or less dragged out to a reception, given by the American Presbyterian minister, at which Longfellow was the principal attraction. Guthrie was weary but some of the women in his party were 'crazed about Longfellow', whom he found simple and unaffected in manners, full of a quiet suavity , although 'neither in his eye nor manner does he exhibit a spark of enthusiasm'.

But the English-speaking communities in Florence were a complex network, not just in nationality but in social composition and theology. Lord Tennyson's brother, Frederick, was one of a group involved in what was called spiritualism but had mystical inclinations and Swedenborgian connections, though he seems at times to have attended the Scots kirk. He also had Tuscan family links, having married a Giuliotti. The Acton family, liberal but Roman Catholic, had Tuscan as well as Neapolitan connections. (Edward Gibbon, who was related to them, recorded in his autobiography how in 1764 he took pity on the first of the Tuscan line, cut off from the society of the other English after conforming to the local religion.)

The literary lions shared the city not only with the Florentines themselves, and after 1865 with the great migration of politicians and officials, princely and petty, but with various flocks of their British and American kinsfolk, as well as with other foreigners. Among them were German Protestant deaconesses who set up a successful school. It attracted many Roman Catholics interested in a liberal education and also made itself acceptable to the Jewish community in Tuscany, which before the coming of religious freedom had been marginally better treated than the few native Protestants. Dr Stewart of Leghorn even suggested in the mid 1850's that the Tuscan Government might be induced to allow Hebrew and evangelical communities the same status.

Florence and some other parts of Tuscany were reckoned good places to live by those who had modest but secure incomes which would go further there than in Cheltenham. Along with the French and Italian Rivieras it had some of the appeal of the Costa del Sol and the Algarve today, as well as a minor role among the many places in Southern Europe where rich British invalids sought refuge from the smoke and fogs of Victorian cities. Soon there was also to be a flow of British visitors in a greater hurry, eager to make the most of limited leisure and new travel opportunities. They were a very mixed lot, socially, culturally, and even theologically. Late in the century the redoubtable Protestant campaigner, the Revd Jacob Primmer of Dunfermline, was delighted to encounter in the cathedral a family from Falkirk with whom he could deplore the innovations in the parish kirk there and 'the Ritualism being forced on the National Church of Scotland'. But as early as 1868, a year before Guthrie's visit, the young Earl of Rosebery, Prime Minister later on in the century, was complaining that Florence was 'swamped with Cook's Tourists'. The element of truth in the slightly snobbish exaggeration was that Thomas Cook was doing well in Italy, after losing money on his first 140 tourists in 1864. The eminent Baptist and teetotaller catered for all denominations, but he was personally rather pleased to combine good business with his 'joy in the resurrection of Italy' and his trips to Rome for Holy Week with pity for what he called 'victims of papal power and priestly domination'.

But Cook was a flexible friend as well as a package tour pioneer. He had made Dr Guthrie's travel arrangements to Italy, supplying tickets and coupons but leaving the choice of return route open. Guthrie sounded quite flattered when he reported home that in Paris he had even been mistaken for Cook himself, 'the great excursionist'. He also conferred on him the more imposing title of The Traveller's Friend.

There was also a permanent British commercial and professional community in Florence to serve the expatriates and visitors - shopkeepers, pension-owners, doctors and other professionals. Dr Guthrie, for example, came across Miss Rimond, a hospital-trained nurse whom he had known in London and who was now also a midwife anxious for recommendations. She was having difficulty with the Yankees, he claimed, because of their prejudices. She was black and Guthrie reckoned her 'a singularly smart woman, rather pretty, having a good dash of white blood in her'. Their previous encounter had been when she spoke at a London anti-slavery meeting which he chaired during the American Civil War.

Not surprisingly this English-speaking community ensured that Florence was well-provided with expatriate churches, including a so-called 'composite chapel', where an American minister offered the Episcopal service in the morning and the Presbyterian style on Sunday afternoons. The Browning family, for example, are recorded by A.L. Drummond as having a pew in the Scottish church. However Elizabeth Barrett Browning died in 1861, the year before the previously rented east wing of the Palazzo Barbenai on the Arno quay was bought and adapted as a permanent church, and her husband left Florence for good after her death. Her last failing weeks had been still further saddened for the Brownings by the death of Count Cavour, in whose leadership Elizabeth saw the future hope of Italy. She appears to have been, quite literally, prostrated by grief on hearing the news.

The Waldensian presence in Florence was impressive. Dr Stewart of Leghorn, who had lobbied for the move of the theology faculty from Torre Pellice and helped secure an adequate building for it, was also involved in a personalised fund-raising project in Britain and Ireland. The Scots Waldensian archives have a pro-forma letter in Stewart's name, based on one to a Miss Jackson in Gurteen, Co. Cork. In this ladies, 'singly or with the aid of friends', set out to raise £90 to cover the cost of a three-year bursary for ministerial students at the new location of the faculty, a college commission having decided that £30 was the minimum annual cost at which 'a student can live in Florence'. The sponsors were not encouraging lavish living.

In 1869 there were 15 students there, who had completed a philosophical and literary curriculum at Torre Pellice before moving to Florence, not only for theology but to perfect their skill in 'the purest' Italian in the heart of Italy. Some of them were alleged to try too hard to lose their valley accents and to emerge from the new college preaching in a purer Tuscan Italian than was ever heard in Tuscany itself.

Its principal was Dr Jean-Pierre Revel (1810-71) who was also fluent in English. Revel is remembered by modern Waldensians not only for the move of the theological Faculty from Torre to Florence in 1861 but as Moderator in the 'decisive years of the *Risorgimento*' (1848-57) and as a leading advocate of the evangelical expansion beyond the valleys. For the last decade of his life he presided over the evangelisation committee which was in effect the Waldensian mission to Italy.

No-one worked more closely with the English and Scottish allies of the Waldensians and no-one leaves a better impression a century and a half later. To read the Scottish correspondence with and about the Waldensians is not always a profound spiritual experience. Much of it was necessarily about money and some of it was about quarrels among Protestants. But from time to time, especially with Revel, the power of the Spirit breaks through and these faded letters in the National Library of Scotland read like tape-recorded conversations of the Communion of Saints. It was a doctrine which, as he wrote on January 27, 1852 to the Scots enthusiast George Freeland Barbour, then gathering funds to build the Turin church, he was experiencing in a new way:

'Je comprends réellement mieux ce que c'est la communion des saints.'

Another of its faculty was Professor Geymonat, who had been imprisoned along with the Madiai before being expelled. The 1856 'memorial' prepared by

Stewart's ally on the spot, Maxwell Hanna, had claimed he was deported chained to a felon. Geymonat comes across as a gentle man who later maintained his contacts across some of the divides that opened up among Italian Protestants.

In some way however the most impressive Italian presence among the Waldensians of Florence at the time was Luigi Desanctis, once a parish priest in Rome but by 1869 (the last year of his life) a Waldensian pastor and theological professor. He had little English but a Scottish wife, née Martha Somerville. He had met her in Malta, where her father was the chief official on the lesser island of Gozo. His own career, or pilgrim's progress, had demonstrated some of the intellectual and spiritual turbulence of the time in Italy. As a young priest he felt oppressed by the moral and religious condition of Rome under Pope Gregory XVI, which he later recorded in *Roma Papale*, one of his many books. He left the Roman Church in 1847 and went to Malta, where there was an Italian Protestant presence in exile. In 1850-2 he was an evangelist among Italian-speakers in Geneva and then joined the Waldensians, serving as a pastor and evangelist in Turin. But there were, as already mentioned, difficulties in Turin over the co-existence of traditional 'valley' Waldensians and new Italian Protestants and there were also the arguments over the site of the first Waldensian church in Genoa. Desanctis broke with the Waldensians, seemed to be won back and settled in a chair at the Torre Pellice faculty but left again.

He was attracted by Alessandro Gavazzi's ideas of a national Italian evangelical Church and worked for several years in Genoa and Liguria with the 'free Italian churches'. He was credited with giving this group their constitution as the *Chiesa Libera*, using formulae which Stewart of Leghorn claimed (in *The Presbyterian*, July 1873) had been prepared by Desanctis as the Italian version of the principles of the emerging international and inter-denominational Evangelical Alliance, and therefore deliberately left rather loose. Dr Guthrie, a biased witness, recorded this spiritual pilgrimage of Desanctis as becoming 'rather entangled with the Darbyites or Plymouthites who have done much mischief on the Continent'. However in his last years, which coincided with the Waldensians' attempt to reach out to the newly united Italy, Desanctis returned to them and brought distinction to the new college and Waldensian church in Florence. After a service there he also gladdened the heart of young Bessie Miller by speaking kindly and knowledgeably about her father's books, especially his *Testimony of the Rocks*.

Alessandro Gavazzi (1809-89) was another example of the interaction in mid-nineteenth-century Italy of religious and political discontent. He came from Bologna in the Papal States and was a Barnabite teaching monk. He has been called 'the greatest intruder of Italian evangelism' and a modern scholar and critic, Daisy Ronco, holds that 'it is impossible to determine when Gavazzi left Roman Catholicism and if he was genuinely converted.' Before he did leave he had caused much trouble for the Church authorities through his radicalism and rebellious tendencies. Pius IX, in his first phase of mild liberalism, had given him a fresh start by letting him out of an enclosed religious house - a form of detention - to become chaplain to Papal States volunteers who fought for Sardinia in the unsuccessful 1848 war with Austria. But he was soon organising hospitals for the short-lived Roman Republic and had to take refuge in Britain, where he won support, raised funds, and attached himself to the Italian evangelical community in London. This was a group with many talents, among them those of Professor Gabriele Rossetti, a Neapolitan of Abruzzese descent who was father of the poet Christina and artist Dante Gabriel, but with even more varied opinions. Rossetti for example not only denounced the papacy of his own day but used his scholarly knowledge of Dante to discover great anti-papal significance in the *Divine Comedy*. The extent of the alienation of the Italian liberals from the Roman Catholicism of their day may be judged from a quite casual reference by a Victorian biographer to Christina Rossetti's decision not to marry an English Roman Catholic, a decision which shaped her life and influenced her art: 'As an ardent Italian patriot she could not become a Roman Catholic, but her devotion assumed a High Anglican character.' Another family connection, Gabriele's cousin Teodorico Pietrocola Rossetti from Abruzzi, spent several years in exile in London but returned to Italy, where he married a widowed governess, a Scots-born Signora Iannetti, née Isobel Steele. This Rossetti, an evangelist and hymn-writer, wore his Protestant liberal nationalism with a difference, becoming a leading but relatively moderate and unfailingly charitable controversialist in the 'Free' Italian disputes with the Waldensians and their British supporters.

The exiled Gavazzi had made a considerable impact on British Evangelicals in the 1850's. When he died an obituary in *The Christian* remembered that 'no such feat is on record of a stranger, speaking in a foreign tongue, entrancing the English-speaking race for years'. But when he returned to Italy, supporting Garibaldi's ventures in Sicily and Rome, he was also committed to the replacement of the papacy by an Italian national Church. At odds with the Waldensians and then with other prominent Italian Protestants, he hived off in 1863 to form a new Free Italian Church. He was encouraged and helped for a time by John R. McDougall, whom Robert Stewart of Leghorn had sought out in the Free Kirk as a Scottish minister for Florence after Hanna's death, but who went his own way in Italian Protestant politics, and raised money in Scotland and Ireland for the independent tendency. McDougall was the author of that fulsome obituary of Gavazzi, thought him a great theologian, and wrote later that 'if ever two men loved and confided in one another it was Gavazzi and myself'. (in his *Open Letter,* December 7, 1895)

The new Church grew and had 22 congregations in 1870. It was supported not only by McDougall and some Scots, English, and Irish but by Americans and Germans, among them Karl Rönnecke, the influential Lutheran pastor in Florence who was later German Embassy chaplain in Rome. It also attracted some people of conviction and integrity who found it hard to fit into the structures and traditions of the Waldensian Church. Among them were Bonventura Mazzarella, a lawyer from Apulia who became a professor of education at Bologna University and then Genoa, entered Parliament, and became notable as a spokesman for the neglected regions of the South as well as for religious freedom, and Count Piero Guicciardini, a Florentine aristocrat. Mazzarella had been influenced towards Protestant faith by the Waldensian J.P. Meille while a political exile in Turin. Guicciardini had been converted as far back as 1836, suffered imprisonment and exile, came to Britain and even took British nationality before the liberation of Italy. In England he enjoyed social contacts with the aristocracy and a welcome from the Plymouth or 'Open' Brethren. His good works included the gathering of a major Italian religious library, bequeathed to the University of Florence, and the revision of the Diodati Italian translation of the Bible.

But despite the individual talents the free churches and the *Chiesa Libera* had attracted, they lost their momentum. The notable names were of those who been young liberals and religious reformers in the days before 1848. Gavazzi himself, its most flamboyant talent, was clearly not a team player at all and his last years were isolated and embittered. The Waldensians had kept him at arm's length. After his death and a further sequence of quarrels, some surviving Free Italian Church congregations joined up with the Methodists, who had been involved in Italy since about 1860, with both British and American connections. Their most significant leader was a British Wesleyan minister, Henry Piggott, a powerful personality but (according to the Methodist historian Giorgio Spini) 'an intelligent and generous man who wanted Italians to create a renewed Church on their own'. He and his American counterpart, the scholarly Leroy Vernon, had an approach not unlike that of John McDougall in Florence but, unlike McDougall, Piggott had the skill or temperament to avoid being dragged down by destructive quarrels among Italian converts.

Congregations of the other stream of free Italian churches continued and developed, but as communities of Brethren rather than an attempt to create a national evangelical Church for Italy. Some of them had moved from being free churches or *chiese libere* into the ill-fated *Chiesa Cristiana Libera in Italia* or Free Church of Italy but reverted to the Brethren name. There are said to be more than 200 such congregations in Italy today. There is also, within the Protestant Federation but as a separate Church, the Baptist Union descended from other British and American initiatives of the age of the *Risorgimento* but later, like some of the Italian Pentecostals, appreciably influenced by the contacts which Italian emigrants made in the United States. However they avoided the worst of the fraternal quarrels of Italian Protestants and in 1901, the year when their old leader James Wall died, the two Baptist movements both joined the Waldensians and others in a Protestant council for Italy which pointed the way to the closer co-operation which developed later and which today raises the possibility of some kind of Waldensian-Methodist-Baptist union.

It is not for a foreigner and a Christian of another age to pronounce with any confidence on the rights and wrong of these minor triumphs and little tragedies long ago, and not for any but the most specialist historian to analyse them in any detail or even unravel the complexities of relations between these new Protestants and the old Waldensian tradition, reaching back for centuries beyond the Reformation.

There were cultural and temperamental difficulties which would have caused problems even if the people involved had not been what they were. One side were Waldensians with the zeal of vindicated traditions and both the strength and difficulties which came with their ethnic character and their little homeland in the Piedmontese valleys. They were strongly supported by the London society in the Gilly-Beckwith tradition and by most of the leaders in the Scottish Connection, especially Dr Stewart in Leghorn and Donald Miller of Genoa, who from the 1870's became a major Waldensian consultant and confidant.

On the other side were people from the mainstream of Italian life and culture, though now to some extent set apart from both by their conversion. Many were simple, humble, and poor people who had felt the power of the Bible's message, life-changing and life-explaining. Others were gifted and articulate Italians, priests among them, who in varying degree saw religious reform as part of the wider reform and unification of Italy. Many converts had the zeal proverbially attributed to that condition, and the determination necessary to sacrifice worldly prospects (as some did) or to set themselves apart from the community, one might even say the civilisation, to which they belonged. There were also human failings on both sides in the course of the quarrel and inevitable hardening of attitudes. In 1875 for example the leading Scots ministers in Italy, Stewart and Miller, were deeply suspicious of a naive attempt at 'conciliation' by an elder statesman of the Free Kirk, Dr Buchanan., though they also urged the Waldensians to avoid unnecessary controversy and polemical sermons. 'What matters', wrote Miller in Italian to the Waldensian Professor Comba (February 10, 1875) 'is that he returns convinced the Waldensians are well disciplined and active'.

In general they were, but ill-natured exchanges developed at some stages of the quarrel, with the Waldensians even being denounced as 'the Jesuits of Protestantism'. When for example the Waldensian church in Rome was opened, with the aged Dr Stewart walking with assistance at the head of the procession, the reports of the occasion in the Scottish Waldensian archives also noted that 'with the exception of the *Chiesa Libera* all the denominations had responded to the invitation.'

Even after the *Chiesa Libera* lost its momentum through internal disputes, there was a thoroughly unseemly quarrel in the 1890's involving its successor, the Evangelical Church of Italy, and the Waldensians, especially Dr Prochet of the mission committee. It seems to have been partly about the secession to the Waldensians, with other ministers and members, of the evangelicals' president, Pastor Damiano Borgia of Milan, and about the church property they took with them. It drew in Dr McDougall of Florence, who had long been the treasurer for the free evangelicals and had once called this Borgia 'the McCheyne of Italy'. He prepared a virulent 42-page pamphlet, an open letter circulated 'privately' but preserved in Scots and Italian archives, which revealed more about the wear and tear on his judgment than about the deeper reasons for the evangelicals' problem in united Italy. For by then McDougall was a frustrated and disappointed man, soon to squander his last energies on wrangles with the remaining leaders of his faction, among them his oldest Italian Florentine ally and protegé, Ludovici Conti. These sad letters have found their way to the Waldensian archive via the Methodist church in Florence, where they were rescued after the Arno floods of 1966.

It may seem self-evident now that it would have been better for Italy and Protestantism generally if all those who left the Roman Church had adhered to the Waldensians, who provided a well-established structure which could and eventually did prove adaptable enough to accommodate new congregations and new trends, even though for more half a century the Waldensians themselves sometimes appeared almost as a federation of the old valley Church and a new Italian mission-Church, or a 'home country' and mission field. The Methodist historian Giorgio Spini suggests that there was a democracy in the valleys with parishes having the right to elect their pastors and be represented in the Synod while the rest of Italy was run by the powerful evangelisation committee which sent in ministers in the way that Governments assigned prefects.

But it was easier to hope for a united Italian Evangelical Church than to achieve it - as is still the case in today's very different conditions - even without that ethnic element and the temperamental problems of accommodating free or rebellious spirits and sometimes flamboyant individualism. There was also, for some Anglicans and others, the prospect that if the Pope resisted all reform in both State and Church some kind of rebellious or schismatic Catholic religious movement might emerge, retaining in a way that no evangelical movement could the ceremony, colour, and the best of the popular styles of devotion for so long associated with Italy.

In the course of writing this book I have not only come to appreciate these difficulties but to see the force of some of the arguments and circumstances which prevented the Waldensians from becoming not just an all-Italian evangelical Reformed Church but The Evangelical Church of Italy.

Most of the printed sources and archival material available to me, as well as the main tradition of Scottish and English friends of the Waldensians, explicitly or tacitly accepted the Waldensians as the chosen instrument of evangelical mission in Italy and lamented the diversion or dispersal of energies elsewhere. These sources were very evidently tinged with suspicion, probably justified, of people like Gavazzi, and in the Scottish dimension of the argument assumed that Robert Stewart of Leghorn and his close Waldensian allies (such as Revel and Prochet) were right and John McDougall in Florence and his allies were wrong, perhaps not heretics but misguided mavericks whose approach was bound to encourage schismatics.

Such a view however should not be maintained uncritically by those who reaffirm (as I do) the importance both of the Waldensian tradition and the continuing Waldensian connection. McDougall's vision was a noble one and his earlier judgment of what might be worth trying with Gavazzi and others was sounder than his later involvement with a cause which brought him and others bitterness and disappointment. But the errors and dogmatism were not only on one side. Hindsight sometimes teaches humility as well as understanding. Perhaps the most effective way to find the right perspective on the damaging mid-Victorian quarrel is to read some of the more restrained and charitable statements of the case for the Waldensians against the enthusiasts for the Free Italian Church. Some of what Robert Stewart, for example, found wanting in it might appear in a very different light today to most reformed Christians, Waldensians included.

He set out some of these worries in *The Presbyterian Journal* in July 1873, a piece which the Scottish Waldensian supporters had reprinted and circulated in a bid to prevent diversion of contributions to Gavazzi's 'Free Church Mission', though the article followed speeches and arguments in the Free Church's Presbytery of Italy and at its General Assembly.

Some of the issues involved were mere debating points at the time (such as the complaint that the *Chiesa Libera* allowed foreigners on their executive committee, one of them being McDougall) or have since been relegated to mere historical interest, such as the defence against the charge that Waldensians 'only speak a sort of French' or the obvious irritation at the way the term 'free Church' was used to attract support in nineteenth-century Scotland.

But other issues were of real theological substance, raising issues on which Presbyterians and Anglican Evangelicals have no more right to insist on their own infallibility than any Bishop of Rome has for his distinctive and sometimes mistaken opinions. One of Stewart's complaints was that the *Chiesa Libera* was too much inclined to independency and congregationalism, and that McDougall in Florence played this down in order to win Presbyterian support in Britain. He also probably regarded McDougall as almost an independent himself. Indeed in a reply prepared when McDougall formerly dissented from a Presbytery rebuke in the long-running wrangle about the summer closing of the Florence kirk, tersely but regularly recorded in the Presbytery minutes, Stewart claimed that 'the pastor, elders and people alike ignored the Presbytery and practically acted as independents.'

There also seems to have a good deal of independency in the way that McDougall organised his time, though like Stewart he had health problems to cope with, and in his fund-raising for the Florence church. He had probably come to Italy too young to become a Presbyterian team-player, and although Glasgow-born with a Scottish home in Bridge of Allan, was ordained in England and never held a charge in Scotland.

In 1860 the Irish-born Methodist analyst of 'Italy in transition', William Arthur, had noted McDougall as a leading supporter of the Italian Protestants, 'especially the Vaudois', and an uneasy partnership seems to have survived well into the 1860's. Stewart acted as session clerk pro tem in setting up the 'Scotch Presbyterian Church' in Florence, the original and proper name which old-timers still tried to insist on as late as 1915. He attended its early session meetings, and presided on occasion at Communion services.

But by 1869 Stewart and McDougall were far apart on policy, even though they were the leading members of the small Presbytery, originally called Leghorn but soon renamed North Italy. . There was particular anxiety on Stewart's side (which was also that of the Waldensians and most of their British supporters) about 1871 regulations which recognised the 'Plymouthite' tenet 'that each particular congregation possesses alone the right, according to Scripture, of recognising among their own members those who are endowed with the gifts of the ministry.' In that year the Florentine kirk's Italian 'town missionary', Ludovici Conti, had demitted his charge to join the *Chiesa Libera*, which was now clearly competing with the Waldensians to be the main instrument of missions to Italy.

However disputes about Church order were of much longer standing. Even from the late 1850's there had been worries about the administration of the Lord's Supper and grumblings about the 'plague of Plymouthites'. British supporters were told of an evangelist at Asti who left the Waldensians, perhaps more in sorrow than in anger, after being convinced that the presidency need not be confined to ordained ministers. But a slightly shocked tone comes into the report (recorded by Wood Brown, whose book used the letters of his father-in-law, Dr Stewart) that in Tuscany an Englishwoman, Miss Johnstone, had gathered converts for the Lord's Supper 'and actually dispensed the bread and wine to them with her own hands'. I hope that I shall neither lose Waldensian friendship nor be hauled to the bar of the Kirk's General Assembly when I confess that when I read that passage I uttered a spontaneous cry of 'Well done, Miss Johnstone!'

Another issue - and also one which has a certain irony today, given current Waldensian practice - was that there was a 'diversity of doctrine, and in practice, particularly concerning baptism, which are utterly at variance with the Presbyterian system.' There was also one familiar to anyone assessing the relations of Presbyterianism with less formal Protestant movements and denominations in many times and places: insistence on a highly educated ministry. That was a tradition which the Waldensians had sustained for several centuries, often in face of great difficulties. It was not such a high priority for those other Italian evangelicals who relied on inspiration rather than tradition, some of them denied the opportunity for higher education, others in revolt against much that they had learned in their seminary days. They might even argue that they had much in common with the mood of Valdo and his early followers.

Modern Presbyterians would engage comfortably if perhaps less dogmatically in that argument. They would also surely accept the wisdom of some of William Arthur's analysis, made at a time before the Methodists themselves had an Italian denomination to advance or defend, in relation to many Italians moved by the Spirit, then and now:

'Perhaps there is in the Italian mind something favourable to teaching which leads them to an abhorrence of every sort of Church government and confounding all forms of ministry with the dreaded Romish priesthood'. The rise of modern Italian Pentecostalism suggests there is still force in that argument.

Both Presbyterians and Anglicans may feel relieved that by nineteenth century standards denominational rivalries were not carried too far, even when Beckwith sulked a little over Calvinism and Stewart manoeuvred to frustrate a Scots Episcopal notion that they might sponsor English-speaking services in the Turin church. But would they all be comfortable with some of Stewart's specific complaints against Gavazzi - for example that in writing and from the pulpit he had been found 'denouncing the doctrines of individual election and eternal punishment'? Many of them would certainly take Gavazzi's side when he argued that historic confessions of faith could be compared to 'hooped dresses of a former century... which no fashionable young lady of the present day would condescend to wear.' That would appear to be the view of many Presbyterians today. Stewart on the other hand was a firm adherent of the Westminster Confession, the Kirk's 'subordinate standard' under Scripture and had from his early Leghorn days been anxious to have it available in Italian, the drafting work being been done by two young women in the expatriate community, Miss Rae and Miss Pate.

To be fair to both Stewart and McDougall, it should be recognised that one was quite sincere when claiming good will towards the *Chiesa Libera* and the other was sincere, dedicated, ingenious, uncomfortable, and ultimately unsuccessful, even embittered, in trying to encourage a distinctive and national new Italian Church which would remain close to the Reformed tradition but require a much looser framework of doctrine and order. This was no farther-fetched than the bid by Gilly and Beckwith to persuade the Waldensians to reach an accommodation with Anglicanism by giving their Moderator an episcopal life tenure or Guthrie's attempt to persuade them to be more sabbatarian.

The awkward fact, as all their British friends recognised, some sooner and more graciously than others, was that Italians had minds of their own and were not going to replace an Austrian temporal domination with a British spiritual one. Again Arthur got near the heart of the matter when he warned in 1860 that 'the last thing that English Protestants ought to think of doing is to impose their own ideas on reformed Italians'. Stewart said similar things, yet in practice both Presbyterians and Methodists found themselves in alliance with kindred Italian groups. Perhaps both also underestimated the inherent difficulties in binding together the frontier Italians who had kept the light shining for seven centuries and the peninsular Italians who had broken with the papacy into a new and sometimes dazzling blaze of light. By the nature of their history, convictions, and experience both groups were likely to be determined and sometimes even headstrong.

The failure and break-up of the *Chiesa Libera* and then of its successor 'The Evangelical Church of Italy' were not the result of Waldensian hostility or lack of foreign support but of internal problems, some of them connected with powerful and conflicting personalities but some of them still unresolved today, even among Protestants. But it is important to record these perplexities as well as to note the quarrels of the time and the hopes which were raised but raised and left unfulfilled.

It is both fair and important to recognise that there are other Italian reformed and evangelical traditions apart from the Waldensian one, even though their late twentieth-century union with the Methodists has brought some descendants of the Free Italian Church into a new and happy relationship with it. In Florence for example the Waldensian congregation which originally gathered in the Palazzo Salviati survives, though it moved across town to the former English Holy Trinity Church. But the other congregation of the united Church, the Methodist one near the Ponte alle Grazie, is the old *Chiesa Libera*.

We should recognise also recognise, whatever may be the future providence of God, that the Waldensian Church, for all its limitations, emerged from the age of liberation and *Risorgimento* not only as a distinctive Alpine community but as a Reformed Church for Italy. However, it would be wrong to misuse the benefit of hindsight to judge harshly any of those involved in the quarrels which accompanied this process. A nineteenth-century union of the Waldensians and other Italian evangelicals (such as was almost concluded around 1885 during an interlude of good feeling) would have created a stronger Church and a greater influence in the new Italy. It would certainly have avoided much wasteful diversion of Christian energies. But it is clear in historical perspective - a more exalted term for mere hindsight - that such a scheme was not feasible at the time. It remains arguable that it might have been better for all concerned if this had been recognised more widely then.

It would also be wrong, even in an account of a very Protestant connection between British and Italians, to ignore the way that the political changes in Italy were to have a tremendous impact of both the style and the claims of Roman Catholicism and the central part played in it by the Papacy. We have to leave the charms of Florence, even though it retained its appeal to Anglo-Saxons for the rest of the century. Latterly it even basked in the favour of Queen Victoria, whose visits were generally informal but who annoyed such ultra-Protestants as Jacob Primmer by her approval of the restored facade of the cathedral, an old enthusiasm of the Prince Consort. However much we would like to linger by the Arno, we have to recognise that in Italian history all roads lead through Rome, a city which was to be vastly changed and expanded after it became the capital of Italy as well as of Roman Catholicism.

King Victor Emmanuel, the politicians, the civil servants, and eventually the Waldensian theological college were to take the same road. Soon after Italy's unification Rome was even to take over from Torre Pellice as the centre for much of the Waldensians' work. The Church's powerful and largely autonomous evangelisation committee was based there, under the presidency of Dr Matteo Prochet, which lasted from 1871 to 1906. It was not until 1915 that this presidency and the Moderatorship were merged and one of Prochet's successors, Ernesto Giampiccoli, became the first Waldensian Moderator to come from a congregation outside the historic valleys. He was originally from the Veneto and a Protestant by conversion, not birth. The nineteenth century British visitors sometimes referred to the 'Waldensian Church proper', meaning the fifteen valley parishes and Turin to which Rosario in Uruguay was added in 1878.

The formal link between the two styles of Waldensianism was the overlapping ministerial membership of the annual synod and the general mission conference, which for a time met every third year. In 1878, for example, this met in Turin in August before the Torre Pellice synod in September.

Long before the Waldensians emerged from this dual system, which they called 'provisional' but lived with for a long time, Rome had become the focus for Italy's political development and the setting of the first general Council of the Roman Catholic Church since the sixteenth-century Council of Trent which created the basis for the Counter-Reformation. If it was not inspired to be a new Counter-Reformation, it did at least do much to counter the threat to the papal prestige from the *Risorgimento.*

Chapter 9

CHANGED DAYS IN ROME

Visiting-time for the 'Prisoner of the Vatican'

Because all roads in Italian history lead through Rome, and because the Roman Church has counted for so much in Italian life, it is necessary now to look at events in which the Waldensians and other Italian Protestants were not directly concerned. However they were events which determined for half a century the mood and style of politics and culture in the new Italy of which Rome was the political and in some ways symbolic capital, though as yet neither the largest city nor economic and cultural centre. Rome had about 226,000 inhabitants in 1870 and just over double that at the end of the century. Only in the Fascist era and after did it really become the Italian metropolis and emerge as a bigger city than Naples and Milan.

From the start of his reign in 1846 Pius IX had hopelessly misjudged the politics of Italy unity and liberalism. He had been welcomed as a moderate man, even a liberal, and in his early years had made gestures of good will, including the release of political prisoners. When T.N. Talfourd arrived in Rome from Naples on September 8, 1846 he mustered enough energy after his tiring journey by diligence to go from his hotel in the Piazza di Spagna to see the illuminations in honour of the new Pope, who had also arrived in Rome that day. He heard ballad-singers sing the papal praises and saw street-traders selling printed sonnets in honour of Pope Pius. Less than two years later Pius was resisting the liberal and national movement and protesting in a most illiberal manner against what he could not prevent, such as the concessions to the Waldensians in Piedmont. But though he stumbled from one political misjudgment to another he also successfully carried through a consolidation of traditional Catholicism and even an extension of the spiritual power and effective authority of the Papacy within its own Communion. The hope of the liberals became the great authoritarian.

In 1854 Rome had made the doctrine of the Immaculate Conception of our Lord's mother an article of faith, much to the satisfaction of popular Italian Catholicism. This action of Pius IX, while it asserted his high view of papal power and authority, probably only made compulsory what had been for a long time a fairly general view in the Roman Church's theology, influenced by a long tradition of Marian devotion which Protestants called Mariolatry. This dogma, now often and absurdly confused even in broadsheet journalism with the Virgin Birth, as well as with the unbiblical notion of Mary's perpetual virginity, asserts that the mother of Jesus was sinless from the moment of her conception. It remains as difficult as ever for twenty-first century Protestants, and possibly many Roman Catholics, to grasp either the importance of the doctrine or the claim that it has any basis in the Bible. One reads the official explanations, turns to the biblical passages mentioned, and emerges not only unconvinced but uncomprehending.

However it is not difficult to relate the enthusiasm for the new article of faith to the situation of the Papacy and of Italian Catholicism in face of the rising tide of Italian liberalism and nationalism. The doctrine aligned the Papacy with a popular cause of a kind, in Italy and some other Catholic countries. It emphasised and enhanced the central authority of the Papacy in an age which tended (as even Macaulay showed in his History of England) to define political trends and choices as those of liberty and those of order. Pius IX was sincere enough, described on the Vatican web-site today as 'benevolent towards all but firm in his principles' and, more debatably, as 'clear, simple, consistent'. He was a man both of faith and great determination, saintly enough in his personal qualities to have his candidature for sainthood, as the Roman Church defines it, promoted by his admirers. (In September 2000 he reached the stage of being 'beatified'.) He also seems to have had a personality which won over some British visitors who were notoriously hard to please. Frances Trollope, for example, found him 'the dear, good Pope'. Gladstone allowed himself to be flattered and ushered into a chair for what, as his biographers describe it, seemed more a dialogue than an audience, although a great gulf remained on Liberal politics and Anglican theology. It was not so much a meeting of minds as an encounter of gifted, opinionated dogmatists, though it is uncertain how far they really listened to each other.

But it suited Pius in mid-nineteenth-century Italy to have a cause which demonstrated that Rome was not fighting a defensive battle or resigned to continuing retreat. He could not be a liberal Pope but he was happy to be, in some respects and for a very traditional sector of Roman Catholicism, a populist one.

That was even more the case when, in the years after the Kingdom of Italy took shape, Pius IX convened a general council of bishops in Rome in 1869-1870 - the First Vatican Council - whose agenda was dominated by the definition and proclamation of the Pope's claim to infallibility when speaking *ex cathedra*.

This doctrine, of course, does not suggest that the Pope is never wrong and cannot make mistakes on matters of fact, science, opinion, judgment, politics, and theology. It maintains that when he defines a doctrine of faith or morals 'using his office as teacher and pastor of all Christians, in virtue of his apostolic office' he has divine guidance and infallibility. Obviously that process involves, as it did in 1870, taking much advice and considering a wide range of opinions, although the temptation for Popes, like others in high office, is to be most impressed by the advice and opinions they find most agreeable. Modern Protestants should also note that the Second Vatican Council of the 1960's refined the doctrine by ascribing this purported charisma of the Pope to his role as head of the college of bishops, though the nuances of the doctrine remain obscure or debatable or both. However Hans Küng, a modern Catholic rebel, has significantly pointed out that since 1870 'the infallible aura of the "ordinary" day-to-day *magisterium* is often more important than the relatively rare infallible definitions.' Whatever the nuances of doctrine, the proclamation emphasised the centrality in the Roman Catholic system of the papacy and increased the authority of the Pope, both as holder of the office and (if he had the will and inclination) as ultimate trend-setter and policy-maker.

In 1870 the demand for the dogma, and the anxiety to declare that the purported infallibility did not depend on the advice and consent of the bishops, had the support of the world-wide ultramontane party in the Roman Church, among them the English Archbishop (later Cardinal) Manning, a convert who had become a zealot in papal matters. However it was, like the Marian doctrine, a cause which had much Italian support, for example from Giovanni Bosco, the Turin educationist, social reformer, and opponent of Waldensian evangelism who founded the Salesian Order. It had Jesuit backing and support was vigorously drummed up by the semi-official Vatican journal *La Civiltà Cattolica* and other Italian Catholic newspapers. But the most powerful single factor may well have been the determination and inner conviction of the Pope himself. Even more than in the case of the Immaculate Conception, he wanted to take a stand against the trend of events and ideas, especially ideas and events in his native Italy. And while the council was truly international (though even Roman Catholic historians still argue about whether it was truly free from improper pressure) it was inevitably dominated not only by the consequences of Italian events but by Italians. In some ways it was the old Italy's rejoinder to the new national and liberal one. Of the 96 key 'consulting' positions on the council's preparatory commissions 59 went to Italians. At a time when Europe remained the dominant political and cultural influence in the world there were also 276 Italian bishops against 265 from the rest of Europe, and 195 non-diocesan bishops of various nationalities, more or less dependent on the Pope and under pressure to follow the party line.

With hindsight we tend to see Pius IX's policy as a decision that attack was the best form of defence, whether against liberal ideas or incursions by Protestant missionaries and such relatively minor irritants as new Waldensian churches in Italian cities. Up to a point that is true, but it would be a mistake to think that the Papacy was clear-sightedly refining and redefining its role to take account of the loss of its temporal power and the creation of the new. Italy. When Pius forced through the dogma of infallibility in July 1870 he did not foresee that by September Rome would be ruled by the House of Savoy. Indeed one of the reasons for the distrust of 'infallibility' by such Catholic monarchs as the Emperor Francis Joseph of Austria-Hungary and the King of Bavaria was an anxiety that Pius might use his enhanced status to intervene even more in temporal affairs. Probably Pius, who was over 70 when he called the council, never really adjusted to the new Italy at all. In the summer of 1870 he was still hoping to hold on indefinitely to his temporal power in Rome, even if he needed foreign troops, while far more perceptive and reasonable men than he was might still have doubts then about the stability and durability of the new Kingdom of Italy, still less than ten years old.

Even in Italy there was some opposition to proclamation of a new doctrine of infallibility, and the Vatican's Secretary of State, Cardinal Giacomo Antonelli, had been against it for political reasons. But at the crisis most of the resistance within Roman Catholicism came from north of the Alps. When the Pope had secured overwhelming victory, winning the vote if not the argument, the continuing protest did not come from the minority among the bishops but from German-speaking academics and other intellectuals, of whom the most notable was Ignaz von Döllinger. He was a Professor of Church History at Munich, at one time regarded as quite ultramontane by Bavarian Protestants and liberals, with whom Gladstone corresponded vigorously on theological matters and tried to define the Real Presence, and in whom he had found a kindred spirit since they first met in Munich in 1845. This resistance was gallant and sometimes determined but given the nature of the Roman system it was also doomed. The victory of Pius IX was, in Hans Küng's words, 'the apogee of the Roman system'.

When some of the most untypically determined of the Catholic opponents of Pius IX's autocracy and doctrinal impositions gathered their resources and resolution they eventually formed the 'Old Catholic' Churches, linking up with an old-established group in the Netherlands, spiritual descendants of the seventeenth-century Jansenists These Old Catholic Churches survive, mainly in German-speaking countries, and in the twentieth century were to develop useful and friendly ecumenical relationships and recognise Anglican orders. But they were always marked by the quality and not the quantity of their support in Roman Catholic communities and never made much headway in Italy, even though there was a Jansenist tradition in Tuscany and a Bishop of Pistoia, Scipione de' Ricci, had been deposed by the Pope after a very independent-minded reforming synod there in 1786. This had advocated use of vernacular language and other reforms, sought a more symbolical role for the papacy, and borrowed both from the Gallican strain in French Catholicism and the reforming outlook of the Habsburg Emperor Joseph II. The Italian Old Catholics did have the nucleus of a Church between 1885 and 1900 but one of their leaders, Count Campello, returned to the Roman fold and another, Ugo Janni, moved to the Waldensians, along with his small congregation in San Remo. There seems to have been hesitation on both sides before Janni made the move and his acceptance by the Waldensians was against the cautious advice - which had been asked for - of one of their leading British friends, the Genoa minister Donald Miller. He wrote (September 27, 1900) to Dr Prochet, the evangelisation committee chairman praising Janni as 'a good man' but worrying about his doctrine and uncertain of his motives. 'I suspect that he still firmly believes the Church of Rome must be reformed from within and that for this bishops with a so-called apostolic succession are necessary'. But the Waldensians went ahead and accepted him.

Janni has been described (by Prescot Stephens) as a man ahead of his time in his vision of an ecumenical movement and of the role of Waldensians in the renewal of the wider Church. But the condition of Italy was hardly propitious for such ideas until long after his time. It is debatable how far it is even propitious today, though when John XXIII called the Second Vatican Council (1962-65) many people in the Protestant world came to value the observation and analysis of the Waldensians, as well as their intimate knowledge of the Roman Church's most important national province.

Meanwhile after September 1870 the Popes became 'prisoners of the Vatican', much to the irritation and embarrassment of the Italian Government, when Victor Emmanuel's troops occupied Rome. The term was effective. It was inaccurate both in fact and theology but it was good journalese and had some appeal both to those who saw the Pope as a martyr and those who, at least metaphorically, would have liked to see him locked up. 'If the Vatican is a prison', wrote a Scots enthusiast for the new Italy, Alexander Robertson, 'the door is locked from the inside and the Pope keeps the keys'. The process was a self-imposed papal retreat from some customary public ceremonials in Rome and a refusal by its bishop to share in the new public life of the city as the capital of Italy and seat of the House of Savoy. Rome was an ancient city which was to acquire some new monuments - notably the massive one to Victor Emmanuel II - but which in its vastly enlarged area and population was itself to become the main monument to Italian unity.

Visitors might be impressed by the new Rome but they still came to see the old one and were sometimes a little disappointed. Baedeker's English edition warned visitors to Holy Week and other great Church ceremonies: since 1870 'the public ceremonies at which the Pope formerly appeared in person (such as those of the Holy Week), the benedictions, and the public processions including that of the Corpus Christi, have been discontinued.' Only introductions from very high quarters could get visitors into the remaining high festival occasions in the Sistine Chapel at which the Pope still officiated. Baedeker's rather more excitable French edition lamented that the great festivals had therefore lost some of their *éclat*.

But the voluntary near-internment did not prevent the exercise of papal authority and influence. Arguably, the combination in 1870 of the final loss of temporal power and aggrandisement of spiritual authority made the papacy even more of an international influence. Nor did it prevent the Vatican and even the Pope personally from retaining their place among Rome's leading tourist attractions. While the faithful still came on pilgrimage and to show solidarity, the expanding Protestant middle-class middle-market tourist trade and cultural interest displayed a equally understandable curiosity, to the annoyance of some evangelicals and anti-clericals. But a visit to the Vatican had been and remained the done thing. For example, Sir Henry Campbell-Bannerman, later the Edwardian Liberal Prime Minister, was the son of a Glasgow merchant but had three months in Rome when he was only 14 to learn languages. Being well-grounded both in Christian charity and Presbyterian preferences, he wrote home to his sister that the Pope was a fine-looking old gentleman but that the smell of incense in St Peter's was 'most sickening'.

Sometimes curiosity was tinged with traces of snobbery. Even in Protestant Victorian Britain a papal audience conferred some social prestige, if only by allowing the tale to be told to eager listeners. (Alas, it was still the same in 1982 when some of us found ourselves exchanging friendly handshakes with John Paul II on his visit to Britain, even when we had ensured that we were not 'in audience'.) In Rome this demand from curious 'heretics' also created a supply of good offices. In 1864, when Pius IX was ill and almost collapsed in struggling to give his Easter blessing, the English travel-writer A.W. Buckland was rather callously 'urged to remain a little longer in order to witness a Pope's funeral and the election of a new pontiff'. The Roman upper classes were ready to act as middlemen and the Roman other classes enjoyed a considerable income from the customary fees and gratifications. Almost every door was open, but every doorman expected his fee.

Critics like Robertson, for whom any recognition of the Pope was an 'insult to King Victor Emmanuel', saw this as part of a papal plan to soften up and win over Protestant Europe and North America, and claimed the Vatican was always eager to know about likely visitors 'of wealth and social distinction'. There is an element of truth in this analysis, but plotting and planning counted for far less than market forces. Eager buyers met ready sellers.

Take for example the experience of four retired or semi-retired Glaswegian Protestant business and professional men who set off - in a year not stated but apparently February to April 1877 - on *A Six Weeks Scamper through France and Italy*. They were to be received in audience by Pius IX, then aged 85, in the course of a vigorous expedition which also took in Monte Carlo, Pisa, Florence, Venice, Milan, Naples, and receptions, with hymns and homilies, given by 'Mr Van Meister, the American superintendent of Protestant schools in Rome'. This was probably W.C. Van Meter, a missionary of the American Northern Baptists who worked with other Protestants and was credited with promoting up to a hundred Sundays schools.

Thomas Cook had arranged the Scots' rail tickets from London at £27 a head, no cheaper than an ordinary return fare, but with bonus provision for breaks of journey and unaccompanied luggage. They chose their own hotels and excursions. Although the book is anonymous, the author or 'diarist' calling himself 'Campobello' was apparently C.T.Bowie of Largs and the Glasgow Saltmarket.

Bowie's account of their visits to St Peter's and the Vatican gives some insights into the practical difficulties and occasional theological complications of this part of the Victorian tour of Italy. John Murray in 1873 was still lamenting the discourtesy of British and American visitors who treated great Roman Catholic occasions 'almost as theatrical performances' or who gave offence by remaining seated at the elevation of the Host. But many Protestant visitors to Rome had also the kind of insatiable curiosity about the tenants of the Vatican which citizens of the great American Republic still display about our British monarchs.

Some had Scruples - the word deserves a capital - about customary procedures and did not find it easy to do in Rome as the Romans did. One of Bowie's three companions opted out of the opportunity to be received by the Pope because, quite literally, it involved bowing the knee to him, following

Murray's advice that 'if as Protestants they cannot conscientiously conform outwardly to the usages of Roman Catholics on such occasions they would do better to stay away'.

They saw the splendours of the Vatican, however, as a party of four, with their entry and easy passage secured by a Florentine and Methodist guide, Antonio Novello, whose Protestantism did not apparently affect his happy diplomatic and pecuniary relations with doorkeepers and custodians of places not formally open to the public.

Access to the Pope himself, however, required a much more exalted intermediary. The Glaswegians had a letter of introduction to the Marchese di Baviera, an officer of the papal bodyguard, the Guardia Nobile, and editor of a Vatican journal. The marquis was happily anxious to be of service and not too proud to step out of his residence into the visitors' carriage to note their names and accept their thanks.

The promised cards of admission arrived and the Methodist Signor Novello's services again came into play. He arranged the fitting and hire of the 'waiters' full uniform' or dress suits which were required, giving the tourists the satisfaction of settling for half the price originally demanded but almost certainly never expected. They did however balk at the price quoted when they were taken to the studio in the Vatican of 'the Pope's principal decorator'. They expected to buy his set of six pictures at £10 each but he tried to get £400 and insisted they be sold as one lot. There was no sale.

The audience itself, in a Vatican reception room which was 'anything but showy', passed off quietly enough apart from the audible ecstasies of a disturbed but well-connected pilgrim who was escorted by a cardinal. The amenities included spittoons for the use of tobacco-chewers, which suggests that the American connection was already established, and what Bowie called a 'chauffer', a brass warming-dish filled with hot embers. The nineteenth-century Vatican, like other Italian palazzi, had the inadequate winter heating which rivalled dirt, leathery beef, tasteless chicken, importunity, beggary, and Popery as causes of annoyance to most Victorian Anglo-Saxons and Scots.

The guests or pilgrims, fewer than twenty of them, got down on one knee. Then the Pope 'with a host of cardinals and attendants entered in an easy way, chatting and laughing in an unsanctimonious manner... and while passing held out his hand for us to clasp or kiss as we felt disposed.' Most of the guests also got a word in their own language, determined from the admission cards held by one of the papal entourage.

The Glaswegians even had the benefit of a follow-up visit from the Marchese di Baviera, well skilled in public relations which might also have been an after-sales service. He offered to help with any further service the tourists might require and, apparently well content, returned to his other duties.

Writing up the day's events Bowie recorded satisfaction that the Pope had appeared 'without any of the pompous insignia of his office about him and noted: 'The ceremony over we felt pleased to have seen the happy and healthy old man who had been chronicled only the day previous as on his death-bed... He left us with the impression that he was a most sensible jolly old fellow, having a jolly set of companions.' In fact the stormy thirty-one year pontificate of Pius IX was drawing to a close. He died less than a year later, a month after King Victor Emmanuel.

Not all those who wanted to meet the Pope were quite so successful as the Glasgow delegation, especially if they were reluctant to go through the usual channels. The Protestant campaigner Jacob Primmer was a minister of the Church of Scotland - the Establishment, not the Free Church, though his views and pungent style make Ian Paisley seem a softly-spoken liberal in comparison. Mr Primmer went through no channels at all but simply set off up the Vatican stairs in the hope, or so he claimed, of having a talk with the Pope (by this time Leo XIII) and redirecting him to proper channels of Grace. He got about eight steps beyond the first-floor landing in the direction of the papal apartments before being persuaded that discretion was the better part of Protestant valour.

Primmer fared better with the Waldensians, and had a long interview with Matteo Prochet, president of their Rome-based evangelisation committee, whom he led into one or two indiscretions. Prochet confessed to having felt some embarrassment at the Church of Scotland General Assembly in 1890 when he was fulsomely, if formally, received by a Moderator, A.K.H. Boyd, whom he regarded as 'the sworn enemy of the Waldensians'. Boyd was a polished and popular writer of the time, and senior minister of Holy Trinity in St Andrews, but he had given offence in a lecture in which he criticised Scottish support for the Waldensians, claiming that they seemed to trade for ever on former persecutions.

Primmer, who had a mischievous as well as a fanatical streak, also induced Prochet to confess to surprise at the 'ritualistic' forms he found when invited to preach at Glasgow's Barony Church, whose minister was Marshall Lang, father of the future Archbishop Cosmo Gordon Lang and one of the Waldensians' allies in the Scottish Establishment,

But Primmer was also the kind of loner who could have insights and raise awkward questions. He remained relatively detached from the quarrels among Italian Protestants, regarding neither the Free Italian Church nor the Waldensians as vigorous enough, but he was also worried that 'the Waldensian Church is weakened, and her liberty invaded by depending on Britain for help', and that Waldensians lived too much on their past. Both points had some validity, if only because they suggested a perception of the Waldensians that, if it misled this most enthusiastic of Protestants, might also occur to the lukewarm, sceptical, and hostile. Indeed there is some evidence in the late nineteenth-century publicity of the British friends of the Waldensians that they had become sensitive on these points, especially the financial one. Unlike the eighteenth-century subsidies, the funds raised were meant not for the Church in the valleys, by now self-supporting, but for the missionary expansion into Italy so strongly urged on the Waldensians by the British from Beckwith's day. It was not unlike the heavy contemporary Waldensian emphasis on the way that their benefits from the Italian tax system are used for social work and good causes (often with an environmental or 'progressive' emphasis) and not evangelism.

Perhaps more than other British Victorian Protestant visitors Primmer also had a sense of the power of habit and custom in Italian religious observance and of the capacity of the Roman Church to co-exist with the secularist, sceptical, and even atheistical trends of the times, even when these were gathering momentum. To read his polemic today is an odd experience, sometimes alarming, sometimes rewarding. He takes too much pleasure in the absurdities of popular Italian superstition, especially those involving dubious relics, and scourges Roman Catholicism with a fury which left him little time or inclination to reflect on the strands of deep piety and social service within it. Nor did he pause to reflect on whether such sustained antipathy to a system might encourage ill-feeling towards those whose birth or culture made them part of it. Yet in a way that more conventional enthusiasts for Italian missions often failed to do, he recognised that the triumph of Italian liberalism did not mean the eclipse of Italian Catholicism, whether as a great force in Italian culture and society or as a political influence with latent capacities for revival. There was some truth in the rather sour view of the conservative Irish Protestant bishop who told Alexander Robertson: 'I for one never desired the overthrow of the Pope's temporal power, for as long as it lasted the world possessed in Italy an object lesson of the degradation to which a dominant Roman Catholic Church can reduce a country and a people.'

The collapse of the temporal power brought immense and obvious benefits to Italy. It later became clear that it has strengthened the international position and spiritual authority of the Roman Church, without destroying its special position in Italy or even the special Italian position within its supra-national organisation.

Chapter 10

A FREE CHURCH IN A FREE STATE?

The new Italy in peace and war

Count Cavour was dead before Italy was fully united but he left the new Italian kingdom and its well-wishers, and not least its Protestants and their well-wishers, the idea of freedom in Church and State. 'We are ready to proclaim this great principle in Italy', he said in an 1861 speech: 'A free Church in a free State.' He did not live long enough to handle the practical problems posed by his splendid phrase.

But after 1870 the apparently impossible had happened. What had seemed diametrically opposed enemies, liberal nationalism and papal authoritarianism, had both won staggering victories in Italy.

The Italian nationalists and moderate liberals had triumphed, uniting Italy and making Rome its capital with international acceptance, though before his death Cavour was one of those who warned that although they had created Italy they had 'still to create Italians'. The triumph of political nationalism did not instantly create a sense of common nationality able to coexist easily with the regional diversities and local loyalties of Italy. Even the Waldensians, enthusiastic supporters of a united Italy and liberalism, were still in some ways learning to be Italians. What they were later to think of as their 'heroic' age was over and had given way to a period of consolidation - sometimes a euphemism for stagnation, but in this case justified - not so much by any great numerical progress but through the successful transition from being an ethnic church in an enclave to being a Reformed Church for Italy.

But in a sense papal absolutism had also triumphed. The Papacy had imposed its claim to infallibility even on the many Catholics who thought it was making a mistake. It also enforced its authority in a Roman Catholic Church which asserted its freedom to differ from the State, and in spiritual things to be above the State. In this situation the idea of what a free Church in a free State must mean in Italian conditions was increasingly difficult to define with any precision or satisfaction. Cavour's great phrase became a slogan and fitted into various agendas. A liberal who served as Italian Prime Minister, Luigi Luzzatti, even used it much later as a delightful line in flattery (quoted by A.L. Drummond) for the Scots minister in Rome. 'There is one country that has satisfied the condition - a free Church in a free State - and that is Scotland.' Luzatti, who was of Jewish origin, had a genuine interest in religious freedom and an amicable separation of Church and State and even appears to have studied the legal problems and eventual House of Lords judgment after the creation of the United Free Church of Scotland in 1900.

In England the enthusiasm of the age of Gilly and Beckwith was not sustained, though a solid base of support and good will remained. In Scotland the enthusiasm that marked early Victorian England probably lasted longer and peaked later. It was not merely the preserve of an élite of leading city ministers and lawyers but a factor in the religious life of small-town and rural Scotland. Waldensian deputies found their way not only to towns like Helensburgh, Kirkcaldy, and Alloa, easily reached from the cities, but to such awkward destinations as Campbeltown. One, Pastor W. Meille, even told the Scottish-Waldensian society annual meeting in 1878 that he had inspected a Roman Catholic church in Dumfries and reported that he found as much difference there from churches in Italy as 'between the Pope and himself'. The Roman system, he declared (among other less complimentary reflections), could even 'put on a Protestant dress in a Protestant country'.

The result of this mingled fraternity and fund-raising was a network of personal connections between the Waldensian ministers and Scotland, not least with the manse families who welcomed, fed, and lodged them. Even in 2000 when a Scots Moderator and son of the manse, Andrew McLellan, spoke at the Waldensian Synod he could testify that he first encountered a Waldensian at the age of six without knowing what a Waldensian was, but readily grasping the sense of brotherly love in which the visitor was held.

For a time the Italian mission campaign was so much a part of Scottish Church and social life that it even attracted criminal attention. In 1872, for example (according to a press cutting in the Scottish Waldensian files), a young woman and 'an elderly female having also a ladylike exterior' operated a scam in Edinburgh, Paris, and Dundee. Part of this was a bogus appeal for schools in Italy when, in the fraudsters' neat imitation of the contemporary idiom of piety, the divine finger 'so evidently points the way to that sunny land'. Edinburgh printers were induced to produce stationery with the names of a local committee of 22 prominent citizens, together with 14 lady presidents and a London committee. When calling on ministers the pair ostentatiously used a well-known born-again cab-driver. Subscriptions, loans, and goods in kind were gathered. A high-class Highland outfitter even supplied a kilt, the role of which in the education of young Italy was not entirely clear. The scheme only collapsed when the tradesmen of Dundee turned out to be more sceptical than those of Edinburgh.

But even without such marginal intimations of Original Sin there were signs that the new era was not to be the brave new world the earlier Victorians had hoped for. Italy was to have its share of illusions, delusions, heartbreak, heartache, and conflict.

One cloud, no bigger than a man's hand, was apparent when the Waldensian minister in Rome, Giovanni Ribetti, brought politics into the fight for the sympathies of the British evangelical public, possibly encouraged by the Rome correspondent of the *Daily Review*, Henry Lowe. Writing to the paper on June 18, 1872, Ribetti denounced the role of Italian Methodists and the *Chiesa Libera*, and especially Pastors Sciarelli and Conti in Roman demonstrations in favour of a 'workmen's society' and of republicanism. Ribetti complained of the 'impropriety of turning our churches into political clubs', and of the Bible society's employee in Rome carrying a banner in the wake of the local freethinkers.

The Waldensian leadership had usually kept radical and often republican nationalism at arm's length. In 1852, for example, Moderator Revel had been suspicious of a proposal for a newspaper which would combine Protestant and 'advanced' ideas. Mazzini, on the other hand, was not only a secular radical but a long-standing opponent of the House of Savoy, having planned an unsuccessful Piedmontese revolution from Geneva and being sentenced to death *in absentia*. Ribetti was certainly no admirer of Mazzini, for he also denounced the *Chiesa Libera* and Methodists for their involvement in a Mazzini funeral demonstration. It was on a Sunday but they had cancelled their services, allegedly because everyone wanted to go to the great liberal nationalist memorial event. 'While they were carrying the bust of Mazzini I was preaching the Gospel in the Waldensian Church', though he admitted that his own congregation had been well below the usual numbers. Gavazzi also came in for special criticism after a rhetorical flourish about Mazzini 'having awakened to new life in the tomb'.

This was one contemporary view, meant to appeal to a section of the British public which was largely Liberal in politics but socially and theologically conservative and inclined to free-market economics, but expressing the now conservative liberalism of the Waldensians. It was partly conditioned and perhaps exaggerated by the widespread revulsion against the destructive and disastrous Commune of 1871 in Paris which Ribetti probably had in mind when he denounced Mazzinians as communists, revolutionaries and allies of the Socialist International. The prevailing modern view of these events, perhaps no less fallible but apparent in such a fine history as that of Giorgio Spini, would be to welcome the signs of Protestant involvement in working-class politics, social reform, and some of the earliest demonstrations that Italy would in time become a very plural society, in its religious as well as its political and economic attitudes. It would also argue that Ribetti's support for the Savoy monarchy was also a form of involvement in politics; and it points to the truth that much denunciation of Church entanglement in politics often reflects concern that the commitment is to the wrong side's opinions, as is sometimes the case. Modern Waldensian historians may have more sympathy with the politically radical elements in the *Chiesa Libera*, some of them later absorbed in Methodism, than with their own leaders of the time, though they naturally emphasise the role of those pastors who in the later decades of the century identified themselves with social reform and even dialogue with Socialism.

These movements of opinion all hinted at the end of the old era of conservative liberalism in the Cavour style; yet there were also signs that the old enemy of liberalism, radicalism, and Protestant missions was reasserting itself. The Roman Catholic Church was to recover much of its political influence. The process began, sometimes gradually, sometimes fitfully, after the death of Pius IX. It became obvious with the encyclical Rerum Novarum from Leo XIII in 1891, which approved of social legislation and trade unionism. It developed further with the extension of Italian franchise to the urban workers and to the peasantry, still very much under the influence of parish priests. For the moment the emphasis in pontifical denunciation was moving from liberal political errors to liberal theological ones, most notably in the condemnation of 'modernism' by Pius X in 1907, even though this tendency associated with von Hügel, Loisy, and others, had been tolerated by Leo XIII.

By the turn of the century, and even more by the First World War, the Roman Church was exercising a considerable influence on Italian Governments and on the election of deputies to Parliament. It also had considerable power over local government in many parts of Italy. The process continued when the Vatican reached a concordat with the State in the time of Mussolini, and the Roman Church in Italy took a very different direction after the dictator's fall by claiming some genuine moral authority in the last stages of the war and the first troubled years of peace and cold war. In John XXIII it also at last - but not till after eleven ballots in 1958 - produced an Italian Pope of unusual and unexpected breadth of mind and appeal, even if where Protestants were concerned his ecumenical success probably owed more to his personal qualities than to any profound understanding or experience of their ways and traditions. As with John Paul II, his natural ecumenical priority was with the 'schismatics' of eastern Orthodoxy and not the 'heretics' of the West. He had spent nearly 20 years representing the Vatican in Bulgaria, Greece, Istanbul before his first serious encounter with Protestantism when sent to France in 1944 at the age of 63.

Yet in the last decades of the nineteenth century it was already clear that Italy was subject to the same pressures of secularisation as the rest of Western Europe. It would be wrong to think of the condition of the Italian Protestants only in relation to the power and influence of the Roman Church in Italy. They too were losing some ground to secularism and uncertain of their response to the new force of Socialism. In theology they were moving away, like Scots and American Presbyterians, from the Calvinist evangelicalism of the *Réveil* and R.W. Stewart towards a synthesis of conservative traditions and liberal tendencies.

It is probably true that in the early years of the Kingdom of Italy the Protestants, and not least the Waldensians, enjoyed the good will of the State, which was anxious to demonstrate its liberal credentials and retain its British good will, while also not averse to reminding the Vatican who now ruled Italy, at least in matters temporal. For example one the great manipulators of Italian politics in this period, the Sicilian Francesco Crispi - the man who had once paid Garibaldi's account with Henderson Brothers of Leghorn - enjoyed reminding the Vatican that if it didn't separate religion and politics the Italian people would 'feel the need for a national Church in whose bosom patriotism and God can agree'. The quotation delighted Wood Brown at the 'Glorious Return' bicentenary celebrations in 1889 but it was a politician's rhetoric, not a spiritual aspiration, on a par with Crispi's suggestion that if the 1878 conclave to elect a new Pope were moved away from Rome (as had been mooted) various cardinals and their civil servants might find it hard to get back into Italy.

The public support from British Protestantism for the Italian mission movements remained strong for the rest of the century. Even if the Anglican patrons of the Waldensians now looked like a bishops' Second XV, stiffened by Irish archbishops, there remained a wide range of support from Evangelicals of most denominations and from all the segments of Presbyterianism. One notable Anglican supporter was Prebendary H.W. Webb-Peploe, one of the moving spirits of the Keswick Convention. There was also a renewed enthusiasm for public demonstration and commemoration of the British connection at the time of the 'Glorious Return' bicentenary, which stimulated a flow of books in several languages, some exhausting itineraries for those who were guests at the celebration in the valleys, and a new burst of publicity and fund-raising which sometimes involved new styles and techniques. The late Victorians perhaps lacked the stamina for the long set-piece orations which their parents had enjoyed.

Scottish-Waldensian archives record that in the brewery town of Alloa for example, 'The Glorious Return' was still being celebrated in December 1890 with what was described as a 'concert and illustrated lecture'. Tickets were half-a-crown (reserved), a shilling, and sixpence. This appears to have been a new edition of a programme previously given in Edinburgh. The reader was David Guthrie, son of the Dr Guthrie who complained that Calvin had set the valleys a bad example of laxity on the Sabbath, but his historical narrative was served up with music sung 'by some of the best amateurs in Edinburgh' and about fifty limelight pictures. These were made from engravings by Bartlett and Brockedon, and from etchings by William Hole, whose biblical paintings influenced generations of Sunday-school children and their teachers. The singers drew mainly on Mendelssohn's oratorios, with items like 'But the Lord is mindful of his own' from *St Paul* fitted between appropriate sections of the narrative. They also rendered the Hymn of the Vaudois Mountaineers by Felicia Hemans and a commemorative piece written by Pastor Giovanni Luzzi of Florence, Not surprisingly the proceedings were rounded off with the great triumphal Psalm 124 ('Now Israel may say and that truly') to the old Genevan tune.

The Waldensians and their friends had good cause to sing about their escape from 'the fowler's snare'. The days were long gone now when they were 'a living prey'. But as their situation became more comfortable in the new Italy, many of their old friends became much less concerned. It is even possible to detect a curious mixture of slight complacency and a little anxiety in the oratorical tour de force in the Edinburgh Freemasons' Hall with which Luzzi commemorated the jubilee of the Emancipation in 1898, dedicating the printed version to the collectors of the Waldensian Missions Aid Society.

There was a change of mood apparent by the turn of the century, not only in many of those who ruled Italy but in the attitudes of the Northern Europeans and Americans towards Italy. There was some mutual cooling-off of the passionate attachments of the mid-nineteenth century, and Italian nationalism no longer needed British moral support. The Italians took up a new diplomatic game, making the dual alliance of Germany and Austria-Hungary a triple one but retaining an eye for the main chance and a good many mental reservations. Meanwhile their intellectuals read Nietzsche; and their politicians thrived in a system where realism and opportunism were sometimes tinged by cynicism.

There was less idealism. In both Britain and Italy there was also less interest in the religious aspects of the mid-Victorian special relationship. The Anglo-Saxons, including the American ones, mustered less evangelical enthusiasm for the conversion of Italy. Far fewer Italians seemed ready to speculate on whether Protestantism was the spiritual corollary of liberalism.

A symptom of the appreciable change can be seen an interesting but minor bit of editorial reworking when the American writer William Dean Howells revised his classic book of *Italian Journeys*. Howells was an Ohio journalist who, still in his twenties, became American consul in Venice under Abraham Lincoln's administration during the civil war. It was his reward for a good campaign biography of the President. He also wrote a fine book on Venice, still eminently readable. Later he moved to New York, became editor of *The Atlantic Monthly*, and a kind of plainer man's Henry James as well as the leading light in the school of 'realistic' American novelists. In 1864 his none too arduous duties in Venice allowed him a leisurely trip to Rome which floods and storms diverted via Genoa and Naples. In and around Naples he made the traditional tourist and literary visits to Pompeii, Herculaneum and Capri but he added to this a newly fashionable one and gave a chapter to the Protestant ragged schools.

But when in 1901 his publisher pressed him to revise the book for a fresh twentieth century edition, 'shedding upon the belated text some light from the events occurring since it was written', the only complete chapter to go was the one on the schools, to which he had been taken by Pastor Amalric Buscarlet, a Swiss-born, Scottish-educated Presbyterian minister who had once been Robert Stewart's assistant at Leghorn and survived long enough to become United Free 'father of the Church' in the 1920's.

The Presbyterian ministry in Naples had originally been a chaplaincy for Scots engineers, though the schools' sponsors were English, Swiss, and assorted Presbyterian, with an American treasurer. Howell's chapter was a first-rate piece of reporting with a good deal of pungent opinion intruded. He wrote that: 'The children are honestly and thoroughly taught and, if they are nor directly instructed in Protestantism, are at least instructed to associate religion with morality, probably for the first time in their lives.' The advance in their condition was 'incalculably great'.

But the older, wiser, or more cautious and discreet Howells had detected in his earlier thoughts on Italy, now almost forty years' distant, that he had 'assumed an omniscience for which I can now find no reasonable grounds'. Too much need not be made of the particular bit of editorial revision, but it was as symbolic as some of the cuts were perhaps expedient, for the New Italy did not enjoy comments, by no means referring only to Neapolitans, about 'the unfathomable, disheartening duplicity of Italians.'

Yet even after his exercise of literary revision and political correctness Howells confessed himself ill at ease. He thought his real problem in yielding to his publisher's plea (which probably was that a revised edition would sell better) was that the conditions he described in the 1860's now seemed incredible to those familiar with the new Italy which claimed the status of a Great Power.

There is something of the same mood in Hehn, the Baltic German who had doubted whether the market for freely imported Bibles would fulfil the expectations of those who had once smuggled them past the customs. He described how in the old Italy the Italian people had really known little of each other. 'It wasn't the custom to travel. No-one could leave his province, even his town without a passport, even without police permission. Several times on a day's journey the coinage changed and the baggage was searched. Since there was no trade or commerce, there was no need for the improvement of transport. As for a customs union, when indeed such a thing was thought of, it ran into a bristling local selfishness.'

But how now things had changed! 'The Kingdom is Italy is so incredible and so suddenly created that the thoughtful observer finds he lacks the words to describe it. And not least among the changes was that everyone can print what he likes and, if it pleases him, get married without priests. And for birth and death there is no more need for either tolling bells or holy water.'

Protestant missions were far from extinct or inactive but they had rather gone out of fashion, both in Italy and in England, even to an extent in Scotland. For the Italians Protestantism had no longer the special flavour of a forbidden fruit. And it had been easier to arouse interest in Italy, cultural as well as religious, when there was political repression and when religious intolerance was a formal part of its systems of law and government. The historical situation has analogies with the cooling of some Western interest in South Africa after the end of apartheid and a similar attitude to Eastern Europe after the collapse of Communism.

In Italy itself there was now a new establishment of conservative liberalism, sometimes challenged by what professed to be radicalism and tending the kind of anti-clericalism which also flourished in the French Third Republic. But Italy's established liberalism was a group of political cliques rather than a structured political party system. The real political challenge of the future was the gradual rise of Socialism.

If the heroic age of Protestant evangelism in Italy had passed, so too had the romanticism of the *Risorgimento* itself. As late as 1890 the French writer Paul Bourget could write in his *Sensations d'Italie* that the great Italian patriots 'had certainly been no braver or persevering than fighters for freedom in many other countries, but they had in this patriotism of theirs a *je ne sais quoi* of something more ideal, like a heroic form of artistic splendour'. But such eulogies were already very much in the past tense. The Italy whose public affairs were successively dominated by Francesco Crispi and Giovanni Giolitti was a much more prosaic place, but one in which the Waldensians felt at home - so much so that a generation of them have been described as *giolittianni*, after their support for the Piedmontese statesman who was pre-eminent in Italian politics in the twenty years before 1914.

The new phase of Italian political liberalism and economic capitalism still had its powerful and vocal anti-clerical tendencies. These included a very secular element in its freemasonry, despite the Christian Masonic strand among the Methodists and some Waldensians (Matteo Prochet, for example, head of the Evangelisation Committee). Masonic connections, of course, often breed suspicions and wild conspiracy theories and 'the craft' has remained controversial in the very different conditions of modern Italy, In its defence, however, it should be recognised that it was one of the few significant parts of Italian society where Protestants were made welcome at a time when Roman Catholicism generally sought to have them ostracised.

But the 'Establishment' of the new kingdom of Italy, with opportunists and self-seekers as well as idealists, was a network of old ideas, liberal assumptions, and new economic interests rather than an ideology. The Waldensians and other Protestants were hardly part of it, and some of them wanted to save the peasantry of the valleys from industrialisation, but they were generally at ease with it. A few went into politics, but as individuals rather than any 'Protestant Tendency'. They felt at home in the new united Italy and with the constitutional monarchy, especially during the reign of Victor Emmanuel's son Umberto I (cut short in 1900 when he was assassinated by an anarchist). Indeed sometimes they gave the impression of being a little too comfortable under the new order, eager not only to show their loyalty to the Italian Crown but to emphasise it in their dealings with friends abroad.

The mood of the time is caught in a deliverance of the Scottish Free Church's General Assembly of 1890 on its Continental Committee report rejoicing in the royal recognition of the loyalty of the Waldensians and their service to Italy. The reconciliation of the Savoy dynasty and the Waldensians was a regular theme of returning British visitors and of contemporary Waldensians It has perhaps distant affinities with a similar, and longer-lasting reconciliation made possible by reform and economic progress in the nineteenth century, the one which turned the rebellious Ulster-Scots Presbyterian community into Irish loyalists.

The hostility of the Vatican and its clerical supporters to the House of Savoy, which added to its credit with the Waldensians, probably made the régime after 1870 seem rather more anti-clerical than it really was. It nationalised many monasteries but certainly did not suppress monasticism and many apparently anti-clerical politicians kept open their lines of communication with the hierarchy and even the Vatican. The régime did not banish Christianity from the schools, though Protestant visitors to the classrooms were never quite sure whether the teaching offered the basis for a non-denominational Christian approach, tempered by the necessities of Italian culture and history, or was still too Roman Catholic by half. Their main worry was it was not biblical enough.

There had also been conflict, as we have seen, among the newly emerging Italian Protestant community that was much wider than the old Waldensian remnant of the valleys, and much confusion among their friends in Britain, as well as among those like Gladstone who had hoped for some reforming and constructive convulsion within Italian Catholicism. But in the new century there was also a new style of radicalism, which was soon to become more concerned with economic grievances than the means of grace, though it still tended to be anti-clerical and even aggressively secularist.

One of its recruits was to be a gifted but excitable misfit called Benito Mussolini (1883-1945), son of an atheist blacksmith in Emilia who chose his first-born's Christian name in honour of the Mexican revolutionary Benito Juarez. Young Mussolini was to develop highly volatile political opinions and became a brilliant self-publicist who later not only enjoyed his own oratory in Italian but his conversations with Hitler in German and Anthony Eden in French. He was also to glorify force and ruin Italy through war and his alliance with Hitler. But while Howells was revising the preface to his travels, Mussolini was a trainee teacher considering whether to flee to Switzerland to avoid military service. Like the Socialists whom he was soon to join, and later reject, Mussolini was anti-clerical, even in those days fiercely anti-religious like his father. This was typical of angry young men from the former Papal States, many more of whom probably had atheist fathers and pious mothers. But this new wave of radical anti-clericalism did not find any attraction or relevance in Protestant doctrine.

The same could be said of most Italians, including notable liberals opposed to both the style and the ideas of the charismatic charlatan, Mussolini. For example the great philosopher and political liberal from the Italian South, Benedetto Croce (1866-1952), for whom history was 'the story of liberty' and liberty a religion of a sort, wrote of the rivalry in his day between Catholicism in its Jesuit style with the 'religions of the Nation, of Race, and of Communism'. He claimed it was a rivalry sustained by a determination such as the reformed Christian religions did not or could not long display, though Croce was well disposed to Protestants and to his honour stood up for full religious freedom when Mussolini's concordat with the Vatican threatened to limit it.

Italian Protestants still had their home missions, their international support, and some grievances. The Waldensians had moved in the later part of the nineteenth century from a situation of mere toleration to one of a slightly circumscribed religious freedom with full civil rights. There were many irritants, but mere irritants do not breed burning resentment or attract passionate support.

One thing which was clear was that there was not going to be any significant new evangelical Church of Italy. That was a victory of a sort for the Waldensians with their belief in the importance of continuing tradition under Scripture and a well-defined and ordered Church structure, but it was part of a substantial setback for the Protestant cause in Italy. It was also clear by the early years of the twentieth century that sooner or later the Roman Catholic Church would assert the great influence in Italian political and social life which its spiritual power and its Italian traditions made possible and even inherently probable. This trend was becoming fully apparent only on the eve of the First World War, which dramatically changed the course. of Italian politics and history.

No-one can say, however, how Italy would have developed if it had managed to avoid the European war which broke out in 1914, when the country was still nominally linked to Germany and the old enemy, Austria, in a defensive Triple Alliance. The sad irony is that, while the other European Powers stumbled into war or were drawn in by alliances, Italy deliberately opted in on the side of Britain, France and Russia. The outcome was to affect not only the future course of Italian history but that old affinity with Britain of which the Protestant enthusiasm for Waldensian and other evangelical missions was one part.

Italy's involvement in the First World War inevitably created a difficult situation for the Waldensians, fervent though they were in the national cause. Like most Italians, they found it easy enough to see Austria as an enemy; but not so a Prussian-dominated Germany. A people with long memories still recalled that in the last war for Italian unity, the 1866 one against Austria, the Italians had been allies of Prussia in Bismarck's triumph. This feeling was even more marked among Waldensians. Like many British Victorians, they had admired Prussia as efficient, Protestant, and 'progressive' - not least during Bismarck's Kulturkampf with the Roman Church. They cherished the memory of Count Waldburg-Truchsess along with that of Gilly, Beckwith, and Stewart and rightly remembered them all with thanksgiving.

Many of their leaders had benefited from the bursaries to study in Berlin which Waldburg-Truchsess had done much to secure as a personal donation from the King of Prussia (later also the German Emperor) and which continued until the First World War. But this unease was not a feeling confined to the Waldensians. Ever since the creation of a united Italy its intellectual leaders had compared their own situation with that of Germany, which had also won national unity in face of Austrian-led opposition. And though Garibaldi's last fling as a general had been an intervention on the French side in 1870, many of his countrymen found much to admire in German success and German philosophy.

When Italy entered the war in 1915 against Austria it was not only in response to the rhetoric of such nationalist zealots as the poet and aviator Gabriele

D'Annunzio but after much calculation on how to exploit the situation to national advantage. It came after public and private argument about commitment or neutrality, most of it on the disastrous assumption that for Italy a war would be short and relatively bloodless.

Waldensian and other Protestant opinion appears originally to have been in favour of neutrality (as Giolitti was) but to have been carried along by the current of opinion in which idealism and opportunism were strangely mingled. Even then the Italians managed for more than a year to avoid war with Germany, which had previously thought of buying them off at Austria's expense.

This complexity in Italian motives may have contributed to what at first sight seems a surprising fact of history: the war in which Britain and Italy were allies seems not to have to drawn the two countries closer together. The alliance of 1915-18 has not remained part of the British folk-memory of the First World War which has survived those who fought in it. If anything, the course of the war and its aftermath, which emphasised the different experiences, motives, and priorities between Britain and Italy, may even have served to widen the gap that was opening up between them and prepare the way for the deeper divisions between them in the Fascist era. The ordeals of the Western Front had made that seem the 'real war' to most British people, though not for the relatively small number of British troops who fought in Italy. They had enjoyed the wine and pasta behind the line but took painful losses in some sharp 1918 fighting on the Piave. But the Italian ordeals on the Isonzo and the Piave and in the Alps and Asiago meant little to the British, with the final break-up of the Austro-Hungarian army wiping away the knowledge of how tenaciously it had resisted for the previous three years.

The Italian disaster at Caporetto in 1917 was caused by a vital tactical break-through and not primarily by a breakdown of morale, though it certainly created one and added to the repercussions which the Russian revolution had on the Italian Left. Yet that military disaster helped to leave a false impression outside Italy of the 1915-18 campaigns as a whole. These campaigns reflected, on both sides, a power of endurance as great as that shown in the trenches of the Western front. And the Alpine war, in the Dolomites and on the Asiago plateau, took its toll on the mountain people of Piedmont even more than the grim campaign on the Carso on the way to Trieste, though one local battalion eventually found itself sent to Albania and was stricken with malaria. The Waldensians valleys have their war memorials, like those of England and Scotland but perhaps closest in mood to the French - except that the suffering, defiant figure is modelled on an Alpine soldier and not the poilu of Verdun. About 500 Waldensian *alpini* are said to have been killed in the war.

Even before the rise of Fascism a gulf had opened up between Italy, as represented both by politicians and in public opinion, and the 'Anglo-Saxons'. The Americans had joined the war long after promises had been made to Italy, and did not feel bound by them. Even to the British, the Italian politicians, who had already seemed mercenary and opportunist, were now perceived as grasping and obstructive. But Italian public opinion was especially hostile to President Wilson and thought the Anglo-Saxons unhelpful and hypocritical. It considered them insensitive to Italy's sacrifices and too susceptible to the claims of Yugoslavia, which included the Croats and Slovenes who had fought tenaciously enough against the Italians until the final break-up of the Habsburg Empire. For the Waldensians this was perhaps an especially confusing quarrel, not only because of their long connection with the British but because their Italian patriotism seemed to be thrust into conflict with their natural affinity for the most determined advocate of a new moral order in world politics, Woodrow Wilson.

President Wilson was a son of the manse and very much a Presbyterian. He was also the kind of moralist whom opponents like to denounce as a hypocrite. His quest for a new moral world order and his advocacy of a League of Nations appears to have had considerable Waldensian sympathy but by a curious irony of history one of his most determined Italian opponents, Baron Sidney Sonnino, Foreign Minister and an ex-Premier, was the Protestant (albeit a nominal one) who had gone furthest in Italian politics. But Sonnino had no Waldensian connections. His father, from the Leghorn Jewish community that had fascinated Bonar and McCheyne, prospered in Egypt and had become Christian on marrying an Anglican, Georgina Terry, and such loose church connection as the family retained seems to have been with the American Episcopal Church in Italy.

This new distrust had partly died down before Fascism sought to revive and inflame it and was probably overshadowed in Italy itself by the ferocity of the internal conflict provoked by revolutionary Socialism, much influenced by the Russian revolution and reaction against it. In Italy, unlike Britain and most of Western Europe, a Communist Party become the most powerful element in the Socialist and labour movements. But the Italian national discontent was a factor in a changing Italian-British relationship also affected by economic and social changes.

The old Victorian links that had survived into the next century were never to be as strong again. Some of the English, Scots and American churches in Italy closed and those that remained had not the kind of ministries they once had, rich in influence beyond their expatriate congregations, both by their contacts with Italians and their contribution to British perceptions of Italy. Yet when the Scottish United Free Church in 1929 became part of the reunited Kirk there were still properties in Rome, Naples, Florence, San Remo, Genoa, and Leghorn to have their new ownership recognised in rather ponderous governmental and legal Italian. The records suggest their relations with the Waldensians were friendly but no longer very close, though when the Scots 'Presbytery of Italy' met a local pastor usually attended the meeting. In 1931 however, that grand if slightly incongruous title faded away, as the surviving kirks were taken into a Presbytery of Southern Europe. Long before that their ministers had concentrated on their role as chaplains to expatriates and visitors.

Perhaps the last of the spectacular personalities was Dr Alexander Robertson (1846-1933), already quoted on the 'prisoner' of the Vatican. He began his Italian career in San Remo, where his good works included a welcome to Ugo Janni, the rebel against 'infallibility', but moved to Venice. His long, scholarly, but sociable ministry there and his encouragement of the Venetian Protestants still left him time for journalism and authorship. Short winter days, and the sea-fogs that gather round Venice out of the tourist season, also gave him time to write a substantial if rather polemical history of the Roman Catholic Church in Italy. But even Robertson, a United Presbyterian later accepted by the Established Kirk, did not fit into the old pattern any more than his independent mission station fitted into the Presbytery of Italy, though for a time it was counted as a charge of the Church of Scotland. He had a great enthusiasm for the Alps but Venice was too far from the Waldensian valleys. He became a great promoter of the Dolomites and wrote what in its time was the best English guide to the area, especially for the Italian side of the pre-1914 frontier.

In his last years he followed his earlier praise of turn-of-the-century Italy and its anti-clerical attitudes - 'the land where one enjoys the fullest religious liberty' - with a favourable book about Mussolini's Italy, claiming that the dictator was 'a man of versatile genius' and that under him Italy had 'realised the true democracy of Christianity'. When shorn of its rhetorical trimmings, this complacent and complaisant attitude to Mussolini probably reflected the mood of many expatriate and italophile Protestants before the dictator's quarrel with Britain and France. The royal Italian honours list even raised Robertson from the rank of *cavaliere* (which he had earned for work with earthquake victims on the Riviera in his San Remo days) to that of *commendatore*; and Mussolini gave permission for the book to be dedicated the memory of his mother. But Mussolini was to become one of the threats to the peace of Europe, and a threat also to the security which Cavour's legacy seemed to have left to Italian Protestants. They had felt reasonably secure and comfortable in the liberal united Italy, but Italian liberalism never recovered from the First World War.

Chapter 11

MUSSOLINI AND AFTER

From the concordat to a new war and new Republic

The Italian writer Enzo Biagi records that in Forli in Emilia, Mussolini's own country, more than 700 boys were baptised Benito between 1922 and 1929. There was no such rush in the Waldensian valleys.

Italian Protestantism and most of its friends abroad did not find much attraction or relevance in the new styles of ultra-nationalism in Italian politics, some of which, like D'Annunzio's seizure of Fiume, were evident before the triumph of Mussolini. Many Waldensians were also, like other Italian liberals and conservative moderates, shocked and alarmed by the Fascist murder in 1924 of the Socialist leader Giacomo Matteotti and other acts of violence or intimidation.

Most Italian Protestants were even less inclined to support the adventures and agitations which marked Mussolini's Fascist régime after he had consolidated power and was affected by the rise of Nazism in Germany and the general instability which came with the economic troubles of 1929 and after. Without any direct political influence, Italian Protestants would probably still have supported middle-of-the-road constitutional liberalism, and were happy with the House of Savoy thanks to its belated but apparently sincere acceptance of religious freedom. They were neither by temperament nor geography susceptible to Mussolini's encouragement of Italians to build an African empire, though some Vaudois-Huguenots from just across the French border (whose history was researched by W.S.E. Pickering) left their bleak hamlets for Algeria. Some Italian Waldensians are also said to have gone there but not to have stayed long. Rather than go to Libya or East Africa, the Italian Waldensian colonists were mostly inclined to head for South America, where there were (and are today) Waldensian communities in Argentina and Uruguay; or to the United States, where in a generation or two they merged into American Protestantism, as at the settlement of Valdese in upland North Carolina. Even the more evident American phenomena of 'ethnic Italian' Baptist congregations, and Italian involvement with Pentecostalists and Adventists, was bound to become less evident as integration progressed. Nor was there ever a 'colonial' Waldensian Church in the Italian Empire, though there was a substantial missionary presence in Eritrea and there is a continuing connection with the independent Protestant community there. (Other countries where Waldensians served through missionary societies include Lesotho, Zambia, and Gabon.)

But the early years of Mussolini's Fascist régime, for all its mixture of fancy dress, bullying, thuggery, and bravado, gave few hints of the troubles that were in store, although its national anthem, *Giovinezza*, not only swore loyalty to Mussolini but claimed that he had restored or remade the Italian people 'for the war of tomorrow'.

> *Li ha rifatti Mussolini*
> *Per la guerra di domani*

Such bombast, however, might be discounted by those, like the Waldensians, who generally preferred a quiet and orderly life and disliked the turbulence and disorder which had preceded the emergence of Fascism and made its success possible. Some Waldensians certainly joined it, though they were untypical and (I am told) tended to be from the cities and not the valleys. Early Fascism was certainly authoritarian but, whatever it claimed, it was not totalitarian in the style of Lenin's régime or Hitler's. It was bombastic and arrogant rather than profoundly and innately evil and it attracted one Italian philosopher of real distinction, Giovanni Gentile, who became Mussolini's Education Minister.

Fascism was essentially, or at least originally, an authoritarian perversion of nationalism and imperialism, not a philosophy of bogus racial 'science'. There were Jews associated with Fascism, as with other Italian tendencies, in its early years, just as there were Protestants who saw it as a defence against Communism, Socialism, and anarchism. Anti-Semitism only preoccupied the Fascists, or some of them, after they became the junior partners of Hitler's Nazi Germany, though the move stemmed from Hitler's emotional impact on the volatile Mussolini and some other Fascist leaders rather than direct Nazi pressure. The controlled press was urged in 1936 to criticise the Jews, whether as Bolsheviks or capitalists. Two years later an official 'manifesto of Italian racism' appeared and 'aryanisation' became Fascist policy. Italy had become an anti-Semitic State and Jews began to suffer discrimination and dismissal from employment, especially in education. Even then parts of the Italian Government were half-hearted or better in responding to the Nazi pressures which began to be felt during the war. For example in the small part of South-eastern France which the Italians occupied after 1940, and extended when the 'unoccupied zone ' was invaded, Jews fared better than in the rest of France, occupied or not. Even after the Germans assumed control many local and refugee Jews on the Riviera escaped to Italy, though in the later stages of the war Nazi pressure and ultra-Fascist fanaticism sent victims from Occupied Italy to the murder-camps of the Holocaust. About 8000 Italian Jews seem to have been murdered at this time.

The initial Waldensian worries about Fascism were more concerned with its inclination to force all Italians into the same mould and its ambiguous attitudes towards Christianity in general and the Roman Church in particular. Some of Fascism's black-shirted adherents spouted what sounded like Nietzsche in translation and it inherited some anti-clerical and even anti-religious tendencies, but it was also politically and emotionally aware of the Roman Catholic Church as a great Italian institution and inheritance. Although apparently committed to religious freedom, it became overtly and increasingly hostile to those Protestant denominations which were regarded as Anglo-Saxon imports. It also had its suspicions of Waldensians who were lukewarm about Mussolini's imperial ambitions in Abyssinia and elsewhere and had historic ties with Britain, France, Switzerland, and pre-Nazi Germany.

In the inter-war years, however, Fascism was hardest on its political opponents and on Italy's newly acquired ethnic minorities, notably the Slovenes in the hinterland of Trieste, the Croats of Istria, and the Germans of the South Tyrol. The Waldensians were out of the direct line of fire because of their political caution, their historic roots in Piedmont, and their long association with the cause of Italian unity.

Up to a point they had even voluntarily agreed to be 'Italianised' long before Fascism was thought of. But the nationalist frenzy of Fascist Italy did increase the pressures on them and they were conscious of being 'political orphans' in the new style of State. It forced Italianisation of many French or Provençal names and in the schools of the valleys, where French was allowed only an inferior status and regarded as a 'foreign language'. It also probably accelerated the final stages of the Waldensian move from French to Italian as the language of worship and Church affairs. There are still today some historic Waldensian churches in the valleys decorated inside and out with biblical texts in French or the affirmation (as at Rorà): *C'est ici la maison de Dieu*. But in the Synod Hall at Torre Pellice the fine decoration to mark the 250th anniversary of the Glorious Return in 1939 is in Italian. Perhaps it would have been anyway, but the trend of the Church and mood of the time settled on a style which was not quite that of Henri Arnaud.

However when Waldensians look back on the Fascist era they think even more of another kind of pressure, and a different sense of insecurity. For Mussolini, the dictator who professed to be pushing Italians forward, made one move which seemed to Waldensians a step backward. He ended the quarrel between the Italian State and the Vatican which had lingered on, though becoming steadily less serious, since the union of Italy after 1860 and the incorporation of Rome ten years later. He also reached a concordat with the Roman Catholic Church, as Hitler was to do in Germany a few years later.

129

Conditions in the two countries were very different. Hitler was concluding an agreement with a very large and influential German minority, to which in a nominal sense he himself still belonged. It involved a large element of mutual distrust and tactical calculation on both sides. In Italy, however, Mussolini was in effect accepting that Roman Catholicism should again be the Established Church of Italy, though he by no means conceded all that the Vatican would have liked. In return he ensured a benevolent papal detachment from politics, now a Fascist preserve, and even a blessing of a sort on what seemed a firmly-established and distinctively Italian régime. The Vatican had already allowed the suppression of the Catholic People's Party, which had briefly flourished after 1918 and added to the pre-Fascist confusion, though it made increasing use of Catholic Action as a lobbying force and power behind the scenes.

The 1929 Concordat and settlement of the 'temporal power' question provide another of the historic occasions about which British Protestants, especially those of rather traditional, conservative, or simply empirical inclinations, need to make an effort to grasp the Waldensians' point of view and the emotions that go with it. They remember it as the beginning of a time of 'dark night'. We may feel a slight tremor of surprise at this, as we may also feel when we hear their emphatic approval of the French Revolution and their two cheers for Napoleon Bonaparte. Few of us would list the Lateran Treaty and the Concordat among Mussolini's acts of stupidity, wickedness, or recklessness, of which there were many. We may even recognise that his agreement in the Lateran Treaty and the Concordat, as far as the settlement of the old quarrel about Rome, papal sovereignty, and temporal power was concerned, was not all that different from the one which a moderate constitutional Italian Government might have reached, given any good will from the Vatican. Even in 1871 the new Italian Parliament had passed a 'Law of Guarantees' which provided for the Papacy to have extra-territorial rights in the Vatican and Lateran, as well as the summer palace of Castel Gandolfo, and recognised its role as an international and supra-national authority for the Roman Catholic Church.

While many Italian anti-clericals no doubt enjoyed twisting the papal tail, the perpetuation of the quarrel had been very much the work of Pius IX and of successors professing loyalty to his inheritance. Now in the very different Italy of 1929, with a dictator who had switched his early anti-clerical rhetoric to denunciation of parliamentary politics, the Vatican took some pleasure in the humiliation of the old-style Italian liberals and secular democrats by Mussolini. It found this a convenient moment to extricate itself from what remained of the legacy of ill-feeling. But in 1929 the Roman Church remained, spiritually as well as culturally, the Church of the great majority of Italians.

At the time Fascism's Protestant admirers, such as Dr Robertson, the Scots minister in Venice, argued that the Papacy had made all the significant concessions, and most Protestants outside Italy probably thought that on balance Mussolini deserved some credit for ending the lingering quarrel. Even the British Waldensian supporters' *Voice from Italy* reacted in April 1929 mainly with a factual summary of what the treaty and concordat involved, though it carried a splendid sting in the tail which made clear that the Waldensians and their friends abroad already shared anxieties. It recalled that the young Mussolini had written about the Czech reformer and martyr Jan Hus as a 'truth-seeker' in a 'book not to be had now for love or money', adding a thought that has the spirit of Waldensian independence in it:

'When Caesar stretches out his hand to Peter, human blood drips from that hand-grip.'

But few Protestants were or are inclined, in the American phrase, to make a big deal of the sovereignty of the Vatican as a city-state within the now far-spread city of Rome. The right to sell philatelists its own stamps, and the other symbols of sovereignty as distinct from mere extra-territorial status, even the broadcasting and occasional ventures into suspiciously creative banking, are a pale glimmer of the temporal and spiritual powers which Popes once sought to combine. Americans are probably more inclined than the British to worry about links between Church and State, having been brought up on a strict constitutional separation that is sometimes carried to doctrinaire extremes by court decisions. But the British, even when Established Churches are apologetic about establishment, retain a sense that the State should express a national recognition of religion as defender of the faith or faiths, the form of which recognition will obviously be shaped by any nation's situation and traditions.

Waldensians, however, look back on the Concordat and Lateran Treaty as the alliance of an authoritarian State and an authoritarian Church, consolidating and even extending those special privileges of the Roman Church which survived after 1870 in the Kingdom of Italy. It had a privileged position in public institutions and in the schools, though children could be withdrawn from religious instruction and the Ministry of Education prescribed passages from Diodati's Protestant translation of the Bible because of its literary quality. On the other hand the law apparently secured freedom of worship, equal rights in public service, and recognition of Protestant marriages, though social pressures and Roman Catholic ecclesiastical law inevitably created problems with 'mixed marriages', as they still do to some extent in the twenty-first century. But the Protestants, whose total number was put at 83,000 in 1931, began to feel vulnerable again, and by no means without cause.

When Mussolini's power and prestige were at their peak in the 1930's, before the German-Italian 'Axis', there was already another axis of mutual support and sometimes mutual flattery uniting the Fascist State and the dominant influences in the Italian ascendancy over the Roman Church. It was natural for a popular writer of the time like Osio Vergani (in his *Bella Italia, Amate Sponde*) to link the themes of Rome's ancient glory, modern revival, and world-wide spiritual influence with conventional homage to Mussolini and emphasis on his restitution of temporal power, however limited, to the 'Vicar of Christ, the Holy Father'. Waldensians were inevitably marginalised when this new style of hyper-nationalist and authoritarian *Risorgimento* linked classical, papal, and Fascist Rome. 'What does the cupola of St Peter's tell you?', asked Vergani. 'It tells you that nothing is great, nothing conquers, nothing rules, if it does not have its foundation in Rome.'

Mussolini himself had set the trend with such oratorical flourishes as one in the Rome Opera House (March 18, 1934) when he called Italy's religious unity 'a great strength of her people. To compromise it or even to allow the slightest fissure in it is to commit a crime against her national greatness.'

The new definitive Italian law on 'permitted religions' and Fascist limitations on press freedom also caused problems for the Waldensians. The State claimed a veto on ecclesiastical appointments, which also applied to Roman Catholic bishops, and made evangelisation difficult, prohibiting open-air rallies and controlling the building and opening of new churches and mission halls. These rules appear to have been exercised with varying degrees of unfairness according to the good will or otherwise of local authorities and police and the determination of local bishops and priests. It was not the condition of the Church under Soviet Communism, but it has some similarities with that of minority Churches and religious groups in post-Soviet Russia, with its tenacious local bureaucracy and its allies in obstruction among the Orthodox clergy.

Things went from bad to worse, especially when the Abyssinian crisis of 1935 and subsequent war opened a great gulf between Fascist Italy and almost all British opinion. The Waldensians were anxious both to maintain their old contacts and to avoid trouble with their own Government. For example newspapers in the valleys record Waldensian involvement, albeit at arm's length, in a troth-plighting propaganda exercise involving soldiers leaving for Africa and the girls they left behind them. Normal fund-raising visits by Waldensian deputies to Britain were suspended in 1936-37, even though British financial support continued. The Waldensians also had no enthusiasm for Mussolini's intervention in Spain on Franco's side in a civil war where the unfortunate handful of Spanish Protestants found themselves at the mercy of events, caught up in a revolution on one side when Communists and church-burning anarchists sought to take over the chaotic liberal Republic, yet liable to be shot by the other side (and some were) as subversive anti-national elements. And though in 1938, at the time of the ill-judged and ill-fated Munich agreement, Mussolini was inclined to pose as a peacemaker and the co-arbiter of Europe, and although he was alarmed at Hitler's eagerness to fight in 1939 and vainly sought another Munich, he was soon looking for an easy war, cheap victories, and a share in the spoil.

The result was that Britain and Italy were at war for more than three years after June 1940, though it was a war for which very large numbers of Italians had no enthusiasm and many privately deplored, among them virtually all the Protestants. They were by now the subject of 'vigilant attention' from Mussolini's Ministry of the Interior, not just because of foreign connections but because they were deemed (in a Ministerial circular of March 13, 1940) to harbour 'a deep-seated hostility against Fascism'.

The war interrupted many long-established contacts between Britain and Italy, among them the exchanges between the Waldensians and their English and Scottish well-wishers and supporters. It destroyed the already much dwindled English-speaking expatriate communities and many of their church congregations were never re-established. The Scottish Presbytery of Southern Europe met sadly in Edinburgh in 1940 to sympathise with members who had lost their 'stations' and their household goods and to note that the last relic of the great connection with Leghorn, the Sailor's Rest, had been put into the care of the American Consul. Yet the war created new contacts, exposed large numbers of British and Italians to a most un-touristic view of each other's cultures, and left some material memorials, from the war cemeteries in Sicily, Salerno, Anzio, and up the peninsula to the makeshift hut-chapel in Orkney which Italian prisoners turned into a thing of beauty. These contacts involved vast numbers of people, far more than even the peak flow of Victorian tourism, as the Allied armies with their high proportion of British and Commonwealth troops fought their way up Italy. They left many memories, fading now as the old soldiers fade away, and stimulated some new tastes, whether for *pasta* and *vino* or the repertoire of the San Carlo Opera in Naples. Yet neither the years of desert and Mediterranean war, nor the confusion of 'co-belligerency' after the armistice with the Badoglio Government which succeeded Mussolini, brought any fundamental changes in the relationship of the two countries.

For the British the involvement of the Italians in the war left no bitter memories of the kind that lingered with post-war Germany and, far more painfully, with the Japanese. It was a nasty business, as all wars are, and left its legacy of grief. Many British friends of Italy were killed or bereaved in the

Mediterranean war and I know of one Waldensian pastor whose father was killed fighting the British in East Africa. But as wars go it was a clean fight. So, at least that part of the wider war seems in British folk-memory. Italian memories are inevitably very different, and not least for the Waldensians. What began for them as a dictator's adventurous and disastrous misjudgment and eventually ravaged much of their country also became in Northern Italy a vicious civil war, as partisans fought not only the Germans but the 'Social Republic' of Mussolini's last phase. It has been estimated that 30,000 partisans were killed in the conflict, plus several thousand civilian victims of reprisals, hostage-taking, and other hazards of the time, in addition to the Jews murdered after deportation. For the first time in 150 years the Waldensian valleys became a battle-ground, with a style of war whose bitterness and tactics both seemed closer to the wars of the seventeenth century than to the clash of French and Austrian armies in the age of Napoleon.

Two experiences during a golden autumn time in the valleys brought this home to me. Waiting for a mini-bus to pick up our weary walking-party at Prali, a village already high in the valleys but with the Waldensian Agape centre even higher on the steep slopes above, I wandered off to look at the war memorial. It was erected after 1918 to commemorate the dead, on the Dolomites or the Carso, of 'the war for the Greater Italy' (*la guerra per la più grande Italia*). The phrase seemed an echo from the distant past, for I also encountered it as the title of a book by D'Annunzio. But that memorial in the quiet village square in front of the modern Waldensian church also commemorated a very different mood, from a different kind of war and a much more recent and lasting pain. A scattering of names after 1940 had also to be added and then the village's eight young men killed with the partisans in August 1944, a year after Italy's armistice and change of sides.

The other impact was made by the Waldensian museum in Torre Pellice, with its long guns and swords from battles long, long ago, its portraits of Calvin and Cromwell, and that most Protestant of relics, General Beckwith's wooden leg, the authenticity of which I forgot to establish. I was being shown round by a pastor whose grandfather had joined the partisans. Suddenly in one room the cruelties of the past were recorded in photographs from the quite recent past. A very young man, who otherwise might still have been alive today, was being led to execution, then hanged by the neck from a balcony and left hanging, by German young men in summer uniform. Some of them may still be alive in Munich or Vienna. The lad, presumably a partisan or sympathiser, was also in shirt-sleeves on a bright day in that August of 1944. His name was Valdo Jalla and the execution was at San Germano Chisone, well down the valleys from Prali. The local Waldensian minister, Pastor G Bertin, was there, presumably to give what spiritual support he could. My recollection (though I made no note at the time and I may be wrong) is that some German, moved by conscience, sadness, or sense of history, may have made over the sequence of snapshots.

That was what war became in the valleys. It was pretty much what war had been like there in the seventeenth century, though the source of invasion and oppression had changed. For the first time indeed the interests and inclinations of the Waldensians put them more or less on the same side as the Roman Church in Italy. By 1944 the temper of Italian Catholicism was being determined by the mood of the people and the judgment of the bishops of Northern Italy, not by the caution and calculation of the Vatican, which now found itself behind the Allied lines. For the moment there was a common cause, in the mountains, and the old alienation and suspicion were never to be as acute again. The partisan movement and the liberation committees covered a wide range of Italian activists, strongly influenced by the Communists and Socialists but by no means confined to them. Among the partisans were assorted democrats and Christians, Italian officers, some of them giving effective leadership, remnants of army formations, escaped Allied prisoners-of-war, mainly British, and - nearer the battle lines - a few stranded aircrew, among them a young Rhodesian called Ian Smith who kept a painting of his Spitfire on the office wall even when many years later he was leading a 'rebel' Government. Among this assortment of unkindred spirits, some of them very anti-religious Italians and many of them Communists, the Protestants and the Roman Catholics were often bound to feel not just allies but fellow-Christians.

The Waldensian valleys became a theatre of war not because there was any mass rising but because they were, as they had been in earlier centuries, good terrain for guerrillas and refugees, and because they were also fairly close to the major industrial area of Turin and the important lines of communications which passed through it. After the liberation of the South of France in the late summer of 1944 they were also close to the inactive front line of the Alps. Many Waldensians, like most other Italians, would probably have preferred to wait quietly until the Germans were beaten elsewhere but life was not so easy. The Germans wanted to secure their rear areas and communications, and proclaimed 'operational zones' in which little attempt was made to conceal their control. The last-phase Fascism of Mussolini, whose feeble Government located itself at Salò on Lake Garda, wanted to assert its remnant of authority with a nervous and often vicious militia. It also wanted to call up young men for its Italian forces, which the Germans were training rather unenthusiastically.

The Germans expected Italian troops to desert and would rather have had more Italian workers for their own munitions industry. As in France, many of the rank and file of the resistance fighters were not volunteer enthusiasts in the simplest sense. Many faced the painful choice of heading for the mountains, where they were likely to be recruited by partisans, or waiting to be carried off either for Mussolini's forces or for work in Germany.

.From the time of the Italian armistice in September 1943 there was no effective government covering the whole of Italy. The constitutional Government, which had to follow Allied directions, looked and was both provisional and transitional, first under Marshal Badoglio and then the old pre-Fascist parliamentarian, Ivanoe Bonomi. Its area of effective civil control under overall Allied guidance only gradually moved north as the British and Americans fought their way up the peninsula. Mussolini's Government of the 'Social Republic' had little substance and its writ hardly ran outside the Po valley, and even then only in so far as the Germans allowed. In the event the remnants of Fascism were themselves bitterly divided and Mussolini had his son-in law and former Foreign Minister, Count Ciano, shot for collusion with those who concluded the armistice.

Meanwhile in the North liberation committees prepared for the end of the war. The Communists prepared to turn their considerable influence and effort in the Resistance to longer-term political advantage and the democratic parties wondered about the future, each other, and the Communists. The liberation committees were in touch with the Allied High Command and the constitutional and still royal Government but were something of a law unto themselves, partly through circumstances, party through inclination. In the Waldensian valleys, where many young men took to the hills, to be joined by refugees from the Turin area and helped by army officers and soldiers, there were new guerrilla skirmishes on historic sites. Torre Pellice was once again the base for an occupying force and punitive expeditions. There was a unit in the valleys of a 'Justice and Liberty' band, controlled after a fashion by the Piedmont National Liberation Committee in Turin - part of a movement which loosely linked the democratic political parties, including the Christian Democrats, and the Communists.

It was against this background that the German command was circulating orders at the beginning of August 1944 - the month when Prali and the Germanasca valley lost so heavily - that 'every act of violence must be followed immediately by appropriate counter-measures... if German soldiers are fired at in villages, the village must be burned. The criminals or else the leaders must be publicly hanged.' So said an order of August 4, 1944 from Field-Marshal

Albert Kesselring, once Luftwaffe commander in the Battle of Britain but then the harsh and skilful commander of Hitler's southern front.

As in every such situation the majority of the population were under pressure from both sides. It came from their own people in the hills, who wanted information, supplies, and shelter, and from the Germans, who not only threatened reprisals and collective punishments but demanded help from 'security squadrons made up the civilian population of the villages themselves.' The Waldensian church leadership, says Prescot Stephens, 'maintained an official attitude of neutrality, but 'each pastor and indeed each church member had to take their own fateful decisions answering for them before God alone.'

Inevitably there was cruelty, destruction, and martyrdom. The two best-known martyrs among the Protestants were Willy Jervis and Giacopo Lombardini. Jervis was a Milan Waldensian of British descent who joined the Turin National Liberation Committee for Piedmont and was a link between the partisans and Allied headquarters. He was captured, tortured, and shot at Villar Pellice. His name is commemorated today in the mountain refuge above the head of the valley.

Lombardini was a Methodist convert who at the age of 50 joined the young men in the mountains after having to flee from Torre Pellice, where he had established a reputation as a Christian thinker about the future of Italy. Although not a pastor, he exercised a spiritual as well as political influence - he belonged to the Republican Party - and conducted worship as Huguenots had done in the Cévennes, Covenanters on the Galloway moors, and seventeenth-century Waldensians in these same mountains. He too was captured in March 1944 and endured a long and arduous captivity before being murdered at Mauthausen in Austria in April 1945, the same month as Dietrich Bonhoeffer was killed at Flossenburg in the last vicious, pointless spasm of hard-core Nazism.

When the war ended Italy was left with many scars, physical, and emotional. Some old scores were paid off and new rivalries developed. For example when the Scottish Horse, who were now also designated 80th Medium Regiment, Royal Artillery, arrived at Pinerolo in June 1945 after the Italian campaign they were given the dual task of patrolling the French frontier to prevent smuggling and gathering in the arms that had been parachuted in to the partisans in the Waldensian valleys. One of their young officers recalled more than half a century later: 'We had singularly little success in either task. The partisans were all preserving their weapons for the coming struggle between the red brigades and the royalists, and we didn't have the resources for effective frontier patrols. But we had a lovely time'. The 'lovely time' no doubt took different forms according to taste and temperament but for Robin Barbour, later a divinity professor and Church of Scotland Moderator, it included many encounters with Waldensians, including at least one minister, 'a magnificent man called Peyronel who was pastor at Prali.' By coincidence Robin Barbour applied the same adjective to that war-tested pastor as Scottish-Waldensian enthusiasts had applied in their obituary tributes to his own great-grandfather's support for evangelism, political freedom, and Christian publishing in the Italy of the *Risorgimento*.

Another Gunner officer and future minister, Malcolm Ritchie, was to be moved by his encounter with the pastor of Venice, Ernesto Ayassot, who had also looked after Udine and the mountain outpost of Tramonti di Sopra. In the mountains he found himself 'the sole representative of the British Empire and the Allies' when Ayassot presided at the unveiling of a memorial to partisans, two of them Waldensians, who had been killed there. He found himself called to speak at the occasion along with Ayassot, the local priest, and the partisan commander. There were many such encounters to sustain and revive the British links with the Waldensians in an Italy where much else was irrevocably changed. There was also resumption of Waldensian visits to Britain and British support for their Church in Italy, though on a modest scale sometimes made even more modest by British exchange controls in that age of austerity.

In this new but scarred and uncertain Italy, political Catholicism and Communism were the two great political powers in the land, with the Crown discredited by Victor Emmanuel III's supine role under Fascism, with liberalism and constitutional conservatism out of fashion, and with the democratic centre weakened by the adhesion of the dominant section of the Socialists to alliance with the far Left. There was no obvious opening for significant Protestant influence in the new Italy.

Many of the energies of the Waldensians had to go into reconstruction in the valleys; many of their inclinations were now influenced by the unhappy experiences of the Fascist era, the war, and the alliances of the liberation movement. There may have been a few passing thoughts about whether the valleys might be better off in France, but both geographically and historically they were part of Piedmont and French policy under General de Gaulle in 1945-46 concentrated on reconciliation with Italy. It exacted only a couple of minor frontier adjustments south of the valleys and promises of cultural rights for the French-speakers of Aosta. Moreover any transfer of the valleys to France would have caused a painful and crippling partition of a Waldensian Church which for a century had been orientated towards Italy as a whole and not just Piedmont.

Along with the burdens of reconstruction the Waldensians inherited a legacy of martyrs and memories. They were the kind of memories that are fixed in the mind. Iain Douglas, the present chairman of the Scottish-Waldensian society (2005) and son of a former secretary, tells of his encounter with one of these memories in his father's Scottish manse. They had a Waldensian deputy to lunch after a Sunday service at which one of the hymns was 'Glorious things of thee are spoken', generally sung in Scotland to a rousing and resonant tune which the hymn-book records as a Croatian folk-song adapted by Hadyn. It is even better known to the words of *Deutschland, Deutschland über alles*. 'The last time I heard the tune', said the Waldensian over lunch, 'I was on my way to join a party of partisans and hiding behind a dry-stone dyke while a German soldier on patrol was whistling it on the other side.'

Perhaps we should add 1945 to those other occasions in history - the French Revolution, the rule of Napoleon Bonaparte, the wave of revolutions in 1848, and the Lateran Pact with Papacy - when the Waldensian perspective is inevitably rather different from that of their closest British friends.

We emerged as a tired but essentially united nation, ready for social reforms but with our political differences kept well within bounds and with no real shocks to our constitutional system. In Italy there had been the dislocation both of battle-front war and civil war. There were punishments, reprisals, uncertainties over the way to restore a parliamentary democracy which had failed 20 years before, and over the constitution. The House of Savoy had collaborated with Fascism until it was too late to save itself, though the majority for a Republic in 1946 was by no means overwhelming (12.7m. to 10.7m., with 1.5m. 'null' votes). If the Roman Church and its new political arm, the Christian Democrats, had not hedged their bets there might have been no Republican majority at all, but the Vatican was not inclined to take risks to save the dynasty which had once infuriated and humbled it. The majority of Waldensians probably voted for the Republic.

The Waldensians had lost their old political moorings from the 1920s onwards and had to look for new ones. Many now supported the Socialist Party, despite its long and disastrous alliance with the Communists. Others pinned their hopes on a 'Party of Action' which seemed for a time to offer a new hope, or hoped for a revival of the secular parties of the right-centre. Some favoured the Social Democrat minority which took a clear pro-Western line but lacked mass support.

To their credit the Waldensians also looked for new opportunities for reconciliation, the beginning of a process which not only restored and modernised their traditional contacts with German Protestantism but made the latter at least as important, in many respects, as the British connection, reinforced by the powerful influence of German-language theologians, most notably the great Swiss-German Karl Barth. One of the first signs of this reconciliation was the German involvement, along with Americans and other Europeans, in the building of the Agape ecumenical centre on the hills high above Prali in what the New York traveller of 1837, Robert Baird, called 'decidedly the wildest and most barren of all parishes of the Waldenses' - though a very beautiful one. The reconciled and more or less united Europe of the early twenty-first century finds it hard to grasp how difficult it was in the years after 1945 not just to help German Christians in their own country's reconstruction, which was clearly expedient from secular as well as spiritual considerations, but to welcome them as partners in countries which had known the bitterness of occupation.

With reconstruction in the valleys and reconciliation in Europe went a renewed Waldensian concern for partnership and national unity within Italy, and for social progress and reinvigoration in the often neglected and sometimes backward areas of the South. The *Mezzogiorno* was subsidised by the political system after its fashion but ill-equipped to share in the economic regeneration of Milan and Turin or the bureaucratic prosperity of Rome. There had been Protestant evangelism and social work in Sicily and Naples from the earliest days of a united Italy - in Palermo, for example, Protestantism seems to have appeared along with 'The Thousand' - but after 1945 it was possible both to undertake more social initiatives and to have a more vigorous Waldensian presence away from the cities. It was an aspect of Waldensian mission much emphasised among British supporters, sometimes in words which echoed the moods and styles of the nineteenth-century move out of the old ghetto into the new Italy centred on Florence and Rome. In 1966, for example, a young pastor, Marco Ayassot, came back to Scotland only three years after being there as a student of the great preacher and theologian Professor J.S. Stewart, who was then chairman of the Scottish Waldensian supporters. In those years Ayassot had been pastor at Catanzaro, a Calabrian town of 50,000 people. This Waldensian described his ministry and congregation to the Scottish central committee on November 12, 1966: 'Most of the people are very poor. Any improvements in the Italian economy have passed the area by and the people are sorely in need of spiritual and material help. The Waldensians are trying to help with all their problems and groups of their young people go out eager to serve the community.' He conducted services each Sunday within a radius of 50 miles; and at open-air services, though there was only a congregation of 80, as many as 300 would gather.

It sounded not only like good work (which it was) but like old times, echoing the mood of the Waldensians who moved out from Piedmont in the age of the *Risorgimento*. It was a picture which could be reproduced for many places in the Italian South and in Sicily and which has significantly altered the style of the Waldensian Church and its ministers, many of them now from central and Southern Italy, even though church growth (as after the first move out of the valleys) has been less sustained than well-wishers hoped for. However there were new moods developing in Italy and affecting the Waldensians as well as the rest of the country and the Roman Catholic Church.

Perhaps there was another date which had to be added to that sequence of different historical perspectives. In British history 1968, when Harold Wilson's Labour Government was struggling along, does not count for very much. Even if we take a wider view of the world we probably think mainly of the Prague Spring and Soviet occupation, or of the turbulence in the United States, with the murders of Robert Kennedy and Martin Luther King, the surge of racial protest, and the campaign against the Vietnam war. Even the one serious riot in Britain, the confrontation with police guarding the American Embassy in Grosvenor Square, is remembered as a 'Vietnam protest'. But in Continental Europe a generation, especially a student generation, remembers 1968 very differently. Student and other rioters in Paris in May thought a new revolution was on the way, and some of their generation, in Italy and Germany as well as France, are still brooding over whether a revolutionary opportunity was missed, sometimes in a way which many British people find bewildering and slightly tiresome.

Italy, which was later to be plagued with revolutionary terrorism on the far right as well as the far left of the 'Red Brigade' movement, was also touched by this revolutionary mood, which the British associated most readily with the Paris Left Bank rioters and such allies as 'Danny the Red', who later turned Green. Even the small Waldensian community, apparently socially stable and devoted to good works, plain living, and high thinking, was affected.

In his survey of discipleship since the Second World War, the leading Waldensian and former Moderator, Giorgio Bouchard, writes of this time, which followed a flurry of ecumenical encounters, dialogue with Marxism, and social initiatives: 'This activity was in full swing when the 1968 student uprisings burst upon the scene. Protestant students interrupted worship services and distributed manifestos, declaring that Western society was rotten and that revolution was necessary. Vietnamese resistance became the symbol of the world's resistance to the "bondage of capitalism". Christian vocation was seen in terms of anti-capitalist struggle. Even the Waldensian synod was disrupted, scandalising the conservative forces.'

A similar point was made to me personally by one of the Waldensians' closest friends in Britain, familiar with them for half a century: 'After 1968

141

many of the young pastors became radicalised and involved in left-wing politics. While this was in tune with their generation, the Church went through a difficult time. As the 1970s went on this violent current of thought weakened as Italian economic life improved and the worst politicians lost power.' Another supporter, looking at the more recent history shaped in part by the turbulence after 1968 and the recovery of consensus with a slightly new emphasis, writes: 'My only concern is that while their academic standards are extremely high and their passion for social justice is unwavering, evangelistic zeal and a vision for Church growth are not so obvious'. On the other hand the Scots Moderator Andrew McLellan, speaking at the Waldensian Synod in 2000, was eager to 'plead' with the Waldensians to 'resist the temptation to retreat into an authoritarian Biblicism which replaces the freedom of the Word with the binding of a legalist literalism'. He seemed to be urging resistance to a none-to-evident temptation, and denouncing sins which most Waldensians had no mind for. He was, of course, correct in identifying the Waldensians as a Church of the Word, a Church 'of the poor', and a Church of ecumenical outlook.

But it is not easy for British observers to assess the long-term significance of 1968, if any, for the Waldensians. Probably we should not exaggerate it, but neither should we ignore it because its violent tactics and its dogmatically misguided opinions - in which we may think we detect more than a hint of a new fascism of the Left - neither appeal to our temperament nor figure in our experience. I confess that the very few occasions on which I have been irritated by individual Waldensians have been when they have interpreted trends of opinion and differences of emphasis in the Church in terms of 'the bourgeoisie' and the rest. I have even been told, and I remain intensely sceptical, that it is mainly among 'the bourgeoisie' that one finds devotion to Waldensian history. Nor am I very impressed when I read suggestions that there was something almost 'aristocratic' in the leadership of those who sustained the Waldensians' attempt to be a Church for all Italy after 1860 and sometimes kept their distance from the more anarchic evangelicals. If it was an aristocracy it was one of talent, vocation, education, and conviction. Whatever errors they made stemmed from conviction.

The important thing is that, as at other times before 1968 when our historical and political perspectives have been very different, the affinity and friendship based on evangelical and reformed Christian experience within the truly catholic or universal church have been both reaffirmed and rediscovered. Karl Barth, not the liberation theologians, was the greatest external twentieth-century influence on Waldensian thinking.

Chapter 12

IN CONTEMPORARY ITALY

From 1984 and all that into a new century

The Waldensians and the Italian Methodists formed in 1979 a united but federated Church, with a single general Synod. Its title is the *Chiesa Evangelica Valdese (Unione dei Valdesi e Metodisti)*. But despite that significant ecumenical date, and despite the impact of 1968 on a section of the Church, for most Waldensians 'contemporary Italy' probably begins in 1984.

In that year the then Prime Minister of Italy, Bettino Craxi, signed an agreement with the Waldensian Moderator, Giorgio Bouchard, which expressed the happy result of extended negotiations between the Waldensians and the Government. The Italian Parliament gave it legislative force later in the year. The Waldensians felt that Italy had at last created the conditions for what, to adapt Cavour, might be called free Churches in a free State, even if there are still worries about episcopal influence on public schools and the idea of a 'Catholic presence' in classrooms.

The agreement came in a rapidly changing Italy. Its prosperity was increasing, its birth-rate falling. Italian society was now a much more complex coalition than the old alliance of large families and (largely) celibate priests. The political power of Christian Democracy, in the Italian sense of the term, was also breaking down, and the old banner-waving solidarity on the far Left had given way to 'Eurocommunism' long before the collapse of the Soviet Union. Italy was reshaping its democracy and reflecting the dominant liberalism of Europe. Despite, or perhaps because of, the previous dogmatic resistance of the Roman Catholic Church to quite moderate reform, it was even doing so in such areas as divorce, contraception, abortion, and pornography. If problems of the use and misuse of freedom and challenges to 'family values' are the characteristics of an advanced society, Italy was proving itself only too well developed.

But it was coping with unhappy legacies from the past. For all their faults, the dull politicians in power held a constitutional and democratic State together in face of the fanaticisms of Red Brigades on the left, a strange and equally terrorist-inclined Nihilism of the far Right, and the tenacity and pervasiveness of organised Sicilian and Neapolitan crime. Politicians of the Right, Left, and Centre continued to be involved in dubious and sometimes corrupt alliances. It was not a glorious time, and it brought such humiliations as the kidnapping, concealment, and murder of the ex-Premier Aldo Moro in 1978 by the terrorists of the Left, but these were the troubles of a free society resilient enough to survive. It had failures. It did not wholly eradicate terrorism. Eventually it produced a new political volatility whose long-term consequences are by no means yet apparent. But it had its successes, and one of them was religious and intellectual freedom.

The settlement of the Waldensians' status and freedom was an agreement but no concordat. It recognised the Waldensian anxiety to avoid any appearance of worshipping and working under licence. One of the most resented features of Mussolini's concordat had been the notion of 'permitted religions'. But it did remove the last ambiguities about freedom of worship and for evangelism. It also provided for Protestant pastoral care in State institutions, including the armed forces, hospitals, and prisons. Even though the courts had already upheld challenges to the regulations surviving from the Fascist era, and though the obstruction from the Roman Catholic Church had greatly lessened after the Second Vatican Council, the formal act and explicit recognition mattered to the Waldensians and Methodists. Two years later there was a symbolic visit from the President of the Republic, Francesco Cossiga, to the theological seminary in Rome.

The Waldensian-Methodist Church in contemporary Italy remains small, rich in faith, works, and example but without much direct influence and without significant direct political or social power. It has also been far less successful (at least numerically) than the Pentecostal Churches in meeting the needs of substantial numbers of Italians, previously nominal Christians or unbelievers, who feel the call of Christ's Gospel and do not find it in Roman Catholicism.

It does what it can and what it must - very obviously with what a hymn about the Church of Jesus calls 'strength unequal to her task'. It has no triumphalist visions but much faith, and it sets its hand to immediate needs.

Some of these needs are very practical, especially in poor areas of the South and Sicily, or in the cities, whether among the homeless and drug-culture victims or the immigrant communities drawn from a variety of east European, Middle Eastern, African, and Asian cultures. Italy's geographical position makes it the most accessible part of the European Union for many illegal immigrants and asylum-seekers, genuine and otherwise, both from Africa and south-east Europe But it does not take long for a visitor to Italy, especially one who visits Waldensian churches, to encounter wider consequences of globalisation and population movement in Italian life, for they are hosts to a variety of African and Asian congregations. It has been estimated that 200,000 of these settlers, expatriate workers, and transients have a Protestant Christian background. A far larger number, along with Italians of many sorts and troubled conditions, provide opportunities for Christian social service and practical help.

But one of the needs, in an increasingly secular Italy of Catholic inheritance, is still to set out the facts about 'what Protestants are and what they think'. I quote the heading on a leaflet I picked up in the church in central Turin, the one on the Via Vittorio Emmanuele which Beckwith was determined should affirm a striking Protestant presence and which British Victorian travellers had visited with something between curiosity and pilgrim devotion. Later I found that it was a local variation on themes emphasised in many Protestant churches and in the literature available in Waldensian or other Protestant bookshops. 'The first thing I had to do in Naples', a pastor told me, 'was to explain that Protestants are Christians'. He found this easier when he moved to Rome!

In former times Protestants expected to find Italians grotesquely misinformed and often blamed Roman Catholic priests for deliberate misinformation, though many of them were probably almost as ignorant of Protestant ways and beliefs as their parishioners. Goethe for example had a travelling companion, an officer in the papal army, who claimed to have been taught that Protestants encouraged fornication and allowed incest, with brothers marrying sisters. In the following century Mrs Gretton encountered a belief in the hinterland of Ancona at Macerata, now a setting for summer opera, 'that the transmigration of human souls into animals was a dogma of the Church of England' - a previous English family there having fondly cherished sick horses and under-nourished sheep in whom they allegedly perceived the spirits of their departed relations. When she tried to discuss such beliefs more rationally she claimed to encounter a immovable obstacle, 'What does it signify after all? You do not pray to the Madonna, so the rest matters little'.

Today's need is not to counter such extravagant fictions, though the Madonna remains a problem where popular religious cultures are further apart than ecumenical theologians allow, but to set out simple facts. Italian Protestants do this in terms and ways which Northern Europeans might emulate in their own secularised societies.

Protestants believe in the one, holy, apostolic, universal Church but do not think any one part of the Church has an exclusive claim to know the truth. They have the two Gospel sacraments; they have a ministry of pastors, doctors, elders, deacons, and others according to the gifts of the spirit. ('Doctors' refer to those who are educated and gifted to lead the community in understanding and explaining the faith.) Even within the Church, however, all have sinned and salvation is by the grace of God through the mediation of Jesus Christ. This is what a casual seeker after truth in Turin would discover, perhaps more readily than in St Giles' in Edinburgh or St Paul's in London.

But much of the emphasis in simple, factual explanations for Italians about Protestant belief and practice has to be an explanation (not a denunciation of others' errors) of where they stand in relation to the Italian religious and cultural inheritance. Most Italians, for example, have never been in a Protestant church and have no idea of how it is set out and why. Most have never encountered the biblical idea of 'saints', which is rather different from the popular Italian conception of them. Most have never encountered the biblical Protestant Christian concept of our Lord's mother as full and grace and blessed among women, though the pious and the sceptics of Italy are acutely conscious of her as an object of veneration and channel of intercession. And for most Italians it is still a surprise that Christians may find no need or occasion to offer intercessions for the dead, since Purgatory has always been very much part of the popular Italian cultural inheritance.

Miracles also have to be discussed still in a very different context from that required in sceptical Northern Europe or France. The problem for vast numbers of Southern Europeans is not that they have lost their sense of the miraculous but that they inherit a culture in which faith, credulity, and superstition are much mingled. Where so many miracles are claimed for so many saints, there can be both devaluation of and diversion from the wonders worked by Jesus, not only in first-century Palestine but ever since.

> His blood can make the foulest clean,
> His blood availed for me.

There is evidence that the work of the Waldensians is becoming better known in a more pluralistic Italy. The most obvious evidence is the benefit which their social work receives through the Italian Government's tax concessions, the equivalent of our covenant and gift aid system. But there may be dangers if a Church is seen only as a social service organisation with a tremendous sense of history, though the core and tenacity of Waldensian belief should make that hardly more likely in their situation than in that of the Salvation Army, which also has a presence in Italy and even in Torre Pellice. But in a sense Andrew McLellan was right to call the Waldensians a Church of the poor, though when one takes account of the talents and initiative within the Waldensian community 'for the poor' might have been a better description.

It is certainly true (to quote a francophile Scot, John Cameron, who has also developed Waldensian links) that there 'is no Italian equivalent of the

French HSP, *Haute Societé Protestante,* made up of bankers, jewellers, senior civil servants, overseas and military élite, politicians, professors, writers, artists, and the like.' Individual Italian Protestants have prospered through education and hard work and may play important roles in commercial, official, and academic life but they have not formed a caste. The 'old' Waldensians are descendants of a deprived and marginalised community in Piedmont. Many of the newer Waldensians of very different Italian origins, like most of the Pentecostal Christians, come from communities which have known other and more modern forms of such deprivation and marginalisation. It is not surprising that they should have a fierce sense of justice and injustice. 'Modern economic and cultural conditions make the feel of French and Italian Protestant communities very different', says Cameron after his experience of both. 'Most Italians do not realise that the Waldensians exist or could possibly be a part of their national tradition. That is not true of the French Protestant community'.

It is probably a mistake to try to understand the Waldensians, or help others understand them, by comparing them with any other Church. They are part of the catholic Church - though when they join in the Creed they call it the *Chiesa universale* - and adhere both to the Reformation and the idea of continuing reformation which, along with the emphasis on the Word, is a mark of the Reformed group of Churches. But, despite their small numbers, history has also made them a distinctively territorial Church - one might say, were it not for the Church of the Emigration in South America, an Italian national Church. There is even a irony of Providence in the way that a community which began as a trans-national one and which then became an Alpine and ethnic one should now in its way be a symbol of the Italian capacity for national unity as well as regional diversity. It is a highly structured Church with considerable diversity but an intensity of identity far stronger than that of the 'national' Protestant Churches of Northern Europe. This comes partly from history, partly from contemporary Italian circumstances, even from the uncertainties about the future.

There are many uncertainties, though probably none of them as threatening as the perils and travails which Waldensians have survived in the past. Some of them are very practical, for example in planning their future role in social service, health, and education. At the time of writing it appears certain that there will be a continuing role for Waldensians in social service but that the noble tradition of Waldensian hospitals may not survive, at least in ownership and management. The practical and financial problems of modern health services seem too great. I have also heard doubts expressed about the long-term future of the most important visible surviving symbol of the great Waldensian school tradition, the *liceo* or college at Torre Pellice.

There are also demographic and political uncertainties. Although the Waldensians have made themselves a small but significant symbol of Italian unity, there are uncertainties about how the Church will develop in a changing Italy. The country is likely to have an increasing immigrant or expatriate population, some of which will be assimilated and some (especially the Muslim part) may not be. One aspect of assimilation may be the absorption of some of the immigrants or 'new Italians' into the Protestant communities, perhaps in such numbers that they will create a new image of Italian Protestantism. Already there are estimates that at least a quarter of the growing Italian Protestant population is from abroad, and even such an old and deeply rooted community as the Waldensian one (which did not share in this growth of the last 40 years) may be significantly affected.

To these social uncertainties must be added theological ones Some are part of the wider uncertainties about the future of the Church, including that of all mainstream Protestantism in its old Western European heartland, but others reflect the particular situation of the Waldensians. No Protestant Church is more affected than they are by climate changes in Roman Catholicism, even though no predominantly Roman Catholic country has more local variations in ecumenical temperature than Italy and some of the co-operation has been with conspicuously liberal, politically radical, and rather untypical Roman Catholics. Moreover some of the more encouraging trends in the mainstream of the Roman Church are comparatively recent and it will take time to discover how deeply they have affected the popular folk-culture of Italian Catholicism. For example it was not till the reign of John XXIII that his Church seemed ready to match its biblical scholarship with enthusiasm for Scripture distribution, though that movement has now gone far and fast enough for the publication of an ecumenical modern translation.

However some of the uncertainties derive from the Waldensians' own variations in attitude and practice, in which tradition and innovation are mixed in ways which can easily baffle the stranger, especially when his or her questions about pastoral experience draw mixed and confusing answers. This seems especially true in areas where theology and pastoral practice are interwoven, such as baptism and marriage.

On marriage, the confusion partly reflects the range of attitudes in the Roman Church towards 'mixed' marriages, which very many Waldensian marriages are bound to be. They may be up to ninety per cent of the marriages in which a pastor is involved, sometimes where the ecumenical climate is benign sharing with the priest in a Roman Catholic ceremony, sometimes (I was pleased but surprised to hear) with a priest present at a Waldensian one. But this remains a sensitive area, with additional problems in some 'mixed' families when there is social rather than religious pressure to conform to Roman Catholic ways, for example when the other children in the street are looking forward to First Communion, more as a family treat and communal celebration than as a spiritual occasion.

Some unusual aspects of baptismal practice also reflect distinctively Italian situations, as well as the way in which both infant baptism and 'believers'' adult baptism are authorised in Waldensian procedures. For example I was surprised to be told that in some marriages between Waldensians and Catholics the choice of infant baptism is influenced by the power of Italian Catholic tradition and lingering popular fear of leaving any child unbaptised. Catholic grandparents, it is said, sleep more easily even if the baptism has been a Protestant one.

But the implications of Waldensian baptismal practice and theology are more significant for the Protestant world and for Reformed Churches. For here is a mainstream Reformed Church, small but historically important, which accepts both forms of baptism in its system, not to accommodate tender consciences and enable some union of different traditions to go ahead but because the two views exist in the Church. This does have some ecumenical implications, for it obviously increases the likelihood that the present friendly co-operation with Italian Baptists will eventually become a closer union, as happened 30 years ago with the earlier co-operation of Waldensians and Methodists. More important, it confronts other Reformed Churches with the question of whether they too should consider this duality of theology and pastoral practice. For some of them, and especially for the Church of Scotland, this would be a major step and a reversal of attitudes which have been quite emphatically maintained in recent decades.

They would perhaps be wise to wait and see how the Waldensian policy works out in practice and how successful pastors are in explaining the options to parents. It must be difficult to do so without some subjective personal attitudes playing a part, though there is no evidence - or none that reached me - that the policy is causing any disharmony in the Church. There probably would be disharmony, judging from the views I have encountered among pastors, if there were any question of reverting to infant baptism as the norm. I am told that it has still considerable support in the traditional Waldensian communities of the Valleys but rather less elsewhere in Italy.

It might also be tempting to speculate whether this open view of the Waldensians on baptismal theology and practice could provide an opening to greater co-operation with independent and Pentecostal groups (far more numerous than the Baptists) and even an eventual union. But it does not seem any easier than it was in the nineteenth century to bring the old Waldensians into the same fold as the new Italian Evangelicals. In one respect the old positions are reversed: for many Evangelicals and Pentecostals the Waldensians' prevailing theology and application of Scripture would now seem too liberal. Many of them are also disinclined to identify themselves as closely with left-of-centre Italian politics as most prominent Waldensians do. Some may also have anxieties about what (according to taste) may be called either the open-minded or unduly lax attitudes prevailing in some Waldensian circles on moral issues, including homosexuality. Some may even worry (as Waldensians and Presbyterians once did) about the full and equal ministry of women in the Church, for the Waldensian-Methodists are now very obviously an equal opportunity Church.

But some older obstacles reappear in the new situation. The Waldensians remain a highly structured and disciplined Church with collective leadership and central authority. They also retain their emphasis on a well educated and thoroughly trained ministry. Other groups set much more store by local autonomy and personal inspiration.

There is dialogue with some of the Pentecostals, as well as friendly relationships and the obvious affinities of Christians who cannot conform to the ways of Italy's dominant Catholicism. The main series of conversations was planned to be a three-stage process, first establishing areas of Christian agreement, then exploring what seemed to be different approaches in matters deemed non-essential, and finally facing up to basic differences. In 2004 these discussions were described to me as faltering a bit about 'stage one-and-a-half'.

There also remain the uncertainties of trends and events, including adverse ones. It would be pleasant to think that the fierce Waldensian devotion to their traditions and inheritance has given them a special dispensation from the problems of ageing and declining congregations which larger Churches know too well. That is not the case. Waldensian pastors speak of the missing age-groups (especially 25 to 40) much as Scots and English ministers do. In Italy too one hears the explanation, that 'people don't join organisations very readily nowadays', as if there were some consolation for the Church in the difficulties of other but less important societies, clubs, and parties.

But the light is still shining in the darkness.

Conclusion:

ON NOT KNOWING EVERYTHING

Reflections on literature, history religion, and catholicity

I might have called this last chapter a postscript, but that would appear to have been something tacked on as an afterthought. It is much more a reflection that has taken shape while the book was being written, and sometimes accompanied the writing of it.

Readers who have journeyed this far, even readers who may have skipped a chapter here and there, will not know everything about the Waldensians and will know only a little more than before about Italy. Many of them, I hope, began by knowing a lot more than I do about Italy, for one of the aims of the book has to make the Italian Protestant tradition better know to people who have been attracted to Italy, Italian culture, Italian opera, Italian cuisine, and the country's vast and varied artistic inheritance. They have probably never visited the Waldensian valleys, which like much of Piedmont are still off the track of most modern tourism and business travel. It is unlikely that elsewhere in Italy they have knowingly encountered the Waldensians or other Italian Protestants in the exploration, which could last a lifetime, of Italy's cultural heritages, classical, medieval, and modern.

But after reading this historical guide-book to another Italian heritage they will now know more about the Waldensians than at least 99 per cent of the British people, and probably also more about them than 90 per cent of the Italian people. They will also, I hope, know a little more about Italy's diversity.

In writing this book I learned a lot of things I did not know about Italy, two of which are important enough to share with the reader.

The first is a paradox. Italy both stimulates and frustrates those inspired to write about it. The English literature about Italy is vast, rich, and yet unsatisfying. There are many fine books in English but I doubt if there is a truly great one.

Many of our greatest writers have either written about Italy or found inspiration in it. One thinks automatically of the great romantic poets and the Brownings but the roll of honour and inspiration is much longer, from Thomas Coryate to John Mortimer, by way of Charles Dickens, George Eliot, and Henry

James. And of course the Roman Catholic strand in English literature offers many a genuflexion to the Eternal City and some epicurean side-trips from those who travelled more comfortably on the road to Rome than Hilaire Belloc. Evelyn Waugh, for example, brought Venice into *Brideshead Revisited* and launches his hero's crusade in the *Sword of Honour* trilogy from a rather vaguely located fishing village, possibly in Liguria, in which a Protestant lady distributes tracts, accommodates stray cats, and demands more humane killing of octopuses. I trust she has found someone to carry on the good work.

There are also a host of lesser but very good books, some of the best of them the least pretentious, such as George Gissing's *By The Ionian Sea*. There are delightful but totally forgotten books like Ion S. Munro's *Beyond the Alps*, written while he was correspondent in Rome of the *Morning Post* and gathering the library of books about the Jacobites there and elsewhere which he showed me in his old age. There are good-class run-of-the-mill books, such as the Batsford *Land of Italy* by Jasper More, a Tory M.P. who got to know Italy in the war and was one of the few twentieth-century travel writers to visit the valleys, even if his suggestion that the Waldensian churches are all Gothic suggests he may not have got beyond Turin and Torre Pellice into the upper valleys. There are also some good but pretentious authors, such as Norman Douglas for those who can take to him. Surprisingly, this enthusiast for paganism rebuked very gently a priest near Taranto who assumed that, as a Scot, he would also be a Calvinist: 'A Presbyterian, I gently corrected'.

There is also an untidy tour of Sicily by Lawrence Durrell and there are the prose hymns in praise of Venice by W.D. Howells and James (now Jan) Morris. There are even important literary relics from D.H. Lawrence's stays in Italy - grotesque when he drags phallic worship into every country festival but well deserving preservation when he shares the pain of unheated winters and the pangs of hunger of Sardinian inns of the 1920's. There are also similar phenomena in other European literatures, from the travels of Goethe downwards.

But I have yet to find that truly great book in English about the Italy of any age. This may be true of other visitors' languages too, though the twentieth-century Italian interpreter of his country to the English-speaking world, the younger Luigi Barzini (son of a great journalist in pre-Fascist Italy), rated Stendhal first among foreign writers, and gave second place to the Anglican Protestant John Addington Symonds. Symonds was a Victorian poet, a contemporary at Balliol of that other but less Christian italophile, Swinburne, and a historian of the Italian Renaissance.

Goethe is hallowed in this case more for who he was rather than what he wrote, and because he expressed a peculiarly intense German longing for the land of sun, wine, fruit, and foliage, sometimes qualified, in Luther's case and many others, with a reaction against dirt, disorder, and perceptions of dishonesty.

But there is nothing in English about Italy to rank in the classics of travel in the way that Richard Ford does with his magisterial 1845 *Handbook for Spain* - a John Murray guide that got out of hand and became a masterpiece - or to match George Borrow's achievement of *The Bible in Spain*, the most eccentric of Protestant literary monuments. There are not even modern equivalents of George Orwell in Catalonia or Gerald Brenan in Andalusia.

But having offered that pontifical pronouncement I also suggest a reason. The emphasis in British and American writing about Italy is on the diversity of its monuments and artistic treasures, not the diversity of the country. Very often the visitors could not see the land for the treasures and antiquities. As Charles Dickens said on the first page of his *Pictures from Italy*, explaining why he wasn't going to write even about the Italian painting and sculpture which he liked: 'There is, probably, not a famous picture or statue in all Italy, but could be easily buried under a mountain of printed paper devoted to dissertations on it.' And of course as the little book gathered pace Dickens forgot his good resolution. Perhaps the tradition of our literature on Italy is a blend of artistic admiration and subjective experience, with the people too often treated either as persistent nuisances (which some of them were) or as picturesque embellishments to the scenery. The better type of English literary gentleman recognised that he must accept the dignity and equality of even the most ragged Spanish caballero. He found this harder with the Italians, who seemed to lack the necessary gravity.

The great and good of English literature who fell in love with Italy, as well as the Grand Tourists and the more modern expatriates or literary holidaymakers, have too often treated Italy as a museum of classical or medieval antiquities, or a demonstration ground for artistic theory (as John Ruskin did) and as a setting or backdrop. They were programmed by a classical education and received culture in which Italy's past mattered more than Italy's people - or in which modern Italians were judged, consciously or not, by contrast and comparison with what their Roman ancestors were supposed to have been in a golden age. That is the second of these discoveries I made while writing this book.

Religion also comes into it. The evangelical Protestant, especially the nineteenth century one, sometimes failed to see the wonders of Italian civilisation behind the layers of dirt, ignorance, and superstition. The moderate Protestant who likes to live and let live concentrates on the art and antiquities, enjoys some of the picturesque splendour of the Roman Church, and adopts a patronising air towards the customs of the natives. The expatriate literary

Roman Catholics, hereditary or convert, can be surprisingly similar in mood once they have risen from their devotions. For them the Italians often don't seem appreciative enough of their role as a chosen people surrounding the supposedly chosen location of the vicarage of Christ. Even the Papacy is sometimes presented by its admirers in a way that reminds me of the veneration of hideous trappings around some dubious holy sites in Palestine where we are supposed to see wonderfully holy things behind a spectacular exterior, unedifying history, and unconvincing claims to authenticity.

The Roman Catholic Church in Italy is, of course, far more than a still powerful institution and a channel for a multitude of good Christian thoughts and words. It organises an enormous part of the social services. It has serious and substantial theologians. It is in touch with important parts of Italian scientific and aesthetic thinking. It is a vast repository of faith and devotion as well as of many beliefs and customs which Protestants must still regard as mistaken and which many modern Roman Catholics, in Italy as well as countries with a Reformation tradition, seem to regard either as extraneous or as optional extras.

But the Roman Catholic Church, quite apart from its international importance, is a tremendous fact of Italian history and in Italian culture. It is not religious bias but realism which almost ensured that anyone setting out to learn Italian (in for example the BBC's *Buongiorno Italia*) would encounter the religious festivals and processions of, say, Orvieto, a town in which I cannot trace the address of a mainstream Protestant church. Roman Catholicism in its Italian style has also a very important role in the international presentation of Italian culture and language. One example I stumbled on by accident while writing this book. It is easy, with an ordinary radio, to keep track of the French and German equivalents of the BBC World Service. The Italians are more reticent, or at least more economical, but not so Vatican Radio, which obviously broadcasts in many languages but also offers the most readily receivable Italian-language world news coverage as well as much devotional material. It is hardly consistently objective, and the commentators have always to declare the Pope the man-of-the-match, but within its obvious parameters it seems well edited and presented. It is also objective and ecumenical enough to have carried (certainly on August 26, 2002) reports of the Waldensian-Methodist Synod meeting in Torre Pellice) with reasonable sound-bites from the Moderator. The modern Vatican is a very impressive institution, and a complex one.

Acceptance of Roman Catholic claims, however, and of the Papacy, is an act of faith, not of reason; and the faith demanded is not all of the essence of Christian belief. It is clear that these claims, as they have traditionally been

154

presented and are still maintained, cannot be reconciled with Protestant ideas of the supremacy of Scripture. We can stand by that view today - we have no choice, as Luther said - without asserting it as stridently as some of our ancestors did, not least when they visited Italy. The modern world, there and here, often forces all Christians to find and hold common ground.

It is also important for Protestants to recognise that tradition too has value, under Scripture. That means having a high regard for many traditions within the Roman Communion, as well as an interest in how they express themselves in contemporary thinking or in a national culture, as in Italy or Poland. But a proper regard for Christian tradition, always subordinate to Scripture, also means resisting the idea that Christian tradition and Roman Catholicism are the same thing. That they are not is perhaps self-evident in the British Isles, Northern Europe and the United States, with their diversity of Christian expression and experience, as well as in the orbit of Orthodox Christianity. But they are not the same thing in the Latin world either, not even in the heartland of the Papacy. Even in Italy - sometimes especially in Italy - there has been a tradition of reform, criticism, constructive dissent, and free exercise of reason within the Christian faith.

The Waldensians are a major part of that tradition, though by no means the whole of it. They were perhaps a little 'Israel of the Alps' but they were not quite the Protestant Shangri-La that some Victorian literature made them seem. Modern Waldensians, thinking of the small scale of their old enclave in the valleys, have suggested it was not much more than a 'religious San Marino'. However the Waldensians were and are an important part of true Christian tradition, more significant than their numbers suggest, because they also express the continuity of the Church, both as the society of Jesus with the faithful of all times, past present and future, and as an evolving institution. They have the fallibility of all human institutions but they also have that authority and continuity which the Church needs.

It is easy to criticise their sense of a particular tradition and their emphasis on a long struggle for survival. A great Scottish Victorian churchman and enthusiast for unity among European Reformed Churches, Principal John Cairns, even let slip an irritated phrase about Waldensian 'ancestor worship', though he also came to admire them and was chairman of their Scottish support organisation. On the other hand much of their work today is in parts of Italy for which the traditions of the valleys mean little but whose spiritual and practical needs are great. It could be that in their anxiety not to be prisoners of their glorious past they are too generous in their welcome for some trends in the modern ecumenical movement, with its enthusiasm for transient social and political ideas. But their proper pride in their past may also be a reproach to those in Scots Presbyterianism and middle-of-the-road Anglicanism who have lapsed towards the other extreme. We in Britain have lost too much of our sense of history. What remains of a common culture in our multi-ethnic, multi-cultural Babel of modern Britain knows only a travesty of Knox, may no longer read Bunyan, and has only a vague acquaintance with Cranmer, Wesley, and Chalmers.

It is for the Waldensians themselves to find the right balance between their past and future. They have also to combine their reverence for the valleys, which mean so much in their history and to those whose lives or roots are there, with the evolving history of their relationship with very different sorts and conditions of Italians, as well as with immigrants to Italy. That is not always easy, for example in relation to preservation and encouragement of the valley dialect (or *patouà*). Its condition is not easy for a stranger to determine, for he may receive apparently contradictory answers to his questions. Yes, it is dying or at least fading away. No, it survives in the home. Look, here it is print in the bookshops, with songs, folk tales, children's stories. Perhaps the most convincing answer I remember, admittedly with a certain detachment from someone originally from Turin: 'It is vigorous today, but a bit artificial.' That seems true as far as literary use is concerned, and it was probably true when Beckwith and Gilly encouraged liturgical experiment with it and Guthrie found Torre Pellice a linguistic frontier town with use of French or dialect identifying the Waldensians and Italian the outward and audible symbol of Catholicism. And no doubt some 'artificial' enthusiasm is needed if it is not to retreat to the upper reaches of depopulated valleys.

But the important thing is that Waldensians must not allow the valleys to seem no more than an open-air museum of religious and social history, or of linguistic survivals. That said, they need to be given credit for the example they set to others with much glorious history of their own and little sense of it.

They also set an example to others in the concern they show for the buildings which are a part of their history - not because they are great architecture enhanced with great art, for they are not, but because (in the Psalmist's sense) the very stones are dear. No-one, of course, would suggest that conservation issues in the valleys are the same as those in Scottish cities or English country parishes. But is it not significant that a Church with a high priority for mission and service outside its traditional areas, and people who in the past often had to be 'a Church without walls', should strike a happier balance than we often do in the dignified conservation of their property?

The Waldensians have also tackled a problem faced by a number of Christian minorities which have strong convictions and inherit intense historical experiences but also reflect ethnic or local identities. There are some in the United States, of whom the Amish people are the most vivid and extreme example. The Waldensians could have chosen the same pious isolation, if not the same ways of showing and maintaining it. If that seems too far-fetched an example, there are a couple much nearer home in Scotland. The Free Church of Scotland, that is the 'Wee Frees' who stood out of the 1900 union, and their kinsfolk the Free Presbyterians, who opted out on points of principle a few years earlier, both profess the Reformed Christian faith. They argue that they are much more loyal to Calvin's insights (and for that matter Chalmers's) than the larger Reformed Churches in Europe and America. In some things that may well be so, though some of them can give the impression that they think they know better than Calvin, as Dr Guthrie did when he lamented the great French reformer's unsoundness about the Sabbath. Moreover even these very small Churches have in recent years been subject to internal splits and discords. But both the ethos of these denominations and the public perception of them is closely linked to their territorial base in the North-west Highlands and the Hebrides. They have city congregations but they may appear as islands of a Highland culture, preaching and singing in a Highland idiom, even when not in Gaelic. It would be unfair to suggest that they are no more than that, but their ethnic character may determine and perhaps limit their capacity for a wider mission.

An outsider might hesitate to make the point were it not for the knowledge that it has at times been forcibly made by Highlanders themselves. And there is enough of a *prima facie* argument to invite a comparison with the Waldensians. They retain territorial roots and an attachment to the valleys at least as strong as any Hebridean's love of Lewis. But they decided to be a Church for Italy, however thinly spread their support and resources might be.

One should not be drawn too far in to speculations about historical might-have-beens. There were late Victorian critics who thought the wider Waldensian evangelical commitment was not wholehearted enough and there were disappointments for the boldest of the Waldensians and their supporters, as well as for those who wanted to create a new Evangelical Church of Italy. Enormous efforts seemed to yield a meagre harvest.

But what if the Waldensians had not made the effort? They would not be extinct. They would survive, as they do, among the changing and in places shrinking population of the valleys and they would have their congregations in Turin, Rome, and other cities made up of exiles from the valleys and at least some of their descendants.

They tried to do much more, avoiding the danger of being no more than a pious and picturesque survival. If they had not tried Italy would have no framework, apart from the small Italian Baptist Union, for a structured Reformed Church. Instead of remaining a historical curiosity they set out to demonstrate a historical necessity; that neither an unreformed Roman Church (as in many ways it still is) nor a secular, anti-clerical rationalism could adequately express the nature and destiny of humanity. And they added to that historical necessity a historical imperative to contribute to the service and development of Italy, including its most neglected areas and peoples, among them immigrants who, legally or not, have come to Italy as a land of opportunity and often also find it a land of difficulties.

For Italy the Waldensians have both a practical and a symbolic importance. They are a small Church with a national framework and sense of mission. They are a channel for Christian faith and works in Italy outside the vastly more powerful currents of the Roman Communion. But they are a vital reminder in Italy and for the wider world that faith does not mean the surrender of reason or surrender to a fallible authority claiming immense power and displaying immense fallibility. They are an important element in the true catholicity of the universal Church and the national and intellectual diversity of Italian civilisation.

They offer, in an Italian idiom, a reasoned critique of the Roman Catholic Church's claim to be the authorised structure of the universal or catholic Church and a succinct statement of where, even after the new mood and real changes of the Second Vatican Council, reform is still awaited on points of doctrine and practice. But they also challenge some assumptions about Italy from very different quarters. D.H. Lawrence wrote much nonsense but he summed up a common Anglo-Saxon intellectual view of Italy when he wrote (in *Twilight in Italy*) about the substratum of things pagan and sensual in its cultural achievement and common life. 'The worship of the Cross never really held good in Italy. The Christianity of Northern Europe never really had any place there.'

There are little bits of truth among his wild exaggerations. Northern European Protestants of the nineteenth century were certainly too sanguine in their assumption that their style of Christianity (and, for that matter, liberal constitutionalism) would suit a resurgent Italy. North American Protestant Evangelicals, far more concerned in recent years than the British about encouraging new growth in Latin countries, probably encounter the same difficulty. The nearest equivalent in the last sixty years to the nineteenth-century missions to Italy is probably the stimulation of Protestant growth, much of it Pentecostal or independent evangelical, in Latin America. Numerically this appears to have been far more successful but it remains to be seen what the long-term impact will be on Spanish and Portuguese speaking cultures, relations with Roman Catholicism, and the harmony of the universal Church. Some of the problems which once beset Italian Protestantism are evident there today. However the parallel should perhaps not be drawn too far there are ethnic factors, non-Christian religious influences, and political complications very different from those of Italy.

But to those, Roman Catholic and secularist alike, who deride the Protestant and Reformed 'intrusion' into a supposedly alien culture, the Waldensians remain an awkward fact of history and contemporary life. For although they provide an important link between Italy and the world beyond the Alps they are not Northern Europeans but witnesses to the universal character both of Christianity in general and of the essentials in its Reformed traditions.

For the world-wide Reformed Communion the Waldensians can also make contributions out of proportion to their small numbers, for example in the work of the World Alliance of Reformed Churches. They also have a quality and quantity of scholarship, in theology, Church history, and Christian social reflection out of all proportion to their apparent strength. This is apparent in the work of those like Giorgio Tourn and Giorgio Bouchard on whom I have drawn heavily for this book. Such names as Alberto Soggin, the Old Testament scholar; V. Subilio, claimed as 'perhaps the acutest Protestant assessor of Vatican II', and Tullio Vinay, the social radical, have also made an impact both beyond the Waldensians and beyond Italy. Giorgio Spini, from the Methodist side of the contemporary Church, is a major contributor in the area where political and religious history overlap. It is astonishing that a small denomination contributes so much, not just in theology and Church history but in contributions to a wider discussion of Italy's past and humanity's future.

Of course one encounters mixed opinions as well as much ignorance about modern Waldensians. One eminent Scots churchman who has said sincere and flattering things about them also told me 'They're very anti-Catholic, you know'. Another told me the opposite, also perhaps meaning it as a criticism: 'My impression of the Waldensians is that on the whole they take a very relaxed line about the huge Roman Catholic dominance in Italy.'

But they can also still make a very powerful impact on those who come to know them and their ways. This book is a testimony to that, in a general way. For a more particular one I quote a Scots minister, Ray Sawers, on the Waldensian Synod: 'I recall with particular appreciation the worship in the great church at Torre Pellice. At one final Communion the service was led by the Synod chairman who happened to be a layman and a lawyer. He was flanked on either side at the Communion Table by two pastors who assisted him. This symbolised in a striking way that the Waldensian Church is not a clerical Church and that the priesthood of all believers is taken seriously. In this they may have much to teach us.'

They add to the diversity of tribes and tongues in the Reformed tradition which, despite the crucial role in its history of a brilliant Frenchman, sometimes seems very Anglo-Celtic in its ethos. They are also a living and historical witness to the continuity of the Church, and a warning against a subconscious Protestant tendency to ignore everything, except some glorious architecture, that Christians did and thought in the centuries between Augustine and the greatest Augustinian, Martin Luther. They also bring insights and experiences of their own which may not be of value elsewhere but deserve consideration - for example their compromise between the traditions of infant baptism and 'believers' baptism'.

It is perhaps worth dwelling briefly, however, on that suggestion that they are 'anti-Catholic' in an age of ecumenical co-operation, good feeling, and an apparent Roman Catholic readiness to co-exist with political democracy.

'I think it is wrong to regard the Catholic religion as a natural enemy of democracy', wrote the French admirer of America, Alexis de Tocqueville. 'On the contrary, among the different Christian doctrines Catholicism appears to me one of the most favourable to equality in condition. The priest alone is raised above the people. Under him everyone is equal.'

And there, Waldensians would say, you have the point exactly. Historically the Roman system has created a priestly caste, an unnatural division in the Christian community where we ought to recognise and use the different gifts of all who are ministers and priests to God. The fallible system is not saved by the great gifts and devotion of some priests and the diligence of most; and it remains to be seen whether ideas of the ministry of the whole people of God and the mood of the Second Vatican Council (which on some points would surely have shocked the liberal democrat de Tocqueville) will profoundly and permanently reshape the inheritance of medieval and Counter-reformation Catholicism. For many Roman Catholic progressives the great struggle was to convince their Church that it could live with political liberalism and democracy. They were, of course, right. Pius IX was wrong and the Church which now venerates him turned its back on his politics.

In Italy the growth of Protestantism was all but halted when it was no longer needed as an ally against a reactionary Church and when those who had a background in traditional Italian religion but no more than the average human spirituality found that their Church could co-exist with Italian unity and new liberties. It was only resumed when Italy, and especially Southern Italy, was influenced by social mission and born-again evangelism.

But most of those Roman Catholic progressives did not address the deeper questions which the Waldensians had faced for seven centuries and with which Protestantism had wrestled since the Reformation: how is a proper sense and structure of order in both Church and State to be reconciled with Christian liberty and the priesthood of all believers?

Perhaps in a world where Christians are very much a minority, and Protestant Christians a much smaller one, the ministry of all the people of God will increasingly be seen as part of a priestly function for all God's world: serving it, loving it, exhorting it, praying for it.

Our perspective is very different from that of the British Protestant Victorians who committed themselves to the Waldensian cause. All of us now have to look back on the turbulence, triumphs, tragedies, and disappointments of history to decide what remains vital and relevant and what can be discarded. It is not easy, in thinking about the future, to decide whether some propositions that once seemed to matter intensely are no longer relevant, or whether they need to be reworded with more charity and humility to meet a new situation in which their truth endures.

I was acutely aware of that dilemma when, looking among a mass of Victorian testimony that sometimes became verbosity, I found a commendably succinct statement circulated by the London friends of the Waldensians around 1890 on 'Why should I support these missions to Italy?' It was probably written by the London society's secretary Major Martin Frobisher, a descendant of the Elizabethan seafarer.

The first reason was 'because Romanism is doing so much evil in our own country and it is important that the evil should be met at the fountain-head in Rome....'. Most Protestants would not put it that way today. Those who do need to ask themselves whether they can adequately defend and extend Protestant Christian truths and insights without accepting the complexity as well as the piety within the Roman Church, as well as a spiritual restiveness not altogether unlike that which led many Italian men and women of the nineteenth century to separate themselves from an institution which embodies much of their history and culture.

But the second reason given was 'because the Waldensian Church, being the ancient Evangelical Church of Italy, has been preserved by God and prepared for this special mission, and he appears so clearly to have put his seal on their work'.

We may - indeed must - respect historical research and different opinions on what we mean by 'the ancient Evangelical Church of Italy', and we may find that God's seal is applied and displayed in much more subtle ways than the Victorians expected. Yet having done that, we may come to essentially the same conclusions.

The first is that the Waldensians upheld truths about the nature of the Church and spiritual authority under God which are not optional opinions but part of the essence and substance of the Faith, perhaps in time to be accepted even within what is today the Roman Communion. The second is that there is divine purpose in history, sometimes more, sometimes less visible, but often clearly visible in the survival and testimony of the Waldensian Church. The reader has the right to disagree. But it seems to me that these are both rational judgments and the evidence of faith.

They are also, for me, the evidence that the Waldensian future, as part of a wider Italian Church and Protestant community, will be secured by a sense of God's Providence in times past and God's continuing guidance through the Holy Spirit. That is not to deny the capacity of Waldensians and Italian Evangelicals, past and present, and of their British friends, to confuse passing fashions and enthusiasms with the Will of God. That happened both in the age of the 'Enlightenment' and the Revival; in the complacency of Victorian Liberalism and the diversions into 'dialogue with Marxism'. The danger confronts not only those Christians enthused for social radicalism and moral liberalism but those of us who react against these trends. I add that last sentence because some British and American Evangelicals today are a little wary of the modern Waldensians. But in that they underestimate not only the importance of apostolic continuity in the Church but the Providence of God and the correcting power of the Word.

In *The Pilgrim's Progress* of John Bunyan, who may sometimes have had Waldensians as well as English dissenters in mind when he wrote of persecution, Christian could not see the gate, set before the way to salvation, that Evangelist pointed out to him. But Evangelist tried again: 'Do you see yonder shining light?' And Christian said: 'I think I do'.

The Waldensians have been a shining light for centuries, before the Reformation and since. It shone in some dark corridors of medieval history, and it was not put out in the age of Counter-Reformation fury and intolerance. It shone on in an age of professed enlightenment when widespread religious indifference gave way to a revolutionary enthusiasm which bred war and tyranny. It glowed brightly in the age of Italian liberation and it still shines in the murk of modern European society, with all its confusion, achievement, and self-indulgence. It will be a light to lighten many kinds of darkness. And, without prejudice to the obligation of humility which falls on every Christian, it may be reckoned in human terms one more among the many glories of Italy.

Most important of all, however, it expresses that dependence on Grace and the Cross which relegates all human glories to their proper proportion. 'My richest gift I count but loss, and pour contempt on all my pride.'

Appendix 1

SCOTTISH WALDENSIAN SOCIETIES 1850-2005
A short historical summary

There does not appear to be any history in existence of the distinctively Scottish part in the British alliance with the Waldensians. As much of this has been maintained by independent societies, there is not even a record to be pieced together from the minutes of Church committees and General Assemblies. This note seeks to fill a gap, though the sources are not as abundant as one might wish. On at least two occasions minutes gave secretaries authority to destroy and dispose of papers and records as they thought fit, and this authority seems to have been used - on one occasion in the 1920's - to save paying storage charges on accumulations of papers.

I have however tried to avoid repeating much of what is important enough to be discussed in the chapters about the British connections with the Waldensians in the nineteenth century and after. This summary is therefore not mainly concerned with the issues involved and the condition of Italy but is an account of the way the Scottish societies involved worked to support the Waldensians and co-operated with them. Some of the personalities and issues involved figure prominently in the main narrative.

The present English Committee in Aid of the Waldensian Church Missions (to quote the title from *The Waldensian Review*) traces its history back to the London Vaudois Committee of 1825, of which Dr Gilly was secretary and moving spirit, though as this book and other histories indicate there is a much longer tradition of support for the cause.

There is also an Irish Committee in Aid of the Waldensian Missions and a Scottish Waldensian Missions Aid Society, though that quite long title is, as this note will show, a short version of an even fuller one.

Formal Scottish support for the Waldensians, on an inter-denominational Protestant basis, appears to date from 1850. This was 25 years before the formation of the World Presbyterian Alliance (now the World Alliance of Reformed Churches, with Congregationalists included) in which Reformed Churches created an international framework for their unity.

An Edinburgh Italian Society, later the Italian Evangelical Committee and afterwards the Italian Evangelisation Society, was formed on June 14, 1850. There was a similar Glasgow-based committee, though it appears later as a Continental and not only an Italian society. The aim was 'the religious improvement of Italy by the diffusion of Scripture truth in that country', with the emphasis on distribution of the Bible and approved religious works but scope for 'such other ways as in the course of God's providence shall appear best fitted to attain that end'. After its first year or two with a Mr J. Hawkins as secretary, the secretaryship was held by David Maclagan, operating from the offices of the Insurance Company of Scotland at 95 George Street, Edinburgh. Some of his correspondence survives. There seem to have been various chairmen at meetings, with the Revd Dr Makellar (sic) taking the inaugural meeting, but the most usual one in the early years was Sheriff Andrew Jameson. Later Sheriff Thomas Cleghorn appears to have taken over.

From the beginning the society was closely involved with the Waldensians, then extending their work out from the valleys to other parts of Piedmont, but much of its attention (as shown in surviving correspondence) was devoted in the mid-1850's to the cause of the handful of Protestant converts in Tuscany, who were under pressure and even active persecution, but who were supported by a London Executive Committee for the Vindication and Promotion of Religious Liberty. The Scottish society worked with this committee in 1856, when a 'memorial' urging British action was presented to the Foreign Secretary, Lord Clarendon There was already close co-operation with Dr Robert Stewart, the friend of the Waldensians and the Free Church of Scotland minister in Leghorn. He was largely involved in advising on how money should be spent and in making suggestions about future plans. In 1856 he strongly supported plans for the Waldensians to be represented at the Free Church General Assembly, hoping that they would be 'as well received' as in Ireland the pevious year and that 'the Vaudois committee will take them actively by the hand'. It is not clear whether he means the committee in London or a group of its Scottish supporters.

The date of the foundation of the Waldensian Missions Aid Society is less clear than that of the I.E.S. There was a magazine reference in 1897 to the society being born in April 6, 1850, but that is the date when the 'provisional committee' for 'the movement on behalf of Italy' met in Edinburgh and started the process from which the Italian Evangelisation Society emerged.

The first distinctively Scottish 'Waldensian aid' meeting I have traced was on October 6, 1851 with Sheriff Jameson again taking the chair. An ad hoc committee was formed to sponsor a public meeting (which set up a formal committee) as part of the efforts throughout Britain to raise funds for the building of the new Protestant church in Turin. The 'manifesto' of the campaign was a letter from Dr W.S. Gilly (Sept 9, 1851) in praise of the project and the Waldensian cause. Close links were established with the Waldensian Moderator, Dr J.P. Revel, who shared in the Scottish campaign. His main Scottish contact was the Free Church layman George Freeland Barbour, who was joint secretary in title but in practice a vigorous lobbyist and fund-raiser, as well as personal contributor. For some time the committee does not record any formal title but a surviving minute of April 6, 1854 calls it 'The Waldensian Committee'. By then the emphasis has switched from the Turin church to one proposed for Genoa.

The minutes of the aid society in book form survive from 1866 and a tribute to the Revd David Guthrie in 1896 suggests that he and his father, Dr Thomas Guthrie, were among the founders of the society under that title after visiting the Waldensian Synod in 1865. (They were both to be chairmen). A memorandum prepared at the time of abortive plans to unite the societies in 1879 also takes this view, describing the W.M.A.S. as about 12 years old.

The 'Waldensian Committee' of the 1850's had been largely run and supported by the same people as the Italian Evangelisation Society, whose minutes of 1857 (quoted by committees proposing a later and successful union plan in 1898) suggest that there were two bodies which regarded themselves as one movement and planned a formal union, being committed to the 'instrumentality of the ancient Church of the valleys' as the main channel for evangelism in Italy. This reflects a decision to back the Waldensians in the many disputes among Italian Protestants about how to use the increased opportunities in an already changing Italy which was moving towards religious freedom. The I.E.S. backed such strongly Waldensian causes as the Claudiana Press and financed bursaries for promising young Waldensians. There is also is a letter from the Waldensian Moderator in 1857 to the Italian evangelical supporters in Scotland asking whether a donation of £400 is for use at discretion or tied to such particular needs as maintaining an Italian master at the Waldensian college. At that time, as minuted on June 10, 1857, the Waldensian committee of the time and the Italian Evangelical Committee (as it then called itself) had agreed to form themselves into one committee under the latter name. By 1861 the committee had become the Italian Evangelisation Society.

An earlier minute of 1854 makes clear that the Scots supported the Waldensian Church authorities in one of the first of many Italian Protestant disputes, involving the secession of Dr Desanctis and Signor Mazzarella and the formation of independent evangelical Churches in Piedmont. Although Desanctis was eventually to return to the Waldensians and become a professor in their divinity faculty, this dispute flared up vigorously again in Scotland as well as Italy in 1857, in the columns of *The Witness* and elsewhere, when a Waldensian deputy, Pastor Leon Pilatte of Nice (then part of the Sardinian kingdom), attacked the 'independents' in a speech at the Free Kirk Assembly. The archives show a public protest from the Swiss-Italian committee in Geneva, much involved in Italian evangelisation, and some private worries among highly-placed supporters, such as the Duchess of Gordon. On the other side there was circulation of extracts from some of the last letters of Dr Gilly, warning Presbyterians how odd it would seem if 'a prelatist' like himself should appear the staunchest supporter of the Waldensians.

In the same year a report from the governing Waldensian *Tavola* (then *La Table*, and today translated into English as 'Waldensian National Board') to friends abroad lamented the dislocation of promising work at Asti by the departure of the lay evangelist, who had been convinced that the Waldensians were wrong in confining the presidency at the Lord's Supper to ordained ministers. There were to be many such problems in Italy.

From 1867 the two Scottish societies certainly had the same secretary, Alexander Brown. He had succeeded the Revd T.B. Bell, who died shortly after taking up the W.M.A.S. appointment. However the formal union was delayed. In 1879 a scheme was prepared but not proceeded with, apparently because of reservations from the powerful minister at Leghorn, Dr Robert Stewart. Despite his Waldensian attachments, he worried about various Protestant but not specifically Waldensian causes which the I.E.S. supported, including schools and Bible depots, and about the risk that some Waldensian deputy would talk the society into switching funds from older causes to some favourite scheme of his own.

Both societies appeared to worry about the campaigning and fund-raising in Britain by independent Italian groups, a matter which was soon to divide the two most influential Scottish ministers in Italy, the pro-Waldensian Dr Stewart at Leghorn and Dr John McDougall at Florence who inclined to the *Chiesa Libera*, though in the 1850's he figures prominently in the I.E.S. minutes as a Waldensian supporter and was secretary of the Claudiana Press in its early days in Florence (In many references, press cuttings, and even the Annals of the Free Church he appears as Macdougall or MacDougall but McDougall seems to have been his preferred style.)

The societies were also on their guard against even more individualistic freelance fund-raising efforts by Italian visitors, though McDougall's fund-rising at first had general approval. He had begun by raising money to build or buy a kirk for Florence but his efforts broadened to seeking funds for missions (one of them originally linked to the Scots church) and then for the 'free' evangelical movement. By 1876 something between competition and acrimony was apparent in letters to the press. There was an Edinburgh-based fund for the Free Italian Church whose supporters suggested that Waldensian subscribers might 'share' their giving with it. However they insisted that McDougall 'had no unkind words for the Waldenses, whatever their friends may have for him'. He made the same point personally in what at times seemed a bombardment of the Scottish correspondence columns by rival friends of Italian Protestantism. For example, in writing from Florence to the *Daily Review* on October 27, 1876 he claimed he was writing about the Waldensians 'without soiling pages with uncharitableness' but he was also wrangling with the Waldensian Professor Emilio Comba about his own role as treasurer of the Free Italian Church.

A good deal of Scottish money flowed in to Italy through the W.M.A.S., the I.E.S., and the supporters of the 'free' Italian movement, which also had a fund-raising committee in Glasgow until the turn of the century. In 1885 for example the W.M.A.S. sent £1450 to Italy in a year when the general income of the Waldensians' mission board was reported as about £10,100.

By the end of the century the Waldensian Missions Aid Society was by far the largest support body for Italy. It then raised an annual average of nearly £1900 - perhaps equivalent to well over £150,000 at modern prices - against about £300 which its smaller I.E.S. partner gathered, mainly for specific objects such as schools in Leghorn. By then the Free Italian Church was dissolving in confusion and unlikely to attract new money. These figures possibly do not include all special collections and not all legacies, and of course exclude the money which was raised for the 'free' Italian movement. The union of the societies did not formally take place until January 1, 1899 under the title of 'The Waldensian Missions Aid Society (for work in Italy) with which is incorporated the Italian Evangelisation Society'. Even after that there was a continuation of funds 'kept in two distinct branches' and raised by separate collectors. Not until about 1950 do references to the two branches of the work or even to the 'two societies' disappear from the records.

The W.M.A.S. worked with a powerful network of local committees and lady collectors. They had areas assigned to them after the style of elders' districts. Good examples of their posters, calling cards, briefing literature, and similar material survive in the W.M.A.S. archive. From the mid-1860's until his death in 1873 its chairman was the formidable Free Church leader and social reformer Dr Thomas Guthrie. He was succeeded by Dr William Robertson of New Greyfriars, who was the Auld Kirk's leading authority on inter-Church relations and was familiar enough with Italy to have written about the events of 1848-50 there.

Guthrie's visit to the valleys in 1865 had apparently been followed by agreement with Stewart and Revel, now evangelisation committee president, on the need for 'more efficient assistance for the Waldensian missions' (IES minute July 6, 1865). By November 14 Guthrie had convened a committee out of which came the aid society.

For a time he also devoted considerable time and effort to work in England, much of it lobbying in influential places, with the aim of establishing a similar style of committee there which would concentrate on fund-raising to assist the new Waldensian mission drive which became possible after the creation of the Kingdom of Italy. On July 27, 1868 it was reported that a central committee for Waldensian aid societies in England had been formed and Dr Guthrie was thanked for his labours there. It was then agreed that 'the efforts of the committee will in future be restricted to Scotland, except in so far as they can give any information or assistance to the committees in England'. This suggests that, although Gilly's London Vaudois Committee had worked since 1825, Guthrie had a key role in getting the English as well as the Scottish arrangements reorganised to respond to the new situation created by a united Italy.

The society had a clear principle and a clearly identifiable partner in Italy. It worked closely with the powerful and apparently even semi-autonomous Evangelisation Committee of the Waldensian Church, based in Rome in the later years of the century with Dr Matteo Prochet having succeeded Revel as president. Such friction as there was does not seem to have been over what to do and where to build in Italy - the Waldensians clearly settled policy and priorities - but over practicalities and occasionally personalities.

In the later decades of the century the successful publicity for the Waldensians and the general British interest in Italy had begun to provide substantial but intermittent legacy income in addition to collections and subscriptions. But the good news of a legacy reached Italy long before the hard cash, much needed to pay ministers in southern and central Italy, to meet the builders' bills, and to ease what may have been a permanent financial crisis. But a mixture of Scots caution, the law's delays, and sometimes the specific provisions of the wills could cause frustrations. This however was part of a wider problem. The Waldensians had from the 1850's been encouraged into a massive mission programme in areas where they had no roots. Some of their letters to the Italian Evangelisation Society (all in French at this stage) survive from the 1850's when their work was no longer limited to the valleys, thanks to the way the law was interpreted in the Cavour era, but still confined to Piedmont and Liguria. Even then they were forced by the pressures on them to show what might seem an unseemly eagerness to know how soon how much would be forthcoming.

As time went on the pressures on the Waldensians continued as their work spread, not only beyond Piedmont but even beyond Italy. The W.M.A.S. ruled in 1869 that it had no legal power to assist the Waldensians in South America, despite a plea from Dr Stewart on behalf of a Montevideo project, though ways round the problem seem to have been found by grants through the Italian Evangelisation Society and (according to a newspaper report in 1877) though an ad hoc fund to which committee members made donations.

The role of Scottish support in Waldensian fund-raising was substantial enough for the Church in Italy to consider the possibility of settling a permanent 'agent' in Scotland. There may be signs of relief in the Scots minute of 1895 which noted a decision by the Waldensians not to pursue the scheme.

On the other hand the societies stood firmly by the Waldensians in recurring disputes in Italy. For example in 1886-87 a Scots minister in Palermo, the Revd J. Simpson Kay, originally a United Presbyterian but serving for some time as a Waldensian pastor, pressed strongly for a continuation of a grant of £50 from each of the Scottish societies even though he had 'resigned his connection with the Waldensian Board of Missions' and declared himself independent. He was turned down in January 1887 but allowed to argue his case in person on March 10. He was still turned down, first by the W.M.A.S. and then by the I.E.S.

The Waldensians were also supported when they were criticised in 1895 for taking in three congregations of the Evangelical Church of Italy in the course of the wrangles which had weakened and divided the new Italian Protestantism of the *Risorgimento*. This had aggrieved the now long-serving Scots minister at Florence, Dr McDougall, who was treasurer of this latest version of the 'Free Italian Church', and the controversy produced letters of complaint and possibly a resignation (the circumstances are not clear) from the committee. The Waldensians had to be advised against circulating an angry 'open letter' replying to his charges which were contained in a 42-page pamphlet of a virulence which suggested that at that time on this issue McDougall's judgment was seriously imbalanced. A sub-committee of inquiry was set up and backed the Waldensians. The Waldensians also felt that some others in the Scottish Churches were hostile to them. The deputy who spoke at the 1890 Church of Scotland General Assembly, Dr Prochet, confessed later to the ultra-Protestant campaigner in the 'Establishment', Jacob Primmer, that he was none too happy about being welcomed by its Moderator, A.K.H. Boyd , whom he regarded as a 'sworn enemy' of the Waldensians. In a St Andrews lecture Boyd, a popular writer as well as minister of Holy Trinity St Andrew's, had criticised the Scottish campaigning for the Waldensian cause.

There was occasional friction over the arrangement of deputies' visits from Italy. This became a substantial organisational task and in 1893 the W.M.A.S. appointed a part-time organising secretary to handle it at £30 a year. But the Revd. James Shiach, who had been a Free Church minister in Dunfermline, was also the convener-secretary of the Sabbath Alliance of Scotland. He organised this linked organisational charge from Portobello, along the coast from Leith, though about this time there also seems to have been an 'Italian mission room' in central Edinburgh, on Shandwick Place, as well as regular prayer meetings there and elsewhere for Italy. (Such prayer-meetings dated from the 1850's and continued well into the twentieth century. The main venue for them in their prime appears to have been the Bible Society Rooms in St Andrew Square.)

The demands of Mr Shiach's two posts seem to have sometimes been in conflict and in 1898 he himself was also in something near conflict with Signor Luzzi, the Waldensian deputy. Shiach claimed, in the kind of letter which is sometimes preserved when it shouldn't have been, that deputies had to work for immediate results while he planned for permanent ones. He resigned at the time of this stramash but was induced or allowed to withdraw the resignation and seems to have extended his duties to include chairing the Western committee in Glasgow. A further resignation was accepted in 1901 after more worries about the demands of Mr Shiach's two jobs, although he reappears a few years later on the committee and chairing one of its meetings.

However the society had a more tactful and enduring secretary-treasurer, the Edinburgh chartered accountant James Forbes Moncrieff, who served from 1883, after a few earlier years as auditor, until 1923. He resumed the work with the Waldensian deputies and was paid £110 a year. He succeeded in retiring at the third determined attempt and was succeeded in 1923 by the Revd Herbert Falconer, followed by an Edinburgh lawyer, Arthur Orr, who served from 1925 to 1952.

Many better-known names had been drawn into the Waldensian work. Professor Archibald Charteris of the Auld Kirk, founder of *Life and Work* and the Woman's Guild, was one. His Life and Work successor, John McMurtrie, was involved in the I.E.S. Another supporter was Lord Balfour of Burleigh, who chaired the W.M.A.S. central committee and acted as 'convener' in 1898 when the societies agreed on their union. The Scottish historian David Hay Fleming was also a considerable influence and eventually elected an 'honorary member'. It was not until 1925, however, that the society seems to have had a chairman in the modern style. In the earlier days there had been much variation and rotation.

Some of the 'big names' seem to have been there partly to provide prestige and broaden the base of work, though there was Auld Kirk involvement at the grassroots too. However annual meetings and large rallies in Edinburgh seem to have been generally in the Free Church Assembly Hall, the Freemasons' Hall, or the YMCA hall. On at least one occasion (1880) the annual meeting was timed to coincide with the Waldensian liberation commemoration of February 17, but this does not seem to have been normal practice.

Sometimes the number of meetings Waldensian deputies had to attend seems to have multiplied in order to emphasise the denominational spread. In the Helensburgh area for example on February 1, 1880, Pastors Meille and Gay were advertised to speak at one parish church, three Free kirks, and the Congregational church. But nationally and locally the Free Church strain (later United Free) tended to predominate, thanks to its powerful Continental Committee, expatriate chaplaincies, Presbytery of Italy, and the involvement of such influential laymen as George Freeland Barbour, who chaired the I.E.S. in the early 1870's. When he died his obituary minute (January 1887) recorded him as a 'magnificent' donor to the establishment of the Claudiana press. It also emphasised his commitment to the political emancipation of Italy. His great-grandson Robin Barbour notes that 'Mazzini was quite a family hero, and I suppose Garibaldi and Cavour were too'.

However the Waldensian committee was non-denominational and also non-political in the British party sense. It was chaired for a time by Principal Cairns and by another eminent United Presbyterian minister, Andrew Thomson, author of one the best Victorian books on the Holy Land. Its supporters also ranged from the Auld Kirk to evangelical Episcopalians. One Edinburgh Episcopalian with Waldensian links and early contacts with the committee was the Revd D.T.K. Drummond of St Thomas's, the 'English episcopal chapel', who wrote a book about his Alpine travels and whose congregation contributed generously to the building of the Turin church. The society also gave women more of their due than was customary at the time, creating the designation of honorary secretary in 1895 for Mrs Ford, previously secretary of the ladies' committee. However in 1905 she opted to be called convener of the ladies' committee so that the honorific secretarial title could be transferred to Dr James Gibson who had been editor of the society's journal *A Voice from Italy* (founded in 1860).

There seems to have been some Scottish involvement too in the London Committee whose treasurer in 1898 was an expatriate Donald Matheson, noted earlier as honorary secretary and a leader in the London-based Evangelical Continental Society. In 1898 it included the Duke of Argyll and the Revd Dr Donald Macleod (brother of 'Macleod of the Barony'), who was also listed on the Western or Glasgow committee of the Scottish society. This committee was formed in 1896, as the 'Glasgow Auxiliary', taking over the Italian interests and Waldensian subscription lists of the evangelical Glasgow Continental Society which had hitherto been the main channel for support in the West of Scotland. The Glasgow committee then also included the great Holy Land scholar George Adam Smith; the Revd Dr Reith, whose son John was to be founding father of the BBC; and Marshall Lang, who went from the Glasgow Barony Church to be principal of Aberdeen University and fathered both a Moderator of the General Assembly and an Archbishop of Canterbury. The Glasgow or Western committee retained its semi-autonomous existence until 1985, when it was merged into the central committee, on which it had always been represented and with which it had worked far more harmoniously than the traditional rivalries of Scotland's two main cities might have suggested.

From time to time visiting Waldensians joined in committee deliberations, as occasionally did Scots ministers on furlough from Italy. The minutes from 1866 show attendances by Dr Stewart of Leghorn but not Dr McDougall of Florence, the advocate of the *Chiesa Libera*, who had been a frequent I.E.S. participant in the 1850s. However in 1900 the society sent condolences to his widow.

The Scots Kirk's congregations in Italy, mainly Free and later United Free, had been an important factor in stimulating support for Italian Protestantism. For example the Mrs Ford who became 'honorary' secretary was married to one of the main laymen of the society who had business links with Italy. Later when she was a widow in poor health she went back there for the winter. Dr Gibson of the *Voice* died in San Remo and was buried at Torre Pellice. But the decline of the expatriate Scottish congregations of the Kirk, which diminished steadily in number in the twentieth century until only Rome was left, was probably one of the factors which reduced the role of the Waldensian connection in the life, work, and thought of the Scottish Church.

By the early years of the twentieth century Italy and evangelical missionary fervour were both going out of fashion, though such supporters as the Hope Trust seem to have been consistent. One or two items in the records suggest that this loss of enthusiasm may have been most marked in the kind of congregations which once had most knowledge of Italy, in the days of leisurely travel and winter expatriates. In 1907 St Cuthbert's in Edinburgh was tackled about a regular donation they had allowed to lapse. Despite repeated approaches and attempts to use personal influence it was not renewed. The same thing happened later with St George's Edinburgh and the remonstrations only managed to get it restored at a reduced rate. By 1921 the society was worried about its grass-roots organisation. 'As vacancies have occurred', the secretary said in 1921, 'I have been quite unable to find a sufficient number of interested friends to take up the work.' He was also worried about the cost of publishing the *Voice* but induced the London committee to increase their annual contribution towards it.

The First World War inevitably dislocated activities and there seems to have been no stimulation of enthusiasm from the wartime alliance with Italy, although there are notes of special contributions to the Waldensian War Orphans Fund. Not surprisingly there was more emphasis on survival than Revival during the Fascist era, although the temper of the times ensured that much of Presbyterian Scotland shared the Waldensian alarm at the concordat between Mussolini and the Pope in 1929. In the pre-war years the Waldensians were suspect and forced to be circumspect, but the old connection did survive, though not on anything like the old scale of activity. There was not the old Victorian sense of evangelical urgency, perhaps on the Waldensian as well as the Scottish side. One senses that the role of 'deputy' to Scotland was no longer such a vital one. Indeed in the 1920's one prospective deputy caused some anxiety and even offence in Scotland by confessing that he spoke very imperfect English but that this wouldn't matter as his wife was coming with him and was Scottish. However deputies continued to come from Italy, most of them effective speakers in English.

Then wars and rumours of wars intervened. The first sign of real difficulty came in 1935 with the Abyssinian crisis when it was deemed 'inadvisable' to have a Waldensian deputy for the following year - for Britain and Italy were moving close to war - although the cautiously written record suggests that the Waldensians wanted to come and were disappointed. This remained the situation in 1937 and even when resumption of visits was proposed there were misgivings, notably in the Glasgow committee. There was then a brief and vain hope of getting back to normal. The last reported visit before the Second World War was that in early 1939 of Pastor Ermanno Rostan, a future Waldensian Moderator.

The outbreak of war in 1939 and the Italian intervention on Hitler's side in 1940 obviously interrupted the connection and disrupted the work. As late as November 1939 the society was seeking permission to remit £738 to Italy but in August 1940 it met to record that there was no up-to-date information on the condition of the

Waldensians and that 'in present circumstances' remittances were impossible. The society, holding funds destined for Italy, had to enter into successful diplomatic relations with the Custodian of Enemy Property and ran into difficulties which appear to have led to the end of the Victorian system of house-to-house collecting for the Waldensian cause, though this was probably already in decay if not terminal decline. New legal controls on such collections coincided with the outbreak of war, though unconnected with it. However they allowed the Scottish Office to 'advise' against Waldensian collections during the war and the society reluctantly conceded the point. There was little to be done for the Waldensians then, though inquiries were made about spiritual care for Protestants among Italian prisoners of war. These found that formal arrangements for Waldensian P.O.W.s had been made in England, but that none had been traced in Scotland.

But immediately the war was over the society, although worried about being almost moribund, rescued its funds from the bank and agreed to send £550 to Italy in November 1945. A year later the *Tavola's* treasurer, Pastor Guido Comba, was able to attend the central committee, though the first formal post-war visit by a deputy - apparently a hurried and frustrating affair - was by Pastor Deodato in 1947. It lasted six days when the Scots were still hankering after old-style visits of six to eight weeks.

In the next few years the society had to wrestle with the practical difficulties of deputies' visits at a time of European and Italian reconstruction and with exchange controls in post-war austerity Britain. Permission to remit money had to be sought and in 1948 only three-quarters of the sum requested was allowed.

However the Second World War and its aftermath of reconstruction stimulated Scottish Church interest in Europe, revived old connections, and reinvigorated existing ones, like the Waldensian society. In 1951 the central committee, then chaired by Dr George Gunn, included such formidable names as Principal John Baillie, Professor T. F. Torrance, and Dr Charles Warr of St Giles'. Gunn was succeeded by Dr Roderick Bethune. By 1968 the chairman was the great teacher and preacher, Professor James Stewart, and the committee included Lord Birsay and the Revd John Brown, father of Gordon Brown, Chancellor the Exchequer when this note is written. A letter from Professor Stewart combined approval for the 'vision and forward-looking attitude of the Waldensians in having women among their ordinands' with support for Waldensian efforts in the aftermath of earthquakes in Southern Italy. Professor Stewart was succeeded by the Revd Thomas Shearer. By this time the *Voice* had been replaced by a Scottish edition of the English committee's latest journal *The Waldensian Revdiew*. The secretary then was the Revd John Douglas, who served for 23 years till 1975, and whose son, the Revd Iain Douglas (a former student at the Waldensian College in Rome), is chairman of the society at the time of writing. John Douglas's interest in Italy had been inspired by his wartime service there as a chaplain. David Lamb, an Edinburgh lawyer, succeeded him and at the time of writing is 29 not out in his secretarial innings. Iain Douglas's predecessors in the chair were the Revd E.A.H. Sawers and the Revd Malcolm Ritchie, who first got to know Italy, from Sicily to beyond Udine, as a Gunner officer in 1943-45. He encountered the Waldensian Church at the end of the war, and had been the last chairman of the former Western committee in Glasgow. This Glasgow committee merged with the central committee in 1985 and the society celebrated its 150th anniversary in 2000, when Professor Paolo Ricca attended the General Assembly and delivered a commemorative lecture in Parliament House. It now circulates *The Waldensian Revdiew* in Scotland with a brief Scottish newsletter instead of a Scottish edition.

The society continues to support the Waldensian-Methodist missions in Italy, which necessarily mean the maintenance of ministries and churches in areas which depend on central support from Italian church funds, quite apart from the costs involved in extensive social work. The contributions - about £3000 from Scotland in a typical year but sometimes up to £8000 - are tiny compared to the needs of the country-wide ministry, mission, and social work of the Waldensians and Methodists in Italy and the support from Italian sources, especially under the recent tax provisions. In real value they are also only a small proportion of what Scotland sent in Victorian times, but they are an outward and visible symbol and token of a common cause as well as a shared history. The society, non-denominational in form but in practice mainly Presbyterian but with Methodist representation, still welcomes Waldensian deputies from time to time, though they are now perhaps more concerned with spreading understanding of the Waldensian tradition than with encouraging financial support. In 2001 it also organised a tour of Scottish supporters to the valleys and to Turin, where David Lamb addressed the congregation of the historic city-centre church in elegantly fluent Italian. Without that tour (followed by one to Tuscany in 2003) this book would never have been written.

Other links with Italy also remain. The Kirk's Moderator, Dr Andrew McLellan, visited the Waldensians in 2000 and addressed their Synod at Torre Pellice. In Rome St Andrew's, which is an overseas charge of the Church of Scotland, provides the city with an English-speaking international Reformed church and ministry. In Turin the English-speaking congregation meeting in the main Waldensian church complex now has (2005) a Church of Scotland minister. There are also still people in the other smaller Presbyterian denominations in Scotland who maintain links with Italy. There is a Free Kirk minister who taught English in Milan before taking up a charge in Glasgow and there is a link between the Free Presbyterians and a small evangelical group in Tuscany whose founders encountered Reformed Christianity in Glasgow.

And although I searched in vain for a Scots name in the roll of the Waldensian ministry (apart from Rob Mackenzie with Turin's expatriates) I was heartened to see that the Baptists of Barletta had a pastor with the rather un-Apulian name of David McFarlane.

Appendix 2
WORDSWORTH'S WALDENSIAN SONNETS AND FELICIA HEMANS' HYMN

These are Wordsworth's three sonnets on the Waldensians which, preceded by one on transubstantiation, form numbers XI to XIV in part 2 of his sequence of 'Ecclesiastical Sonnets' Two of them were published in 1835 and probably all four were written in the early 1830's, when Gilly and others had made the Waldensians a popular cause in Britain. Wordsworth used his creative imagination in the sentiments he ascribed to Valdo and accepted the historical theory that the Waldensians were not just followers of Valdo but a surviving pure Church of 'the unadulterate Word', retaining the pattern of apostolic times.

XI Transubstantiation

Enough! for see, with dim association
The tapers burn; the odorous incense feeds
A greedy flame; the pompous mass proceeds.
The priest bestows the appointed consecration;
And, while the Host is raised, its elevation
An awe and supernatural horror breeds;
And all the people bow their heads, like reeds
To a soft breeze, in lowly adoration.
This Valdo brooks not. On the banks of Rhone
He taught, till persecution chased him thence,
To adore the Invisible, and Him alone.
Nor are his followers loth to seek defence.
'Mid woods and wilds, on Nature's craggy throne,
From rites that trample upon soul and sense

XII The Vaudois

But whence came they who for the Saviour Lord
Have long borne witness as the Scriptures teach? -
Ages ere Valdo raised his voice to preach
In Gallic ears the unadulterate Word,
Their fugitive progenitors explored

Subalpine vales, in quest of safe retreats
Where that pure Church survives, though summer heats
Open a passage to the Romish sword,
Far as it dares to follow. Herbs self-sown
And fruitage gathered from the chestnut-wood,
Nourish the sufferers then; and mists that brood
O'er chasms with new-fallen obstacles bestrown,
Protect them; and the eternal snow that daunts
Aliens, is God's good winter for their haunts.

XIII

Praised be the rivers, from their mountain springs
Shouting to freedom, 'Plant thy banners here!'
To harassed piety, 'Dismiss thy fear
And in our caverns smooth thy ruffled wings!'
Nor be unthanked their final lingerings -
Silent, but not to high-souled passion's ear -
'Mid reedy fens wide-spread and marshes drear,
Their own creation. Such glad welcomings
As Po was heard to give where Venice rose
Hailed from aloft those heirs of truth divine
Who near his fountains sought obscure repose,
Yet came prepared as glorious lights to shine
Should that be needed for their sacred charge:
Blest prisoners they, whose spirits were at large.

XIV Waldenses

Those had given earliest notice, as the lark
Springs from the ground the morn to gratulate;
Or rather rose the day to antedate
By striking out a solitary spark
When all the world with midnight gloom was dark, -
Then followed the Waldensian bands whom hate
In vain endeavours to exterminate,
Whom obloquy pursues with hideous bark:
But they desist not; - and the sacred fire,
Rekindled thus, from dens and savage woods
Moves, handed on with never-ceasing care,
Through courts, through camps, o'er limitary floods;
Nor lacks this sea-girt Isle a timely share
Of the new flame, not suffered to expire.

Hymn of the Vaudois Mountaineers by Felicia Hemans (1793-1835)

For the strength of the hills we bless Thee,
Our God, our fathers' God,
Thou hast made thy children mighty
By the touch of the mountain sod;
Thou hast fixed our ark of refuge
Where the spoiler's foot ne'er trod,
For the strength of the hills we bless Thee,
Our God, our fathers' God.

We are watchers of a beacon,
Whose light must never die;
We are guardians of an altar
Midst the silence of the sky.
The rocks yield founts of courage,
Struck forth as by Thy rod....

For the dark resounding caverns
Where thy still small voice is heard,
For the strong pines of the forests
That by thy breath are stirred,
For the storms on whose free pinions,
Thy Spirit walks abroad....

The royal eagle darteth
On his quarry from the heights,
And the stag, that knows no master,
Seeks there his wild delights;
But we for thy communion
Have sought the mountain sod....

The banner of the chieftain,
Far, far below us waves;
The war horse of the spearman
Cannot reach our lofty caves,
Thy dark clouds wrap the threshold
Of freedom's last abode....

For the shadow of thy presence,
Round our camp of rock outspread,
For the stern defiles of battle,
Bearing record of our dead,
For the snows and for the torrents,
For the free hearts' burial sod:
For the strength of the hills we bless Thee,
Our God, our fathers' God.

BIBLIOGRAPHY (with notes on sources)

I was reluctant to include source-notes in a book not mainly intended for the academic readers, though I hope it will have some. On the other hand I do not want to make assertions without evidence. I have compromised by integrating into the text references to all the more important sources and even some of the minor ones and by adding the very full bibliography which follows this note. I hope this, without burdening the more casual reader, will appease those anxious to know where I got my facts and some of my notions. There are some minor problems about dates in the Scottish Waldensian Missions Aid Society archive where press cuttings and other items are not always precisely dated and attributed, and some similar problems in the Scottish Church papers in the National Library of Scotland (NLS).

Manuscript and unpublished sources:

(a) In Scotland:

Scottish-Waldensian archive: Surviving correspondence and papers of the Italian Evangelisation Society 1852-99. Minutes of the Italian Evangelisation Society, and of the committees which formed it, 1850-1899. Minutes and papers of the Scottish Waldensian Missions Aid Society 1866-99 and of the society after its incorporation of the Italian Evangelisation Society, 1899-2004.

Press cuttings books, (nineteenth century) and publicity material of W.M.A.S. and I.E.S.

Minutes of Western Committee of the W.M.A.S, 1896-1929 and 1958-85.

At the time writing the possibility is being explored of transferring these archives to the NLS. This has been agreed in principle.

Thomas Guthrie Family Letters: Letters from the Continent to his family from Thomas Guthrie, 1869. Printed for private circulation 1871.

Donald Miller Papers: Letters and papers of Donald Miller: A family collection, mainly of letters from Genoa 1874-1910, which are also in the Waldensian archive, Torre Pellice. However some material, including notes about Garibaldi's Sicilian campaign of 1860, may be exclusive to the family collection.

NLS: Church of Scotland foreign and continental archives, now transferred to the NLS in its Manuscripts Division (Acc. 7548 G87 etc.). These also contain material from the Free Church and United Free Church, as well as some early Waldensian committee papers and correspondence, including that of G.F. Barbour. The collection includes records of the Scots Presbyteries in Italy and of the kirk in Florence. The records of the Presbyteries of Leghorn and North Italy up to about 1870 consist of several hundred letters, memos, and loose minutes crammed into a large file cover.

Private communications to the author from various sources.

(b) In Italy:

Waldensian archives: The excellent *Archivio valdese*, a Church institution located along with the Waldensian Museum and Cultural Centre in Torre Pellice, contains a wealth of material about the international connections as well as the internal life of the Waldensian Church. It also now provides a home for material about Italian Methodism and the nineteenth-century *Chiesa Libera* movement. Much of this appears to have come via the Methodist Church in Florence, once a stronghold of the *Chiesa Libera*, and has been preserved or restored after damage in the Arno floods of 1966.

I have drawn on Waldensian and Methodist files for R.W. Stewart (which include his sermons, sundry papers, and his mother's diary) and for John McDougall. His last embittered correspondence is well preserved, but painful to read. The Waldensian files also provided me with much additional material on Alessandro Gavazzi.

The Waldensian Museum at Torre Pellice, part of the Waldensian Cultural Centre, also provides many insights and much interesting material.

Books:

Anon. (possibly Goldwin): *A Brief Account of the Vaudois* (London, 1753)

Anon. (C.T. Bowie?): *A Six Weeks' Scamper through France and Italy* (Glasgow, 1879)

Acquaviva, Sabino: Italy section in *Western Religion*, ed. H. Mol (the Hague, 1972)

Allix, Peter: *The Ancient Churches of Piedmont* (Oxford 1821, with add. section on Languedoc, new ed. of 1690-92 works: Gallatin, Tennessee 1989)

Arthur, William: *Italy in Transition*, Lon. 1860

Baedeker, Karl: *Handbook for Travellers*, (Leipzig, various editions of Italian vols.)

Baird, Robert: *Sketches of Italian Protestantism Past and Present* (British edition, Glasgow 1847)

Barzini, Luigi: *The Italians* (London, 1964)

Beattie, William: *The Waldenses* (Lon., 1838)

Biagi, Enzo: *Italia* (Milan, 1975)

Bonar, Andrew and McCheyne, Robert Murray: *Narrative of a Mission of Enquiry to the Jews* (Edinburgh, 1842)

Bost, Charles: *Histoire des Protestants de France* (Carrière-sous-Poissy,1924)

Bouchard, Giorgio: *I valdesi e l'Italia* (rev. ed., Turin 1990)

Brown, David: *The Life of Rabbi Duncan* (Glasgow, 1986 edition)

Brown, J. Wood: *An Italian Campaign* (London 1890)

Buckland, A.W.: *The World beyond the Esterelles* (London, 1884)

Deakin, William : *The Last days of Mussolini* (London, 1966)

Drummond, A.L.: *The Kirk and the Continent* (Edinburgh, 1956)

Drummond, D.T.K.: *Scenes and Impressions in Switzerland and the North of Italy* (London, 1853)

Fabre, Rémi: *Les Protestants en France depuis 1789* (Paris, 1999)

Gilly, William Stephen: *Narrative of an Excursion to the Mountains of Piemont* (London, 1824)

Gilly, William Stephen: *Waldensian Researches during a Second Visit to the Vaudois of Piemont* (London, 1831)

Gretton, Mrs G.: *An Englishwoman in Italy* (London, 1861)

Hasler, August Bernhard: *How the Pope Became Infallible* (English translation, New York, 1981)

Hehn, Victor: *Italien* (Berlin, 1912 edition)

Henderson, Ebenezer: *The Vaudois* (London, 1845)

Hibbert, Christopher: *Florence, the Biography of a City* (London. 1993)

Howells, W.D. : *Italian Journeys*, pocket edition (Edinburgh 1887)

Howells, W.D.: *Italian Journeys*, revised edition (London 1902)

Jackson, James: *Remarks on the Vaudois of Piemont during a Journey in the Summer of 1825* (London, 1826)

Jenkins, Roy: *Gladstone* (London 1995)

Luzzi, Giovanni: *The Waldensian Church and the Edict of Emancipation* (Edinburgh, 1898, reprinted Turin 1998)

McLellan, Andrew: *Gentle and Passionate* (Edinburgh, 2001)

Madaule, Jacques: *Le Drame Albigeois et l'Unité Française* (Paris, 1973)

Magnus, Philip: *Gladstone* (London 1954)

Maselli, Domenico: *Storia dei battisti italiani* (Turin, 2003)

Miller, William: *Wintering on the Riviera* (London, 1879)

Murray, John: *Handbook for Travellers in Switzerland and the Alps of Savoy and Piedmont* (London, 1838)

Nelli, René: *Les Cathares* (Paris, 1972)

Pickering, W.S.E.: *What the British found when they discovered the French Vaudois in the nineteenth century* (Privately pub. Cambridge, 1995)

Platoni, Giuseppe (ed.): *La Bibbia e l'Italia* (Turin, 2004)

Primmer, J.: *Jacob Primmer in Rome* (Dunfermline, sixth edition, 1912)

Religious Tract Society: *Sketches of the Waldenses* (London, c1846)

Richards, Charles: *The New Italians* (London 1994)

Robertson, Alexander: *Mussolini and the New Italy* (London 1930)

Ronco, Daisy D.: *Risorgimento and the Free Italian Churches* (privately published, printed by University of Wales, 1996; also notes in New International Dictionary of the Christian Church)

Rouse R. and Neill S.C: *A History of the Ecumenical movement 1517-1948* (London, 1983 edition)

Spini, Giorgio: *Italia liberale e protestanti* (Turin, 2002)

Stephens, Prescot: *The Waldensian Story* (Lewes, Sussex 1998)

Stewart, Robert W.: *On the Present Condition and Future Prospects of the Waldensian Church, from Lectures on Foreign Churches* (Edinb., 1845)

Talfourd, T.N.: *Supplement to Vacation Rambles* (London, 1854)

Tourn, Giorgio: *Italiani e protestanismo* (Turin, 1997)

Tourn, Giorgio (ed.): *Viaggiatori britannici alle valli valdesi* (Turin,. 1994),

Tourn, Giorgio, & assoc.: *You are my Witnesses: the Waldensians across 800 years* (Turin, 1989) with an account of Methodism in Italy (Giorgio Spini), post-war discipleship (Giorgio Bouchard) and S. American Waldensianism (Roger Geymonat)

Wylie, James: *Wanderings and Musings in the Valleys of the Waldenses* (London, 1858)

Wylie James: *History of Protestantism* (London, 1880) Includes as Book XVI his *History of the Waldenses*, also pub. separately *Dictionary of National Biography* (DNB) and new Oxford *DNB* (2004)

New International Dictionary of the Christian Church; Concise Oxford Dictionary of the Christian Church *Valli Nostre Indirizzario 2002* & later eds.

Periodicals: *The Waldensian Review*, Scottish edition; *The Waldensian Review* (to 2005); *Riforma; Life and Work*; other periodicals as quoted

INDEX